D1165807

EMPIRES

AND

ANARCHIES

A HISTORY OF

OIL

IN THE MIDDLE EAST

MICHAEL QUENTIN MORTON

REAKTION BOOKS

Published by Reaktion Books Ltd
Unit 32, Waterside
44–48 Wharf Road
London N1 7UX, UK
www.reaktionbooks.co.uk

First published 2017
Copyright © Michael Quentin Morton 2017

All rights reserved

No part of this publication may be reproduced, stored in a retrieval system,
or transmitted, in any form or by any means, electronic, mechanical,
photocopying, recording or otherwise, without the prior permission
of the publishers

Printed and bound in Great Britain by TJ International, Padstow, Cornwall

A catalogue record for this book is available from the British Library

ISBN 978 1 78023 810 4

CONTENTS

ARABIA AND THE GULF

THE MIDDLE EAST

AUTHOR'S NOTE

IN THE PROCESS of writing this book, it has been necessary to settle on certain geographical definitions. For the Middle East, a term variously interpreted, it seemed sensible to focus on Iran, Iraq, Arabia and the Gulf states, these being the main oil-producing countries, and to bring in others as and when required: Algeria, Libya, Egypt, Lebanon, Jordan and Palestine, for example. Turkey is mentioned because of the Ottoman Empire's former control over parts of the region. As for the use of historical names, I have kept the name 'Persia' for Iran in the opening chapters because that is how it was recognized in the West until 1935, and the term 'Persian Gulf' for a similar reason; Iraq is referred to as 'Mesopotamia' because it was known in the West as such until the kingdom of Iraq was created in 1921.

Empires and Anarchies is aimed at a general audience, therefore spellings are derived from Western sources and I have not included any diacritics. Many places and individuals are named as they appear in the UK Foreign Office and India Office documents. I have omitted the definitive article from Arabic place names unless in common usage.

Of course, the book is not primarily about names or transliteration, but about the wider perspectives of history. More than a century has passed since the birth of the modern oil industry in the Middle East and, while its final impact is yet to be revealed, we can only strive to understand the story so far.

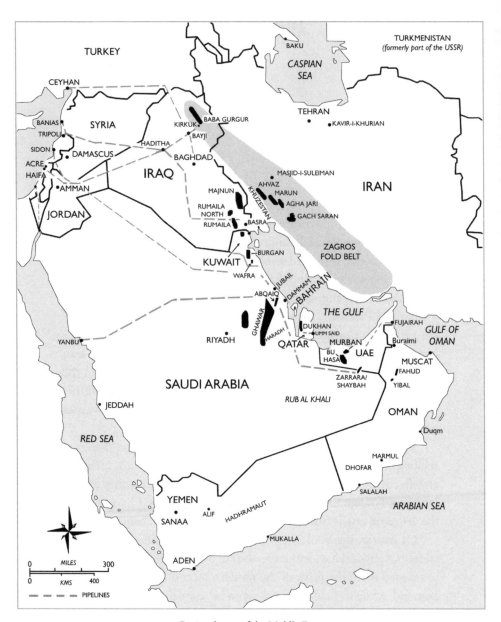

Regional map of the Middle East.

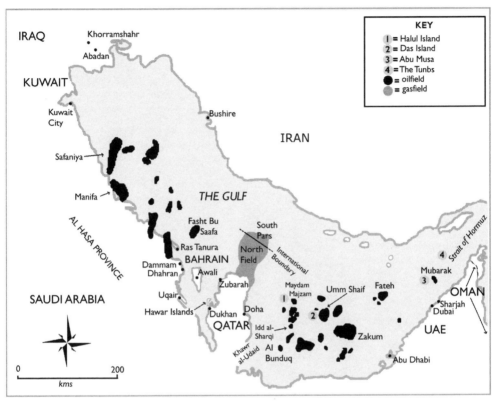

Major gas and oilfields on the Arabian side of the Gulf.

Even then it took another fourteen years before IPC's assets were nationalized. After that, the brakes were taken off. The fact that Saddam
Hussein was able to plunge the region into a prolonged period of inse-
curity and conflict from 1980 onwards through the Iran–Iraq and Gulf
Wars was in a large part due to the oil revenues that brought him the
weaponry necessary to do so – otherwise, in the pre-oil days, he would
have simply been another sabre-rattling despot. It also explains why he
was able to challenge the West and provoke it to invade the country in
2003, resulting in the destruction of his regime, the dismantlement of
the Baath party and the descent of Iraq into the discord and warfare
that continues to this day.

In Saudi Arabia oil did not bring revolution but validated the
existing tribal structure, investing it with affluence and providing the
necessary resources for its leaders to spread their largesse widely. While
the oil wealth rolled in, and the motor cars of the West kept running,
this did not seem to matter so much in the capitals of Europe and
from the days of King Faisal's rule in the 1960s, oil revenues enabled
the Saudis to export Wahhabi teachings of Islam across the globe; and
(together with the United States) to provide funding to the Mujahidin
in their fight against the Soviets in Afghanistan. But in the aftermath
of the 9/11 attacks in the United States, perceptions changed. Today,
speculation about the role of Saudi officials in the 9/11 plot persists
and is unlikely to abate: the decision of the u.s. Congress to override
President Obama's veto has allowed relatives of the 9/11 victims to
sue Saudi Arabia, raising the prospect of many lawsuits in the years
to come.

Phrases such as 'the curse of oil' and 'the paradox of plenty' are
often applied to the experience of the oil-rich nations, and not only
in an economic sense. Certainly, a great deal of the oil wealth has
flowed into the hands of powerful elites and dampened the incentive to
develop other sources of income, though some countries have tried to
address these issues by redistributing the wealth through generous welfare schemes and by diversifying their economies. But it goes further
than that: for good or bad, oil has shaped the political structures that
exist in the Middle East today. It has brought prosperity and power to
its countries and propelled them into the first rank of nations, but left
others behind. The failure of governments to meet the expectations
of their people has led to the demands for democracy, and the brutal
repressions, of the Arab Spring.

It has also provided the revenue to support many of the conflicts that disfigure the region today. Witness, for example, how oil wealth has empowered the Shiite Iranians and Sunni Saudis to battle it out on a regional scale through their proxies in Bahrain, Syria and Yemen.

On another level, it might be said that what makes oil so important in the world today is the West's reliance on petroleum and its many byproducts – hence an obsession with oil prices and the cost of petrol. It is true that the affairs of the Organization of the Petroleum Exporting Countries (OPEC) are often in the headlines and that the price of oil is clearly important to the economies of the West, though not as much as it used to be forty years ago since alternative forms of energy are being more widely used. But it goes beyond a simple matter of price: the statistics that are often crammed into standard works on the oil industry will not be found here because arguments about price and production figures are not only arguments about money and profits, they are struggles for power through the control of oil.

To those who make the claim that the Middle East is not oil, it is its people and its land, this book counters that the history of oil *is* about all these things, and is an important part of their past, present and future. The fact that oil is a passing phase is undeniable; that the effects of oil will disappear with it is an illusion. Although we might prefer to think of oil simply as a thick, black substance that oozes out of the ground, the central argument of this book is that oil creates empires and anarchies in the same way that wealth, power and greed have always done. The themes of foreign control and dominance, of the powerful and the dispossessed, and the struggle between the few and the many, all these will be found in the history of oil.

IRAN

• bitumen: A black viscous mixture of hidrocarbons obtained naturally or as a residue from petroleum distillation. It's used for road surfacing/roofing. (16)
↳ AKA: asphalt

ONE

A SCRAP OF PAPER, 1849–1918

THE SMOKY LAMPS THAT burned in the night, the walls of the ancient temples bound with (bitumen) and the seepages that wept like open wounds: these were simple clues to the presence of oil. And yet it seemed that nothing could disturb the timeless patterns of this land nor prepare its people for what was to come. The country was wild and rugged, its tribes watchful and jealous of intrusion. Here, in the foothills and on the plains of Bakhtiari territory in southwest Persia, great (khans) ruled by dint of sword and custom, and the shah in Tehran held little sway. When the geologist William Loftus ventured onto these lands in the 1850s, he did so with the permission of the khans, though quite what the tribes made of the wandering Englishman is uncertain. Even if the bristling warriors of the high passes watched his progress with suspicion, they surely had no inkling of the future.

For his part, Loftus was as wary as the watchers. The apparent tranquillity of the land was deceptive, for it had been fought over for many centuries. In 1849 he had joined the Turco-Persian Frontier Commission, a body appointed to demarcate the boundary between what are known today as Iraq and Iran. Members of the commission spent the next three years surveying the territory and drawing up a definitive frontier line, with the British party extending its work as far as (Shiraz.) As the mapping work wound down in the latter stages of his survey, Loftus was able to travel about the interior more freely. As well as being a geologist, he was an archaeologist and carried out several excavations in the area. One of his discoveries was of a different kind, however, for among the many places he visited was Masjid-i-Suleiman,

Part of a noble rank; it's a title given to rulers + officials in Central Asia, Afghanistan, and other muslim countries.

5th most populous city in Iran and the capital of the Fars Province.

16

the ancient Temple of Solomon, where dark rivulets flowed and eternal fires burned from the earth.

Despite its religious connotations, this was the very playground of the devil – there was an almost unbearable stench of sulphur in the air. In that remote and barren terrain, Loftus could see a narrow ravine plunging between the contorted rocks. A small stream rose high up in the ravine, and gathered speed, volume and an oily liquid – a mixture of black bitumen and white naphtha – on its downward charge. Once caught in a man-made dam below, the oily liquid was gathered, dried in the sun and reduced to the consistency of soft mud. It was then placed in a large cauldron, gently simmered and then allowed to cool and harden – the bitumen was now ready to be used. In a pattern that was to be repeated throughout the history of oil, an elite group of people had control of the product, in this case the *seyyids* at Shuster, who had the sole right to make bitumen at that location.[1]

Bitumen, like its close relative crude oil, had several uses; there was a local demand to use it for waterproofing, mortar and caulking boats. Oil seepages were a common sight in certain parts of the Middle East but, in the West, they were a geological curiosity and little more. Oil had limited applications: in a refined form it might be used for lamps, though the most prized type of lamp oil came from the sperm whale. More than twenty years would pass before kerosene would become the main oil for lamps, and more than thirty before the motor car would make a significant impact on the demand for oil.

Even so, as Loftus dusted off his boots upon his return to London in 1855, he thought the matter important enough to include in his report to the Geological Society. Sadly, he would not live to see the day when commercial oil was discovered in Persia. He ventured abroad once more but, weakened by a fever developed in the swamps of Assyria, he collapsed from sunstroke. On 27 November 1858, while making the return voyage to England aboard the *Tyburnia*, he died from an abscess of the liver.

Meanwhile life went on: the Bakhtiari tribes carried on their twice-yearly migrations as the Great Game was played out between Great Britain and Russia over the northern provinces of Persia. The primitive Persian oil industry (such as it was) played second fiddle to Russian oil from Baku, which was imported to supply the lamps of Tehran, and the occasional European traipsed across the country in order to study the country's ancient ruins.

*Dervish: A sufi Muslim who has taken vows of poverty and austerity. First appeared in 12th century. They were noted for their wild/ecstatic rituals and were known as dancing, whirling or howling dervishe according to practice

Muhammed Karim Khan, Aziz Khan and Ali Agha with their tribesmen
at Qasr-i-Shirin in 1911.

Westerners found Tehran remote and difficult to reach. A Hungarian traveller, Arminius Vámbéry, made the arduous overland ride from Tabriz in 1862, a journey that left him feeling like – in his own words – a 'half-boiled' fish by the time he saw his destination.[2] As the horses drank water from a nearby stream, he looked on the city below, glimpsing its glittering domes through shrouds of blue smoke rising upwards. Vámbéry, as it was, had no interest in oil beyond noting trading boats on the Caspian Sea loaded with supplies of naphtha and pitch. He left the hustling, bustling city disguised as a dervish in order to travel around central Persia; but others would later come in search of oil.

THE SIGHT OF CRUDE oil seeping out through cracks in the ground was never a sure-fire guarantee of an oilfield below. Oil is the product of natural processes over millions of years, formed from the debris of organisms and plants that fall to the ocean floor. It then becomes buried deep in the earth where, under great heat and pressure, it 'cooks' to form hydrocarbons – oil and gas. Since oil is lighter than water, it rises upwards. In the absence of impervious rocks to halt its progress, some oil leaks to the surface as seepages. Otherwise, the oil becomes trapped and accumulates, and this is how the great oilfields of the Middle East were formed. Yet the natural processes were unpredictable enough to make early oil exploration a hit-and-miss affair, and its history is littered with false hopes and broken expectations.

There is something in the geology of the region, however, that makes it exceptionally rich in oil and gas. The secret to Persia's abundance of oil resources lies in what geologists call the Zagros fold-belt. The ancient movements of the Arabian tectonic plate, which collided with the Eurasian plate over millions of years, compacted the western land mass and created mountains, including the Zagros range. One byproduct of this process was great folds in the earth, natural receptacles for oil in the ground known as anticlines – a treasure chest for the petroleum geologist. Taken with the region's proximity to the ancient Tethys Ocean, from which the major oilfields of the Middle East arose, these Zagros fold-belts presented geologists with the one of the most prolific oil-producing areas of the world, the so-called 'Goldilocks Zone'. They lie south and west of the mountains and a few were evidenced by the oil seepages Loftus had seen and mentioned in his reports.

[handwritten margin note: Also called the Tethys Sea & the Neo ethys, existed during the Mesozoic Era and located between the ancient continents of Laurasia/Gondwana]

The modern oil industry developed first in and around the Caspian Sea and then across the United States. Some basic techniques have barely changed: the primitive oil derricks in Texas, for example, are unmistakably related to the structures of today. As knowledge of oilfield management grew, so the forests of oil wells that once blotted the landscape were replaced by rigs more generously spread apart. Drilling equipment was little more than a heavy chisel on a rope that was repeatedly dropped from the top of a wooden derrick to smash the rocks below. Oil tended to be found in remote areas, in places where it was difficult to transport supplies and set up drilling equipment to build rigs and pipelines.

Traditionally, entrepreneurs or a foreign state sought permission from the government of the day – whether it was headed by a shah, sultan, king or sheikh – to carry out their activities. Although there was a long history of trade with foreigners through the ports of the Persian Gulf, it was an uphill struggle to persuade anyone from Europe to invest in Persia. For the British, it was part of the imperial narrative to describe the interior parts as wild and rugged, and filled with lawless and primitive tribesmen beyond the control of central government. That apart, Persia did have one advantage over many other countries of the region – it was independent, free from Ottoman control – and its Qajar rulers were looking for new sources of revenue to support their lavish lifestyles. A number of breathtaking opportunities arose.

One entrepreneur to show an interest was a German-born British subject, Baron Julius de Reuter, founder of the famous news agency. On 25 July 1872 he obtained a wide-ranging concession from the ruler, Nasir al-Din Shah. The agreement virtually gave away Persia's entire economy by allowing de Reuter and his syndicate the right to run industries, establish a national bank, print currency, build railways and more. Outraging the Russians, who considered the country within their sphere of influence, and embarrassing the British, who had not been consulted during the negotiations, the concession caused such a commotion that the shah was forced to cancel it only a year later.

De Reuter was not quite finished with Persia, though. In 1889 he established the Imperial Bank of Persia, which went on to become the British Bank of the Middle East. An oil concession was also awarded to the de Reuter group, which proceeded to drill two wells at Daliki in Fars province and another on Qishm Island before abandoning operations. A simmering resentment over the scale of foreign investment boiled over in 1891 with the Tobacco Revolt, when Persians stopped smoking in protest at the monopoly held by the British Imperial Tobacco Company over the production and distribution of tobacco in their country. In these events, we can see a Persian antipathy towards foreign domination that would later have far-reaching ramifications for the oil industry.

Elsewhere, the seeds of the future had already been sown with the development of the internal combustion engine. By now, the first automobiles were puttering out of Carl Benz's factory in Mannheim, Germany, heralding the start of the modern automobile age. This in turn gradually triggered a growing demand for oil and attracted the attention of entrepreneurs and speculators to the nascent oil industry, which would make Persia an area of prime interest. In the latter part of the nineteenth century a number of geologists surveyed and reported on the stratigraphy of the Zagros Mountains. They included a French geologist and archaeologist, Jacques de Morgan. In a paper in the *Annales de mines*, published in 1892, and the second volume of his book *Mission scientifique,* published in 1895, de Morgan reported that there were many oil seepages in western Persia and postulated that it might be possible to establish an oil industry in the region. That was more easily said than done, of course.

AT THE TURN OF the century William Knox D'Arcy alighted on the petroleum scene. An Englishman who had made a fortune from the Mount Morgan gold mine in Australia, D'Arcy progressed from small-town solicitor to millionaire and bon vivant of London society in the space of a couple of decades. Looking around for new investment opportunities, he became interested in oil. According to one account, the 51-year-old was lunching with a friend who pointed to a passing motor car, a new-fangled device at the time, and suggested that the oil business might be worth a look. D'Arcy was subsequently told that an Armenian by the name of Antoine Kitabchi Khan was trying to attract investors to an oil concession from the Persian government, and the two men met in Paris on 8 January 1901.[3]

A person who enjoys a sociable and luxurious lifestyle

After the meeting, and having read a copy of Jacques de Morgan's report, D'Arcy was suitably impressed. He may also have sought the advice of Sir Boverton Redwood, the author of *A Treatise on Petroleum* (1896), who ran a petroleum geology consultancy in London. Redwood was perhaps the most authoritative figure in British petroleum circles at the time. He would later become an adviser to D'Arcy's exploration company and recommend early sites for drilling. As it was, the science of petroleum geology was fairly rudimentary at the time, relying more on sightings of local oil and gas seepages – though Persia appeared rich in both.

D'Arcy's representative arrived in Tehran in April to discuss an oil concession with the Persian government. On 28 May 1901 an agreement was reached whereby the Persian ruler Muzaffar al-Din Shah (1896–1907) received £10,000 and a promise of 16 per cent of future profits. In return, the D'Arcy group gained exclusive rights to produce and transport oil from the southwestern provinces of Persia, an area of approximately half a million square miles. It sounded grand – and it was for D'Arcy – but in later years the Persian press could barely suppress its contempt for 'the D'Arcy scrap of paper'.[4]

At first, it was a huge gamble. Even though the First Exploitation Company was formed to operate the concession with D'Arcy holding a half share, other major investors such as the banking family of the Rothschilds and the chairman of the oil company Royal Dutch shied away. Nevertheless, on the advice of one of Redwood's geologists, drilling began in November 1902 at Chiah Surkh, in an area previously mapped by Jacques de Morgan where oil springs had been found.

It would take a man of rare qualities to see the project through, and in George Reynolds they found such a man. His powerful physical presence, gruff temperament and brooding appearance belonged to the era of the early oil pioneer, and yet he had a certain way of dealing with problems that matched the conditions he faced, though he did not always please his masters. He had graduated from the Royal Indian Engineering College and served in India, teaching himself geology and gaining experience of working in the difficult conditions in the Dutch oilfields of Sumatra. This was a valuable grounding for the challenges awaiting him in the frontier lands of southwest Persia.

With a team of Polish and Canadian drillers, an Indian doctor, an American engineer and others, Reynolds worked in a harsh environment of mountains and plains where lugging materials to drilling sites could take weeks and disease could take a heavy toll; freezing winters and rainy seasons, scorching heat and surging rivers all added to the hardships. The later drilling sites were remote and far from any major cities (apart from Ahwaz), with all the difficulties in obtaining supplies and communicating with the outside world that entailed.

The tribes had to be placated, too. At Chiah Surkh, Reynolds dealt with Kurdish chieftains for the right to use their land and recruit local labourers and then, when drilling moved to the southeast, he

A shooting party at William Knox D'Arcy's country house, Bylaugh Hall, Norfolk, in 1897 (D'Arcy is third right).

negotiated with the Bakhtiari chiefs. A precedent of sorts had already been set with the Lynch Road, which had been built by a British firm, Lynch Brothers, to connect their steamer route on the River Karun with Isfahan. The consent of the Bakhtiari khans had been obtained for that road, but the British consul often had to intervene in disputes over payments and repairs.

As was often the case in the early oil industry, there were many false dawns. Oil was encountered at Chiah Surkh at a depth of about 238 metres (780 ft), but it was 'heavy' oil, which was thick, sulphurous and expensive to refine, making the oilfield unprofitable to develop. According to one account, in late November 1903 a despondent Reynolds was to be found in Kuwait attempting to book a passage back to England. By chance, he encountered a British official, Louis Dane, who was accompanying the Viceroy of India, Lord Curzon, on his famous tour of the Gulf. Dane was compiling a gazetteer of the region and, in the course of his research, had heard about a place called Maidan-i-Naftun ('Field of Oil'), which reminded him of oil-rich Baku. He strongly suggested to Reynolds that it was a place worth surveying; not that they knew it at the time, but it was the same area that William Loftus had investigated more than fifty years before. That conversation in Kuwait was enough to persuade Reynolds to visit the location three months later, and find the reputed seepages of oil.[5]

That site would have to wait, since drilling was still in full swing at Chiah Surkh. In the summer, oil was struck in a second well but, again, it was not commercially exploitable and lacked the ring of certainty that might attract serious investors. Both wells were closed down in mid-1904. With the cost of operations high, the D'Arcy group was anxiously looking around for sources of finance to extend their Persian adventure. The Treasury refused a loan and, in search of funds, D'Arcy travelled to Cannes to meet Alphonse Rothschild of the famous banking family, and even discussed terms with the American oil company Standard Oil. All the time the Foreign Office looked on with a rising sense of alarm.

It was not as though Persia could be ignored. There was a growing interest in the geology of the area and, after Lord Curzon's famous 1903 visit to the Gulf, arrangements had been made for a survey of the region. Guy Pilgrim, the deputy superintendent of the Geological Survey of India, visited both sides of the Gulf during the 1904/5 season. British fears of French and Russian interest in Persia endured, and there was a strong feeling that the D'Arcy concession should not be allowed to fall into foreign hands. All these factors militated towards having a British oil company operating there; perhaps the party with most to gain from having a supply of Persian oil was the Admiralty, which was in need of new sources of fuel for the Royal Navy.

So it was that the Admiralty took up the baton, acting through its financial secretary Ernest Pretyman, and an 84-year-old wealthy Scottish-Canadian businessman, Lord Strathcona, who was to act as a figurehead for the venture. Pretyman brought a new player into the equation: the Glasgow-based Burmah Oil Company. The two companies were a good match: Burmah had a proven track record in the oil business through its oilfields in India and the Far East, while D'Arcy held access to potentially vast reservoirs of crude; Burmah was the prosperous oil company, D'Arcy the near-bankrupt investor. When Strathcona also offered to make a hefty financial contribution, the financial prospects looked even brighter.

Although the Royal Navy was a possible customer for Burmese oil, the Burmah directors were worried that their existing oilfields might not cope with the navy's demands, and that the Persian fields – if and when they came on stream – would flood the Indian market with cheap oil. It was far better, then, to use the Persian fields as a form of insurance against failure as well as a means of controlling the amount of oil on the market. Upon the British government giving an assurance that it would protect the oilfields, Burmah agreed to go ahead. On 20 May 1905 Burmah bought D'Arcy's rights in the concession and the shares of the First Exploitation Company, which now became a subsidiary of Concessions Syndicate Ltd. With Lord Strathcona and Burmah as its main shareholders, the new company was to provide the finance for the future exploration and development of the concession; the Persian oil project was back on the rails again.

BASED ON THE REPORT of D'Arcy's geologist, W. H. Dalton, the drilling crew planned to move southeast to drill at Shardin, in Bakhtiari lands. Since they would encroach on the Bakhtiari winter grazing grounds in Khuzestan, it was the task of John Preece, the British consul in Isfahan, to smooth the way and obtain the consent of the tribal leaders. On 15 November 1905 the four Bakhtiari khans signed an agreement. Among the signatories was Sardar Assad, who was to play an important part in future events. The khans would receive £2,000 (£200,000 today) a year for the rent of the land and providing guards, £1,000 to protect a projected oil pipeline and a 3 per cent share in the company – a considerable reduction from the 20 per cent the khans had originally sought – once the oil started to flow. At last, in August 1906, drilling began at Shardin.

With guards to protect them, the drilling team toiled under the hot summer sun and froze in the snows of winter, and their horse and mule trains struggled up the mountain passes to the next wells to be drilled. Reynolds gained the trust of local chieftains, and the presence in the party of a doctor who tended to the needs of local people also helped improve relations: a ragged queue of tribespeople waiting for treatment outside the medical tent, its black goatskins flapping in the breeze, was a common sight. The doctor was not only required to dispense medicine and advice. Dr Morris Young, who arrived in 1907, was a skilled practitioner and moderator, acting as a calming influence on the khans.

Affairs were not entirely trouble-free, however. When the Persian government in Tehran denounced Preece's agreement with the khans, Sardar Assad backtracked, claiming that he knew nothing of business matters and had only signed it out of respect to the consul. The company had never been entirely at ease with the arrangement, with D'Arcy himself muttering that it was 'blackmail'.[6] In the field, security was often chaotic, with the tribes arguing between themselves, and logistical headaches and the harsh terrain only adding to the troubles. As equipment was transported through the tribal lands, there were incidents of petty theft and blackmail along the route. A few months after the arrival of Dr Young, the British government sent a detachment of Bengal Lancers under the command of Lieutenant Arnold Wilson to protect drilling operations and replace the Bakhtiari guards.

In the same year, while drilling operations were still ongoing at Shardin, Reynolds revisited Maidan-i-Naftun, where he had seen oil seepages three years before. He prepared a report that was enthusiastically received in London by Sir Boverton Redwood. Accordingly, the company decided to drill the next wells at Masjid-i-Suleiman and an access road was built through the mountains. Once the two test wells at Shardin had proved dry, drilling began at the new site in January 1908, but four months later there was still no sign of subterranean oil and the syndicate was ready to admit defeat. Reynolds received a telegram from the head office in Glasgow ordering him to stop work, dismiss the staff, dismantle anything worth keeping and come home. He delayed responding, claiming that telegrams were unreliable, or perhaps through sheer cussedness – for whatever reason – he decided to wait for the orders to be confirmed by post.

He struck lucky. Early in the morning of 26 May he was woken by a dull rumble and looked out of his tent to see oil spurting out above the derrick to a height of 24 metres (80 ft), drenching the site in oil. He was witnessing the birth of the first commercial oilfield in the Middle East. According to legend, Arnold Wilson immediately jumped on his horse and galloped to Ahwaz in order to telegraph the news to the Foreign Office in London. The drillers were less than impressed: the first question they asked was whether it was time to go home.

Sardar Assad was just stepping off a boat at Marseilles on his latest European tour when he first heard of the oil strike. Despite the earlier

The first oil strike in the Middle East, at Masjid-i-Suleiman in 1908.

disruptions, the Bakhtiari, like the British, would profit from the flow of oil, the former enjoying the wealth that came from their share of the revenues and the latter receiving their precious oil. At some point, however, the company would have to choose between local chieftains and central government.

In 1909 the Bakhtiari tribes took the city of Isfahan and marched on Tehran in support of an uprising against the shah known as the Constitutional Movement. Ostensibly this had nothing to do with the oilfield and was about securing greater freedoms from a dictatorial ruler, but the discovery of oil had given the autonomous khans a new-found confidence to take on Tehran. The shah was removed in favour of his young son, Ahmed Shah, and the *Majlis* was confirmed as the parliament of the country. Britain, fearing that renewed Russian influence in Persia might threaten its interests in India, lent its support to the new shah. Persian oil was, in the words of Winston Churchill, 'a prize from fairyland beyond our wildest dreams'.[7]

That fairy tale would have a dark side, though, and in these events the seeds of future trouble in the country's oil industry were sown. Oil would remain a difficult issue between the oil company, the Tehran government and the *Majlis* for many years to come. A distrust of the British, a feeling among Persians that they were not being treated fairly, reinforced by a strong sense of national pride, and the seemingly unbreakable hold that the British had over their oil industry, made for a volatile recipe.

The Constitutional Movement marked a high point of the khans' power and influence. Oil did not bring universal happiness to the Bakhtiari, who saw their incomes fall in the 1920s as various local activities such as guarding and tolls were taken over by a strengthening central government. Many families struggled to repay loans taken out when times were good. Sardar Assad, for one, had large gambling liabilities. The khans' oil revenues grew, but were not enough to release them from their indebtedness. In the end they would be abandoned by the oil company and forced to sell their oil shares to the Tehran government.[8] Sardar Assad, having risen to the post of minister of war under Reza Shah, ended his days in prison.

All that was yet to come. On 14 April 1909 the Anglo-Persian Oil Company, the forerunner of British Petroleum (BP), was registered with Lord Strathcona at the helm. The new company, in which Burmah held the majority of shares, bought up the Persian operation lock, stock and oil barrel: the concession itself, the First Exploitation Company and the Bakhtiari Oil Company (which had been created to distribute payments to the khans) were included in the deal. Boverton Redwood devised the geological puffery for the prospectus, declaring 'promising areas' in this 'unique concession'.[9] When shares in the company went on sale five days later, the Glasgow branch of the Bank of Scotland was overwhelmed by eager customers. It was not all good news, though. D'Arcy became an honorary director of the new company, but effectively had no influence on the board. George Reynolds was sacked in Persia two years later; he nevertheless went on to forge a notable career for himself in Venezuela.

Despite the glowing prospectus, Anglo-Persian's future was by no means assured. D'Arcy and his associates had already spent an estimated £400,000 (£43 million today) to get this far, and the cost of exploring and developing the concession would prove almost ruinous. As the company lurched towards its next financial crisis, an entirely different problem faced workers on the Masjid-i-Suleiman oilfield. Conditions were primitive: there were a few basic structures used for offices, workshops and dwellings, and caves cut into the hillside used for workers to shelter from the midday sun. The dispensary was attended by a long queue of local workers suffering from a variety of ailments, such as dysentery and malaria.

One aspect of the site was particularly striking: it was drowning in oil. As new wells were drilled, there was nowhere for the crude oil to go other than collecting in pools on the ground. A *Times* correspondent visiting the site in January 1910 described the following scene:

> Eight wells have been drilled to a depth varying between 300 ft. and 1,600 ft., and in some of them the pressure is so great that the oil spurts up between the ground and the iron casing. A large quantity now runs to waste, and in time of flood passes along the local streams and floats down the Karun in ugly brown floes.[10]

Fortunately, Burmah Oil had experience of building pipelines in difficult places, having completed a pipeline in Burma to its two refineries for the production of kerosene and paraffin wax for candles. Plans for a refinery on Abadan Island were formed, and Anglo-Persian set about building a 15-cm (6-in.) pipeline from the oilfields (known as 'Fields') to the site of the refinery, transporting pipes along the Karun River and then overland by mule train across the intervening hills.

By July 1911 the final 138-mile pipeline ran from Masjid-i-Suleiman via a pumping station at Tembi to Abadan Island. But labour problems and disease dogged work on the new refinery, and costs were rising. Upon completion, the installation proved unreliable and produced oil that smelled of bad eggs due to its high sulphur content, which company scientists struggled to remove. One despairing director described the whole thing as a 'scrap heap'.[11]

Meanwhile Burmah had encouraged the use of managing agents to deal with local affairs in its oilfields, a practice that was replicated in Anglo-Persian's use of Lloyd, Scott & Co. as its managing agents in Persia. The system had more than a hint of empire about it, having been developed by European companies trading in the East over many years. Its application in Persia was a new complication since the agents brought no technical skill to the business, providing only an extra layer of management sandwiched between the men on the ground and the board in Great Britain. These 'gentlemen' agents remained a feature of local operations until they were terminated a decade later, by which time Anglo-Persian had grown up and eclipsed its ageing parent, Burmah Oil. That, though, was for later; for now money was running out and things looked bleak for the company.

Bakhtiaris laying pipes in Persia, *c.* 1912.

There was only so much that the directors could do to save the situation, and they were fast running out of options. They had aimed to make Anglo-Persian a going concern only to find themselves on the brink of failure. Others waited in the wings for the outcome. In the event, it would take the meeting of two minds to bring the great project to fruition.

'THEY'RE ALL BITTEN! Internal Combustion Engines Rabies!' was how John ('Jackie') Arbuthnot Fisher described the enthusiasm of his colleagues on the Royal Commission on Fuel and Engines.[12] As First Sea Lord, Fisher had been an early proponent of converting naval ships to run on oil rather than coal, an idea that he shared with the First Lord of the Admiralty, Winston Churchill.

In May 1912 Churchill pursued Fisher to Naples in order to persuade him to come out of retirement and return to London to head the commission. 'This liquid fuel problem has got to be solved,' Churchill told Fisher, knowing that it was a challenge that the energetic admiral would naturally relish.[13] The commission was the outcome of a long-standing debate in government and naval circles, one that had engaged the far-sighted Fisher from the start, the case of oil-versus-coal. Converting the Royal Navy's ships to oil would bring great advantages over coal-powered ships, such as increased speed, convenience and endurance, and render obsolete the numerous coaling stations dotted about the world.

It was a daunting task. The first attempt to switch from coal to oil had been a disaster: the ship used for the experiment, HMS *Hannibal*, was enveloped in black smoke caused by faulty burners. Once the technical problems were overcome, the whole issue of oil supply then had to be addressed – where might Britain obtain the necessary supplies of crude oil safely, reliably and cheaply? The only domestic source of oil was in Scotland where it was distilled from oil shales, but these were becoming less productive and more expensive to process. A new and reliable source of fuel oil would have to be found abroad.

Once the Royal Commission had decided in favour of oil, Churchill appointed Rear Admiral Edmond Slade to lead a fact-finding mission to Persia. Slade reported on a 'sound concession' that could be exploited to a 'gigantic' extent.[14] If the oilfields were under British control and kept out of foreign hands, the admiral opined, the navy's future oil supplies would be assured. Slade recommended that Anglo-Persian was the ideal vehicle for such a scheme. Although its chairman, Sir Charles Greenway, had already made a deal with Royal Dutch Shell to market its oil, the company was still in contention for an Admiralty contract, and the quality issues that had dogged the Abadan refinery appeared to have been ironed out.

In May 1914, therefore, the British government acquired a 51 per cent stake in Anglo-Persian for £2 million and, by a secret contract, the Admiralty would receive fuel oil at a preferential rate for twenty years. Parliament approved the agreement the following month. Slade was one of two government-appointed directors on the board, and then its vice chairman, carrying a veto over non-commercial matters. As it happened, none of these directors ever exercised their veto during the long period of state involvement.

For the company itself, the deal was a golden opportunity to start expanding its refining activities and to branch out into transport and marketing operations; it also lifted the threat of bankruptcy and a takeover by Royal Dutch Shell, at least for the time being. Sir Marcus Samuel, the founder of Shell, could barely conceal his bitterness at the outcome: 'It is a curious moment that the Admiralty have chosen to subsidise a company operating in a foreign country, and where their own advisers tell them that they are subject to very grave disturbances on the part of the natives.'[15]

It was a moot point. During the First World War a number of the Bakhtiari tribes sided with the Germans, providing an escort for the German agent Herr Wilhelm Wassmuss. In February 1915 the Bawi tribe sabotaged Anglo-Persian's oil pipeline to the Abadan refinery. This brought British troops to Khuzestan, another sign in nationalist eyes of Britain's military and economic dominance of the country. The company's claim for damages and loss of profits from the damaged pipeline opened up a long-running battle with the Tehran government over finances generally, and stoked a suspicion among Persian politicians that the company was short-changing the country.

In the drive to increase oil production during the war years, the Abadan plant was run to full capacity, and in the post-war years there was a series of strikes, which led to an 80 per cent pay rise and many Indian workers being replaced by Persians. The living conditions of local workers remained poor in comparison with those of British employees, however. This did not bode well for the company, but

Professor John Cadman being carried onto the Gulf shore during the Slade mission, 1914.

nationalists saw an opportunity for change. In the post-war years Persia was an independent country and, unlike Iraq and Syria, not mandated to Britain or France. This meant that other foreign oil companies could, in theory, apply for oil concessions. Perhaps here Anglo-Persian's monopoly might be broken but, as will emerge, when the theory was put to the test in the 1920s, a rather different picture appeared.

TWO

CIRCLING SKIES, 1918–45

I N 1926 SIR JOHN Cadman was riding on a journey from Masjid-i-Suleiman to Isfahan when he came to the Tembi River. The surrounding plain was dominated by 'the great rounded mass of the Asmari Mountain', from which the oil-producing rock formation took its name, and was dotted with the black tents of Bakhtiari tribesmen and their herds of sheep and cattle.[1] At sunset his party reached their camping ground at the foot of the mountain and, after dinner, they looked across the dark hills into the distance where a brilliant red glow lit up the northwestern sky, the reflected light of flaring gas from the oilfields.

There seemed to be no escape from this apparition. On another occasion, a great storm of wind and rain burst out, clearing the sky and leaving the lights of the oilfields plainly visible, even though they were 80 kilometres (50 miles) away. Where once there had been darkness, there was light. Here was the great aorta of the British Empire pumping lifeblood into the ships of the Royal Navy. Cadman – a tall, professorial figure – was a member of the Anglo-Persian board and soon to become its chairman. Perhaps at these moments he had time to reflect on his company's achievements, from the early days of the D'Arcy concession to the construction of the refinery at Abadan. Surely he would have called it a great endeavour, but it was also a tragedy in the making.

Persia was a nation with a proud heritage, its empires now crumbled yet not forgotten. In the early twentieth century, under the Qajar shahs, the country had slipped into poverty and its political life was dominated by Anglo-Russian rivalry for influence and control. The

British hardwired the D'Arcy concession to their imperial ambitions, making oil their central concern and restricting the shahs to a paltry 16 per cent of profits; and they created many enemies in the process. Then, while Britain dominated the oil business in the southwest corner of the country and was influential in the east, Russian influence suddenly fell away after the Bolshevik revolution in 1917. The Soviet government abandoned its claims to northern Persia and wrote off the country's debt. The withdrawal of British troops from Baku in 1918 signalled a lack of long-term ambition over the Russian oilfields as Britain settled for the greater prize in Persia. Overall, these events left the British firmly in the driving seat with regard to Persian oil.

There was trouble ahead. In 1919, amid public unrest, the British attempted to dispense with the pretence of Persian autonomy and impose military rule. The Anglo-Persian Agreement, signed by a weakened shah and immediately opposed by the largely toothless *Majlis*, allowed the British to take charge of the army, treasury and communications. In these circumstances, the appearance of the Americans with their Monroe Doctrine and commitment to democracy chimed well with the Persians. As the chargé d'affaires at the u.s. mission in Tehran would observe:

> From the Persian point of view, neither concessions nor loans are as important as American financial and other advisers whose presence it is believed would protect Persia against unfair political influence, even under an all-British loan.[2]

An American, Morgan Shuster, was a financial adviser to the Persian government and held in high esteem. In broad terms, the United States was well regarded at this time.

✶ Britain had the resources, military might and know-how to dominate the Persian oil business for many years to come, but the appearance of the Americans, much like their entrance onto the Iraqi stage, set alarm bells ringing in the corridors of Whitehall. Foreign Secretary Lord Curzon was clearly unaware of the irony when he described Standard Oil of New Jersey (Jersey Standard) as 'that omnivorous organization [that] was endeavouring to secure a foothold on Persian soil'.[3] He warned the Persian minister in London against any attempt to introduce the company to Persia. To some extent that was bluster since Anglo-Persian would soon be discussing with Jersey Standard

En route to Isfahan on the Anglo-Persian's main road to the oilfields, 1926.

the possibility of joint working in the north of the country, if only as a means to control American involvement there. All the same, it was Curzon's view that set the scene, reflecting British antipathy towards similar approaches by U.S. oil companies in Iraq and Palestine.

Deep-seated feeling of dislike; aversion

The post-war years brought a fresh drive by U.S. companies to extend their reach abroad. Jersey Standard vied for oil supplies with its great rival Royal Dutch Shell; these two firms were the dominant oil companies in the world at the time. Shell's fortunes, based on its Dutch East Indies oilfields, were in the ascendant. But a favourable deal with the French government had brought a forceful reaction from the Americans, who launched a counteroffensive against both Shell and Anglo-Persian. They had the support of the U.S. administration, which sought equal access for American firms to oil resources across the globe; this was the so-called 'Open Door' principle. Jersey Standard's push was to have some success, forcing a deregulation of the French oil market and giving them access to the Dutch East Indies and Iraq. Their attempt to enter the Persian arena was another story.

Rising in power or influence

A U.S. ... rm in ...eign affairs ...r a policy ...tablished late 19th nd into ...rly 20th entury

It began in August 1920 when the U.S. firms were invited to bid for concessions in northern Persia. Officials passed the invitation on to Jersey Standard, which took up the challenge and opened talks in Tehran. But it soon became apparent that this was not going to be a straightforward exercise in foreign relations. Another U.S. firm, Sinclair Oil, declared an interest, immediately presenting Jersey Standard with a rival bid and ensuring that the State Department could not provide any meaningful support: tied by a policy of neutrality and the 'Open Door', officials were unable to favour one firm over the other. This was a major disadvantage since the British Foreign Office would single-mindedly push the interests of their protégé, the Anglo-Persian Oil Company, in any negotiations that might follow.

The First World War had demonstrated the importance of Persian oil to Britain, and the British were unlikely to allow the Americans in without stiff resistance. At face value, Britain's financial clout gave her the whip hand vis-à-vis the Persian government, outweighing any financial inducements that the u.s. firms could muster. But relations had entered choppy waters. The Persian government hired a British adviser, Sydney Armitage-Smith, to review the D'Arcy concession, which was riddled with ambiguities. He in turn hired an accountant who discovered that the company had underpaid royalties. Anglo-Persian settled by paying £1 million (£41 million today) in compensation; the debt was paid, but the mistrust remained. In December 1920 the Armitage-Smith Agreement confirmed Tehran's 16 per cent share of the company's net profits on all operations involving Persian oil.

As for the Americans, Anglo-Persian officials thought they had a degree of leverage against them. The Khostaria concession covering an area in northern Persia and originally granted to a Russian, Arkady Khostaria, was supposedly owned by Anglo-Persian. Although the legality of the concession was disputed (it had never been ratified by the Persian government), the British still insisted that it was sound. In this they had the support of the Foreign Office, which informed the u.s. Secretary of State via its Washington embassy that, since the Khostaria concession belonged to Anglo-Persian, Jersey Standard's bid was unlawful.

Nothing was ever certain in the circling skies of Persian politics, however. In 1921 a coup brought Reza Khan Pahlavi to power. Having the tacit support of the British, he had arrived in Tehran with about 3,000 men and arrested the prime minister and his cabinet, and in due course persuaded the debauched and ineffectual Ahmed Shah – the last of the Qajar rulers – to go abroad on the pretext of his health. Reza Khan did not stop there. After the coup, he ousted the new prime minister, the pro-British Zia Tabatabai, and eventually took over the office himself. In the space of two years the 45-year-old outsider had become commander of the Persian army, minister of war and prime minister.

For a man from a relatively modest background, having been born into a military family, this was a remarkable achievement. His rising influence would become manifest in every area of public life, including oil negotiations. In the tradition of the great rulers of the past, Reza Khan ruled Persia with a rod of iron and ruthlessly suppressed any domestic opposition. His general appearance reinforced the impression of strongman and dictator: tall, sullen, with a large nose and grizzled hair. That, at least, was how the poet and traveller Vita Sackville-West saw him, as 'a Cossack trooper'.[4]

For the time being, the matter of oil rights grumbled on. Public opinion was mixed, with a mistrust of foreign interference tempered by the idyll of the Americans 'with their flourishing wealth'.[5] In November 1921 the *Majlis* granted Jersey Standard the right to negotiate a fifty-year concession with 15 per cent of gross – as opposed to net – profits. Clearly, Persian politicians had realized the shortcomings of the D'Arcy agreement and were determined to break the company's monopoly; it was a signal that the board of Anglo-Persian would ignore at its peril.

Nevertheless, it was evident that Jersey Standard was struggling. An American company operating in Persia faced formidable obstacles: Anglo-Persian controlled the pipe-laying rights and therefore access to the Gulf, which was the only realistic oil outlet for any oil discovered. Routing the oil through the Soviet Union was not an option because the country was still perceived to be unstable after the Bolshevik Revolution of 1917 and essentially anti-business. Britain, France and Russia strongly opposed the concession. And, as a precondition of the concession, Standard was required to loan $10 million to the Persian government, but was not prepared to do so until a full concession was granted.

Faced with these difficulties, the company did a deal that reflected the realities of working in the Middle East of the 1920s. There was a rapprochement with the British across the region: in return for American companies being allowed to participate in Iraq and Standard Oil of New York (Socony) being allowed back into Palestine, Jersey Standard agreed to work with Anglo-Persian in the northern provinces of Persia. It was a pragmatic solution to a knotty problem, but unlikely to win any plaudits in the *Majlis* and beyond.

Indeed, this was where Standard's Persian scheme hit the buffers. As the company was now identified with Anglo-Persian, so the initial warmth of the Persian press turned towards hostility, one newspaper describing Britain and the United States as 'worshippers of gold and stranglers of the weak'.[6] In February 1922 the *Majlis* rejected the proposal. This in turn presented Sinclair, which had been biding its time, with an opening. Despite the fact that the British government strongly backed Anglo-Persian (and by association, Standard), the strength of Anglophobia among the deputies of the *Majlis* worked in Sinclair's favour. And yet the deputies were in no hurry and discussions dragged on, descending into chaos as allegations of bribery filled the air.

Eventually in June 1923 the *Majlis* arrived at a decision. It would offer terms to whichever of the two American companies was prepared to accept them: a forty- to fifty-year concession in four out of five northern provinces for a minimum 20 per cent share of the profits and a loan of $10 million. Jersey Standard dropped out of the running, leaving Sinclair free to make a slightly amended offer. At this point, Reza Khan was prime minister and the *Majlis* moved swiftly to accept the company's offer; a new concession was signed on 20 December.

To get around the logistical problem of exporting the oil, Sinclair planned to transport it across the Caucasus to the Black Sea; the company had good relations with the Soviet government and believed this to be a viable option. Meanwhile Jersey Standard found itself defending the legality of the Khostaria concession as a means of blocking Sinclair, but then another fault line opened up: back in the United States Sinclair was implicated in the notorious Teapot Dome scandal, having used bribery to gain a domestic concession, and was now accused of bribing Persian officials.

Heads were spinning. Whether or not the allegations were true, press speculation made it more difficult for Sinclair to raise money, thus jeopardizing the $10 million loan and the concession itself. For many Persians, the mere suggestion of bribery was outrageous and, assisted by a seething media, engaged a strong sense of national honour, inflaming feelings against the company. It has also been said that Sinclair's good relations with the Soviets relied on a promise to secure recognition for the Bolshevik regime in the United States: this was not forthcoming, and hence the scheme to export oil through the Caucasus was in doubt. But for the *Majlis*, the whole bribery storm smacked of British intrigue, and the deputies moved quickly to confirm the terms of the concession, apart from the loan provision.

Sinclair executives were in a quandary: should they stay or cut and run? Then, unexpectedly, they were presented with a pretext to withdraw from Persia, even if it was in tragic circumstances. The incident seemed unrelated to oil at first. In June 1924 there was a rumour that a Persian of the Bahai faith had been blinded at a well in central Tehran. The well became a shrine (*saqqa-khaneh*) visited by Muslims who started anti-Bahai demonstrations. Another rumour then circulated that Bahais had poisoned the well, bringing even larger crowds and great excitability to the vicinity. One Friday morning in July, Robert W. Imbrie, the u.s. vice-consul in Tehran, and Melvin Seymour, an oilman, visited the location to take photographs for the National Geographic Society. As they returned to their carriage a shout went up that they were the Bahais who had poisoned the well. A great tumult ensued, and the Americans were dragged from the carriage and assailed with sticks and stones. They were taken to hospital, but the crowd renewed its attack and killed Imbrie in an operating theatre. Seymour survived after the crowd missed him alone in a side ward. In the confused aftermath, it was said that the incident had been motivated by oil, with the mob mistakenly believing it had attacked Ralph Soper, the Sinclair representative. Taking the hint, Soper left Tehran ten days later.

A decision of the Soviet government to block the export of oil through its territory was the final straw for the beleaguered company; in 1925 Sinclair withdrew from the concession, and Standard followed them two years later. As much as that left the field open to Anglo-Persian, it also removed distractions and allowed the spotlight of Persian frustration to focus once more on the company and the unpopular D'Arcy concession.

IN 1926 A BRITISH spy, Reginald Teague-Jones (alias Ronald Sinclair, no relation to the oil company), was travelling across Persia in his dusty Model A Ford on a journey from Beirut to India. It was the first occasion that a single driver had attempted the route. Having combined an economic study of Persia with his travels, Teague-Jones's real mission was to study and report to a group of British businessmen about trading conditions in Persia.

Curiously, he was in Tehran on 25 April when Reza Khan was crowned and the modern state of Persia came into being. The Western community in the city, such as it was, was caught up in the preparations. Here he found the British chargé d'affaires, Harold Nicolson, and his wife, Vita Sackville-West, helping to design symbols and heraldry for the ceremony, with Vita occasionally visiting the throne room to criticize the shades of its peach-coloured, distempered walls.

Having abandoned his republican ideas in the face of opposition from clerics, Reza Khan was now invited by the *Majlis* to assume the Peacock Throne, proclaiming himself Reza Shah. He had broken the hereditary continuity of the Qajar line and was about to create his own dynasty. Nevertheless, he was at pains to emphasize the link between his reign and the rulers of the past, hoping to acquire greater legitimacy by doing so. He also had the reputation of being a ruthless man, a shah who would not hesitate to move against foreigners in general and Anglo-Persian in particular. He might have owed the success of his coup to British money, but since then he had achieved supreme power through his own efforts. Beyond keeping the oil revenues flowing, he had no particular affiliation to Britain.

In Tehran life went on much as before. Camels arrived with boxes and bales from Baghdad and petrol from the south, with the words

Reza Shah in military uniform, *c.* 1926.

'highly inflammable' on the crates they carried. Although many miles from the flag-decked streets of Tehran, the grimy, smoke-filled oilfields to the south were the key to it all. Reza Shah was well aware of their importance to the economy and realized that any action against Anglo-Persian had to strike a balance between the demands of the reformers and the progress of oil operations in the country. Needing money to finance a programme of public works, including the construction of roads and railways, the new shah directed his government to open discussions with Anglo-Persian and renegotiate the 1901 agreement, that infamous 'scrap of paper'.

Four years later and they were still talking. The Great Depression had begun to bite and royalties from the oilfields fell by £1 million. In protest, the Persian government broke off the talks and promised a set of counter-proposals, but none was forthcoming. Reza Shah was growing increasingly frustrated. When his visit to the oilfields and refinery was arranged, he flatly refused to go. He attended a meeting of his council of ministers and berated the court minister Abdul Husayn Khan Teymurtash, who was leading the talks, for not bringing them to a conclusion. In a fit of pique, it is said, the shah threw a file on the negotiations into a burning fire.

That was the least of it. On 27 November 1932 Reza Shah cancelled the D'Arcy concession, effectively ending Anglo-Persian's right to operate the oilfields. Exactly where this left the company and the British government was to be seen: perhaps the company could continue pumping oil and Whitehall could send in the troops, but these measures hardly amounted to a long-term solution. There was a mulishness about the company that seemed to defy common sense. *The Times* was only making an obvious point when it later noted:

> A state which has just emerged from a secular torpor which is
> fired by an ardent desire to make the most of its resources, and
> is ruled by an energetic reformer, cannot be denied the right
> to review the terms of a concession granted a generation ago.[7]

[handwritten annotation: A state of physical or mental inactivity; lethargy]

The company pressed on – protests were made, diplomatic remedies sought. The dispute went to the Council of the League of Nations for arbitration, only to be referred back to the parties for more talks that became bogged down. On 11 April 1933 Sir John Cadman arrived at the shah's palace in Tehran in order to resolve the matter once and for all.

The atmosphere in the city was tense. The press was hostile and ministers, fearing for their necks, did not dare to be seen talking to the British delegation; at meetings they sat around like statues while the shah held forth. Almost two weeks later the talks were deadlocked and the engines of Cadman's aircraft were warming up for his departure. Finally, an agreement was reached. This fixed the Persian government's royalty at an annual minimum of £750,000 (£49 million today). The company was required to pay a minimum annual sum of £225,000 for the first fifteen years of the new concession, and £300,000 for the next fifteen while exempted from taxation. Other claims were settled, the concession area was reduced to 100,000 square miles and the concession itself would run for sixty years. Finally, the company's name was to be changed from the Anglo-Persian to the Anglo-Iranian Oil Company, recognizing the official name of the country, Iran.

The company might have put a gloss on the outcome, calling it just and fair, but Cadman had different thoughts, writing in his diary: 'I felt we had been pretty well plucked.'[8] The new agreement settled the arrangements between Iran and Anglo-Iranian for the remainder of the shah's reign and saw a major increase in state revenues. The surrender of territory was not such a hardship for the company, since the new concession area would still be larger than the United Kingdom. For others, the outcome was not so good. Teymurtash met an untimely end, having lost his office, been put on trial for corruption and then murdered in his prison cell.

The shah became very grand, being proclaimed as 'Most Lofty of Living Men' among sundry other titles.[9] In 1938, at celebrations of the twelfth anniversary of his accession, he stood and acknowledged a dutiful procession of diplomats, ministers, army officers and notables, all bowing their heads as they traipsed past the seventeenth-century Peacock Throne. The shah was at the height of his powers and had embarked on an ambitious programme of public spending, including the building of the Trans-Iranian railway, all financed by oil revenues.

Relations with Britain were in decline, despite Cadman's best efforts to keep them on an amicable footing. The shah took slights easily and did not quickly forgive criticisms of his country in the British press, although Cadman was able to persuade Geoffrey Dawson, the editor of *The Times*, to print a series of favourable articles about Iran. But Cadman's health was failing – he was preparing to hand over to others in the company and his ability to influence relations between Britain and Iran was fading.

In the same month as the anniversary celebrations, Tehran Airport saw the arrival of a large Junkers monoplane with swastikas on its tail, inaugurating Lufthansa's new commercial route between Iran and the rest of the world. This was more than simply a flight, though, since the plane's arrival marked a leaning towards the fascist nations of Germany and Italy; Lufthansa had gained the air route in the face of stiff opposition from Britain's Imperial Airways. Ships were ordered from Italy, with Italian officers being dispatched to train Iranians in their use. Under a clearing agreement, German goods began appearing in Iran and one hundred German warplanes were delivered for the Iranian Air Force.

There were many who thought that the shah was a charismatic leader on the verge of true greatness – but in reality, he was heading for a fall.

AMID THE DARKER UNDERCURRENTS of the Iranian oil business, Arkady Khostaria cuts something of a dash. A Russian from Georgia, quaintly described by the Russian consulate as a 'gentleman' of that province, he was a wheeler-dealer and an agent for Russian interests in Persia.[10] He also had an eye for the exotic: when Reginald Teague-Jones visited Tbilisi in 1922, he stayed with Khostaria and noted that his house was decorated with the heads of a leopard and an elephant ordered from a London taxidermist. Apart from the Khostaria concession, his dealings included the Kavir-i Khurian concession in north-central Iran for ten rudimentary sulphur and oil mines that had originally been granted by royal firman in 1880 to an Iranian official. Khostaria acquired a part interest in that concession through some of the heirs of the first owner, and hoped to develop or sell it on.

In 1924 the *Majlis* decided to regularize various claims for oil rights throughout the country and, during the bureaucratic process that followed, only one out of 23 requests was registered – the concession for Kavir-i Khurian (probably on the payment of large sums of money). It appears that the Ministry of Public Works then sold the concession to Khostaria, who transferred it to the Russians.

Despite protests from the heirs to the original concession and Anglo-Persian, which regarded the area as within the D'Arcy concession, a syndicate of Iranian and Russian shareholders was formed to develop the Kavir-i Khurian concession. Khostaria, who was on its board, was highly active on behalf of the new company and persuaded the Russian Bank to furnish the bulk of its capital. He offered a holding in the company to French and Italian interests, resulting in a party of geologists being sent to examine the concessionary area. Their report was unfavourable, even if a prominent Soviet geologist had different ideas. Between 1925 and 1932 two wells were drilled without any success and the concession remained unproductive at the outbreak of the Second World War.

A Franco-Belgian syndicate began negotiating for a concession in northern Iran in 1927 and initiated a survey, the results of which led to the creation of a new company, Société Franco-Persane de Recherches. A party of geologists and engineers was dispatched and a shallow well drilled, a few miles from the Caspian coast at Naft Chal. Later that year, however, all operations ceased because of 'difficulties' encountered with the Persian and Soviet governments.[11]

In 1937 the Amiranian Oil Company, a U.S. firm based in Delaware, gained a concession for northern and eastern Iran for a period of fifty years. This was abandoned after two years, the company having spent $2 million during that time. Its geologists examined some promising indications of petroleum in one province and less encouraging seepages in another. Although the company intended to drill, it abandoned its plans because of the difficulty and expense of developing such a remote area, and the high cost of marketing any oil that might be found. In May 1939 a Dutch firm, the Algemeene Exploratie Maatschappij, obtained an exploration licence for the five northern provinces. The outbreak of war, however, suspended operations and the licence was cancelled in 1944.

Anglo-Iranian went from a faltering start to growing strength. At first there were concerns about how long the Masjid-i-Suleiman field would last. The Hungarian geologist Professor Hugo de Böckh was asked to choose new drilling sites, resulting in the discovery of the Haft Kel field, some 56 kilometres (35 miles) south-southeast of Masjid, which started producing from six wells in 1930. Production was limited to these two fields before the outbreak of war, though four more oilfields were discovered for future exploitation. In the interim, the settlement around the refinery at Abadan had grown into a small city of some 100,000 people, housing British staff in well-appointed houses and Iranian workers in less salubrious accommodation. A form of segregation applied to the population, with Iranians barred from certain amenities such as shops and cinemas.

Anglo-Persian geologist G. M. Shaw plane-table mapping in the field with the Asmari Mountain in the background, 1925.

Writers such as Stephen Longrigg would describe how well the workers were treated in comparison with their agrarian counterparts, and point to the company's plans to bring skilled Iranians into the industry, a policy of 'Iranization'. Yet this was not a serious attempt to transfer the wealth of the company to the Iranian people, and the fact remained that the major profits of the business flowed with the oil out of the country. Longrigg betrayed little conviction when he wrote: 'The training of Iranians for higher posts in the company was encouraged by common sense, by economy, and by policy.'[12]

ON 22 JUNE 1941, when the Germans launched Operation Barbarossa and invaded Russia, the picture in Iran changed. Britain and Russia were already deeply anxious about Reza Shah, who had refused to expel German personnel from Iran with the result that their agents were still active – there were some 2,000–3,000 German 'tourists' in the country at that time.[13] Faced with the German advance into Ukraine, Whitehall and the Kremlin hurriedly signed an Anglo-Soviet Agreement for Mutual Assistance. On 25 August their troops crossed into Iran, the British coming from the west to seize the oilfields and the Russians moving down from the north. Within three days the allies had declared a ceasefire and installed a new government in Tehran. The shah abdicated in favour of his son, Mohammad Reza Pahlavi, and went into exile.

British troops at the Abadan refinery, 1941.

Reza Shah, who died in Johannesburg in 1944, was a mixed blessing for the country. His rule was an absolute one and was remembered as a time when democracy was suppressed and nationalists went into hiding. His departure was greeted with relief and celebration in many quarters. He was criticized for the terms of the 1933 agreement with Anglo-Persian, especially for the extension of the concession for sixty years. Of the legendary incident when he threw a file about the oil negotiations on the fire, it was said – somewhat implausibly – that he had done this in order to cover up evidence of his own collusion with the British.

Yet Reza Shah imparted a degree of security to a country once wracked by division and tribal rivalry. If he did not exactly make the trains run on time, he did bring Western modernization in the form of roads and railways, and reformed the banking system. Whether that was a good thing is still debated today. At least, when he was removed from the political scene, the nationalists emerged from the shadows, blinking in the light of a new dawn.

THREE

INTO THE GREAT UNKNOWN, 1945–71

I N THE SPRING OF 1946, as the snow still lay thick in the mountains above Tehran, a dangerous stand-off began. The Second World War had ended six months before, yet the Red Army remained in northern Iran, despite an agreement made in 1943 to withdraw its troops. The Soviet Union demanded oil rights and supported dissident groups seeking to establish independent states in the provinces of Azerbaijan and the Kurdish republic of Mahabad. In April, amid American protests, the Soviets departed on the promise of an oil concession for the area. In 1947, however, the deputies of the *Majlis* debated the issue and refused to ratify the deal, and the Iranian army defeated the dissident forces.

Despite the international ramifications of these events, the real winner was Iran; and it was in this victory that another idea took root. Their success in thwarting the Soviets without incurring any retaliation led the deputies to turn their minds again to the Anglo-Iranian concession. In October they passed a 'single article measure' that effectively scuppered the proposed Russian concession and flagged up the possibility of attacking the 1933 agreement:

> In all cases where the rights of the Iranian nation in respect of the country's natural resources, whether underground or otherwise, have been impaired, particularly in regard to the southern oil, the Government is required to enter into such negotiations and take such measures as are necessary to regain the national rights and inform the *Majlis* of the result.[1]

Qajar Dynasty; Irani royalty from the Qajar tribe, which ruled Iran from 1789-1925.

...ians may have inserted this provision in order to ...ir treatment of Britain and Russia, the reference to ... highly significant in the atmosphere prevailing at

The nationalist movement was gaining momentum. Its fortunes had been variable in the past, often rising and falling with the character of a particular shah – was he a reformer, a suppressor or simply weak? The strongest shah of recent times had departed and his son, the unimpressive Mohammad Reza Shah, sat on the Peacock Throne. Now the nationalists were on an upward curve – those who once bided their time, waiting in the wings in exile or living in quiet rustication – had *being sent down or expelled temporarily* reappeared. Political parties flourished and the press revived.

A key figure in the debate was Mohammad Mossadegh. He was the son of a former finance minister and a Qajar dynasty princess. Born in 1882, he had studied abroad and was first elected to the *Majlis* at the age of 24. He served as finance minister and foreign minister before retiring from politics upon the inauguration of Reza Shah in 1925. In 1940 he was imprisoned and released without charge a few months later. His thirteen-year-old daughter witnessed his arrest, and was so traumatized that she spent the rest of her life in psychiatric hospitals. Although strong moral values and deep study of corporation, constitutional and parliamentary law in his thirties no doubt contributed to his anti-British attitude, it was an unbending passion to free his country from foreign interference that drove him on.

In 1944 he was elected as a deputy to the *Majlis* and three years later he was in the thick of the political scene. By his own account, he became a convert to the cause of oil nationalization when a radiant figure appeared to him in a dream. The figure, which he believed had been sent from God, told him to tear the chains from the feet of the Iranian people. In the broad sweep of Iranian history, such an image was entirely in context: there was numinous passion about the nationalist movement that defied the Western mind.

On a more immediate level, the oil refinery at Abadan defiantly spewed its smoke and sulphurous fumes across the surrounding landscape. The refinery, by this time the world's largest, was Britain's prime overseas investment and processing almost 17 million tons of crude oil at the war's end. And yet, while being a source of great pride to that country, it was a constant reminder to most Iranians that foreigners were controlling and depleting their country's natural resources. It was a recurring theme: they felt they were losing out, and assertions that they were getting a good deal were regarded at best as mere platitudes and at worst as downright lies.

Events elsewhere reinforced that impression. Royalties paid to neighbouring governments were greater than those paid to Iran – the Iraq Petroleum and the Kuwait Oil companies paid more than three times as much, for example. And then a *Majlis*-commissioned report found numerous shortcomings in the company's accounting practices, adding fuel to the fire. Actions and slights, some real and others imagined, conjured a vitriolic atmosphere of recrimination – and yet had little impact on the apparently serene progress of the mighty oil company.

The war years had been good for Anglo-Iranian, bringing a massive rise in oil production, while keeping it safe; and yet life for the ordinary Iranian was little changed. From 1930 to 1950 the company's gross profits rose from around £6.5 million to almost £85 million, with the Iranian government receiving a royalty of four shillings per ton of crude and 20 per cent of the dividend paid to the company's ordinary shareholders. By the late 1940s the company was the largest foreign investor in Iran, with a workforce and contractors of some 80,000 people.

The company had implemented training schemes for local workers, employing local artisans, technical and commercial staff, and was now considering workers' committees so that grievances could be aired; but it was not enough. The results of Iranization were slender: according to the *New York Times*, the highest an Iranian had risen in the managerial structure was to assistant general manager and, on the technical side, to assistant chief chemist; there were no Iranians on the board. True, between 1930 and 1938, Iranian nationals in the company increased from 2 to 12 per cent, although the British remained predominant in the higher management roles.

The company remained an enclave within the country, a state within a state, a colonial preserve in a foreign land where never the twain should meet. In the 1930s the company had attempted to address concerns about housing by building the Bawarda Estate, a garden city for supervisors, artisans and their families. Nevertheless, among the 200,000 Iranian oil workers, many of whom lived in the slums known as Kaghazabad, or 'Paper City', grievances against the company ran deep.

View of the Shatt al-Arab waterway with the Abadan refinery in the distance taken from the Bawarda Housing Estate, 1949.

On 2 July 1946 workers at the refinery went on strike over pay and working conditions. In response, the British encouraged Arab workers to join their own trade union and march against the protestors, with the inevitable clashes erupting between them: in one such disturbance, two workers died. The strike ended and some concessions were made, but the company was not overly distracted from the main business of extracting and exporting oil.

There was more to come. The nationalists possessed a steely resolve verging on fatalism; they would brook no compromise. The nationalization of the Mexican oil industry (albeit unsuccessful) in the 1930s had set a precedent that many Iranians would staunchly follow. Mossadegh and others were not too troubled by details such as Iran's lack of technical staff to run its own oil operations: the moral argument in favour of nationalization far outweighed any practical risks or economic harm. It was an attitude that would leave sober-minded shareholders of Anglo-Iranian spluttering in disbelief. What they missed was the simple fact that, in Mossadegh's mind, the dispute had nothing to do with oil; it was all about getting rid of the British from Iran.

In other circumstances, a more amenable approach might have brought a fair solution to the dispute. Set against the nationalists, however, was an Anglo-Iranian chairman who was determined not to budge. Sir William Fraser began his career in the Scottish shale oil industry before joining the Anglo-Persian board in 1924. He was very experienced, having been closely involved in the 1933 renegotiation of the D'Arcy concession.

On the other hand, Fraser did not always display the tact and diplomacy required to steer the company through the political rapids. His guiding principle was that commercial matters should be kept separate from political ones. In the swirling cross-currents of Iranian politics, it was presumptuous to think that the dispute could be confined to commercial issues, but such was his tenacity that a Foreign Office minister compared him to a 'Glasgow accountant'.[2] He was generally disliked in government circles, a feeling that was entirely mutual, with Fraser holding senior civil servants in contempt, dismissing them as 'West-End gentlemen'.[3] He gave the Americans short shrift, too.

At one level, then, we might see the dispute that followed as a contest between two main protagonists, the 'fire-eating' Fraser and the 'slippery' Mossadegh; but this would be a rather too convenient gloss.[4] The nationalist movement was hardly a homogenous mass of people seeking the same outcomes. While most could unite under the banner of oil nationalization, the commonality of their cause went no farther.

There were the clerics, conservative mullahs who opposed the liberalization of society and who had forced Reza Khan to abandon his plans for a republic. There were the secularists, those who sought to model Iranian society along Western lines. There were the communists united under the Tudeh Party, who were effectively supported and controlled from Moscow. And finally there were the armed forces and the police force, which contained various sections that were open to bribery and persuasion. In many ways, Iran was a political saboteur's dream, since these elements presented great opportunities for sowing discord and misrule – opportunities that a foreign agency such as the CIA would exploit to devastating effect.

Clearly the British government was not prepared to abandon its golden egg. By 1949 Anglo-Iranian was paying the UK Treasury £26 million in taxes and providing £92 million in foreign exchange, as well as supplying the Royal Navy with 85 per cent of its fuel at a discounted rate. Opportunities to soften the financial burden on Iran were ignored: when the u.s. government allowed a generous tax break to Aramco in order to mitigate the impact of a profit-sharing agreement with Saudi Arabia, the Treasury would not agree a similar provision for Anglo-Iranian.

As a result, the company maintained that it could not increase Iran's share of the oil revenues on account of its British tax liabilities. And when the pound was devalued, the Treasury refused to make up the subsequent loss to Iran's revenues. It certainly suited British politicians and officials to cast Fraser as the scapegoat, since Whitehall was implicated in the affair. The uk government remained the majority shareholder in the company, vetted the company's proposals before they were submitted to Iran and was nominally involved in the management of the company. Even so, by taking the official line that the Iranian negotiations were strictly commercial and to be settled between the parties, Whitehall could maintain a degree of independence – or virtue – if things turned sour.

For their part, the Americans had no particular desire to rescue Anglo-Iranian from its troubles. Any pressure from u.s. firms to participate in Iranian oil had dissipated since oil discoveries in Iraq, Saudi Arabia and Kuwait. Whereas the sympathies of President Harry Truman and his administration (1945–53) might incline towards nationalism vis-à-vis imperialism, their main focus was on preventing the spread of global communism. In this regard, Iran, with its northern border fronting the Soviet Union, was considered a prime hot spot. Washington was quick to read a communist plot into the events of 1946, and stepped up its military and financial aid to Tehran accordingly. The Americans were not completely oblivious to the oil dispute, naturally, and looked on with exasperation at Anglo-Iranian's intransigence towards Iranian demands. But an Iran without Anglo-Iranian was one thing; an Iran under communism was quite another.

It is often said that this was Mossadegh's bluff, playing up fears of communism in the expectation that the Americans would step in to support Iran once the British had gone; if that were the case, he was seriously mistaken.

IN 1949 WATER RAN through Tehran along the *jube* system, a network of open water channels that began as fresh clear streams in the mountains and turned muddy brown as they flowed alongside the streets. The northern flank of the city rising up the mountainside was mostly open ground and the southern part was a swarming slum. The summer heat was oppressive, reaching temperatures of 48°c at midday, and visiting officials could find no relief in air conditioning, which was not available then. 118.4°F

Beyond the confines of the u.s. embassy, Presbyterian preachers dominated a small American community and freely travelled the countryside. It was a time when the United States was still respected in Iran, and against this background Washington entered the fray as a self-professed honest broker, hoping, in the words of one diplomat, to 'reconcile logic and feelings'.[5] It was a worthy ambition, but a fatuous one, too. As events turned out, it was not long before 'Yankee go home!' slogans were appearing on the walls of the capital.

The Anglo-Iranian talks were going nowhere. In response to Iranian demands for a revision of the 1933 agreement, a document entitled the Supplemental Oil Agreement had been drawn up, agreed with the Iranian government, and signed off by the finance minister. This would have guaranteed a doubling of the country's income over a three-year period, but the *Majlis* oil committee refused to endorse it on the basis that it did not serve the country's best interests. When it came before the *Majlis*, the deputies used delaying tactics to make sure it did not pass before the end of the parliamentary term. A frustrated shah responded by priming the *Majlis* with his own supporters for its next term, but this only prompted widespread civil unrest that forced him to back down and cancel the results of the election he had so obviously rigged.

Manucher Farmanfarmaian, the shah's petroleum minister and author of an autobiography that described these events, felt everyone except the shah was to blame. But clearly the shah had more than a walk-on part: he was no longer the marginal figure that the British had been reluctant to back in 1941. He was now aligned with their interests, and eager to seize back power from the political parties whenever he could: the failure of an attempt on his life in 1949, for example, was a pretext for suppressing the Tudeh Party.

Since the only real power he possessed was his command of the armed forces, it was only natural that the shah should seek a military solution to the wave of popular unrest that confronted him. He persistently asked the United States for military hardware; his particular obsession was tanks. The strategy did not impress the Secretary of State, Dean Acheson, who considered that economic and social reforms should take priority, drawing a parallel with recent civil war in China where the superior forces of Chiang Kai-shek had lost soldiers through lack of morale. There was no agreement, and the shah left Washington in December 1949 with only a vague promise that the Americans would look into the matter of military aid.

At this juncture it was apparent that the Supplemental Oil Agreement was in deep trouble. Opposition in the *Majlis* had melded together under the leadership of Mossadegh, who was now 67 years old and the leader of a new group, the National Front. He commanded wide and enthusiastic support among the population, possessing a charisma that belied his appearance as a bald, sickly old man who was prone to weeping and taking to his bed. His tactics often perplexed visiting diplomats, but behind Mossadegh's idiosyncrasies lay an iron determination that would not buckle or break whatever the pressures on him.

Pitched against the nationalists was the shah's choice of prime minister, General Ali Razmara, who was a hardliner in the mould of Reza Shah. He also possessed a degree of finesse not found in his role model: brutal and tough yet educated, he had a well-developed understanding of international politics. He worked closely with Max Thornburg, a former Standard Oil executive with an extensive career in Middle Eastern oil that had taken him from Saudi Arabia to Bahrain and now to Iran as a U.S. special adviser to the Iranian government on economic reform. Thornburg was convinced that Anglo-Iranian's presence was detrimental to the country's progress. After British protests, the State Department ordered him to return to the United States.

Upon his appointment, Razmara set about appeasing the foreign powers, assuring the British that he would see through the Supplemental Agreement – only, that was, if he could offer a few sweeteners to the *Majlis*, such as opening up the company's books for inspection, progressing Iranians to senior positions in the company, paying royalties in advance and parity with Iraq. In return for a £25 million advance, Razmara would ensure that the agreement went through in six months' time.

With hindsight, these seem unremarkable proposals: clearly the power balance between company and state was tilting in the latter's favour. A Venezuelan 50–50 profit-sharing deal, which included a provision to inspect the oil company's accounts, had received widespread coverage. Rumours of a 'bombshell' 50–50 profit-sharing deal between Aramco and Saudi Arabia were already circulating.[6] Anglo-Iranian was

Sir William Fraser (left) with Shah Mohammad Reza Pahlavi during the latter's visit to the Anglo-Iranian laboratory at Sunbury-on-Thames, 1948.

prepared to make some concessions, though Fraser refused to agree to the advance, taking the view that the Supplemental Oil Agreement had already been settled between the company and government, and that it was for the British government, not Anglo-Iranian, to agree loans with Iran.

At this point Fraser appears to have had a change of heart – not exactly a Damascene moment, but rather a practical recognition that further resistance to 50–50 profit-sharing was futile given the impending Saudi-Aramco deal. He promised to consider such an agreement in the future, but only after the Supplemental Agreement had gone through. In the circumstances it was too weak a gesture to have any meaningful effect. The dance went on; the Iranian ambassador in London carried details of the proposal back to Tehran and no more was heard from Razmara on the subject. A reduced loan of £8 million was paid, and another loan of £25 million was made to the Iranian government early the following year. None of this could save the Supplemental Agreement, however: Razmara could not deliver on his promise to see the agreement through the *Majlis* and it was withdrawn on 26 December 1950.

For the nationalists, this was the perfect storm. Among the opposition groups jostling for position were the clerics who at first glance had little in common with Mossadegh's secularist ambitions. One leading cleric, Ayatollah Abul Qasim Kashani, had survived early encounters with the British in Iraq to become a deputy in the Iranian *Majlis*. A supporter of Reza Shah, he had remained in contact with German agents after the shah's fall in 1941 and was subsequently exiled until the end of the war. He suffered another period of exile in the late 1940s before returning to Tehran on June 1950 to a warm public reception. Nationalists and clerics united as another mullah, Muhammad Taqi Khonsari, issued a decree that nationalizing the oil industry was in accordance with the principles of Islam.

Thus the movement gained an evangelical zeal, having not only political weight but the power of religion behind it as well as the charismatic figurehead of Mossadegh. Kashani summed up the strength of feeling on the issue when he said that Britain had created all the sorrows of Iran and that nationalization of its oil industry was the only remedy for their troubles.[7]

On 19 February 1951 the end game began. Mossadegh formally proposed to the *Majlis* oil committee that Anglo-Iranian be nationalized,

[handwritten margin note: An important moment of insight, which typically leads to a dramatic transformation of attitude or belief.]

and when Razmara appeared before the deputies to oppose the proposal he was shouted down. By now the company had offered a 50–50
agreement, though the beleaguered Razmara dared not disclose this.
Perhaps he feared that disclosure would simply open the way for the
Majlis to degrade the offer by further haggling; he was also anxious
not to reveal the £25 million advance in case it was interpreted as a
bribe. Anyhow, his personal standing was beyond salvation in the eyes
of the nationalist deputies, who accused him of being in the pockets
of the British.

The oil committee was a strange creation, more a political body
than a technical or economic one – an 'emotional jousting field' that
often degenerated into attacks on a weak government.[8] Mossadegh
dominated the proceedings, commenting sarcastically on anything he
disagreed with. In these circumstances, if the outcome of these sessions
seemed inevitable to the seasoned observer, what happened next was
truly shocking. On 7 March, a few days after informing the committee that nationalization would not work, Razmara was murdered.
His assassin was a member of Fidaiyan-i Islam (Devotees of Islam), a
religio-political group with links to Ayatollah Kashani. Shortly before-
hand, a strange silence had fallen over the normally bustling bazaar of
central Tehran, as if people knew what was about to happen.

Next day, amid scenes of wild euphoria outside the parliament
building, the oil committee recommended nationalization, followed
by a bill in the *Majlis* a week later. A nine-point law nationalizing
the oil industry was duly passed and became law on 1 May 1951. Thus
Mossadegh, who had been elected prime minister a few days before,
achieved his immediate aim. Oil operations were to be transferred
to a new company, the National Iranian Oil Company (NIOC), with
all revenues belonging to the Iranian government and 25 per cent of
the net revenues to be paid to Anglo-Iranian as compensation. It was
decreed that company directives were not valid unless countersigned
by an Iranian official. British protests were met with indifference,
with responses like 'It's just the same old nonsense. We've heard all
that before.'[9] Mossadegh maintained that the action was a legitimate
exercise of Iran's sovereign rights.

How nationalization would work remained to be seen; there was
precious little detail in the plan. When Basil Jackson, deputy chairman
of Anglo-Iranian, later asked Ali Varasteh, the finance minister, how
the Iranians would export oil without any tankers, his question was

shrugged off – it was being considered by a committee of experts, he was told. In June, after the ritual slaughter of a sheep and the ceremonial raising of an Iranian flag, a committee of deputies, senators and government officials purported to take over oil operations at the company's main office at Khoramshah. Husayn Makki, one of the deputies on the committee, called for the flow of oil from the oilfields to be shut off and only changed his mind after much persuasion. The committee demanded that tanker captains should sign receipts showing the oil belonged to the NIOC and not the company. Finding his position untenable, general manager Arthur Drake was forced to escape across the Shatt al-Arab river to Basra.

Mossadegh remained in frail health. He gave an impassioned speech to the *Majlis* and promptly collapsed but, as the deputies knew, he was prone to such episodes. He told the press that he went in fear of his life, not daring to go home or to his office, and would work in the parliament building until the oil dispute had been settled. 'Dark hands are intent on my destruction,' he gloomily declared.[10]

More details of the nationalization project emerged. Kazem Hassibi, the minister of finance, was an engineer and the only member of the oil commission who had any experience of the oil industry. He announced that an immediate plan to run the oilfields would be carried out whether the British were willing to work for Iran or not: 'Anything we cannot manage, we will close down.'[11] The Iranian government was ready to take over the concessions, using the present British staff and, possibly, American and other experts. There was an element of brinkmanship in this: if the British would not cooperate and some operations ceased, production would be lost and Iran as well as the West would suffer.

It was not a plan that inspired confidence. Oilfields closed down one by one, refining operations declined and then ceased, tankers stopped loading oil. In Tehran, foreign diplomats and politicians came and went, their attempts to moderate failing to elicit any meaningful response. Expectations were running high among the restless population, and the visit of Averell Harriman at the head of an American mission was greeted by an angry mob. In August Sir Richard Stokes arrived in Tehran with a delegation of British civil servants and Anglo-Iranian officials. Despite accepting the principle of nationalization and discussing a possible settlement with the Iranian government, however, Stokes saw his proposals rejected.

Protestors trample an Anglo-Iranian sign brought down from the company's
information centre in Tehran, June 1951.

The shah dared not speak out against nationalization, still less
dismiss Mossadegh as he had done with prime ministers in the past.
A British appeal to the International Court of Justice at The Hague
was denounced by the Iranian government, which maintained that no
one else had the right to claim ownership of a nation's resources. In
due course, the court decided that it had no jurisdiction to adjudicate
between Iran and a foreign company (rather than the UK itself), a
ruling that Iran interpreted as a victory over the forces of imperialism.

In its imperial heyday this would have been a minor inconvenience
for a power like Great Britain. Now, with the United Nations and
International Court of Justice providing worldwide arenas, charges
of imperialism could no longer be swatted away. The reality was that
Britain's power and influence was in decline and, in the case of Iran,
global opinion was largely against her. Mossadegh's story struck a
populist chord in the Western press, particularly in the United States
where parallels with the American War of Independence were drawn –
a connection that Mossadegh was happy to mention.

There were good practical reasons for avoiding a military intervention, besides. Whitehall might rattle its sabre by sending its ships
and troops to the region but a cold, hard analysis of the situation

deemed a seizure of the oilfields too risky – there was no guarantee of American support and a danger that any such action might trigger a Soviet invasion from the north.

That was that, then. Talking had failed, and by 4 October all company personnel had left the country and oil production had ceased altogether. The recently completed £100 million refinery at Abadan was abandoned, an event that Churchill called 'the Abadan scuttle'.[12] The smoke stacks that had once seemed so invincible were idle, the plant becalmed and the signs of busy activity that had once characterized the site now consigned to the past.

WE NOW SEE A greater tragedy unfolding. In attempting to mediate in the crisis, the Americans found themselves cast in the same mould as the British. It was a role that did not sit well with them, since from the outset they had been far more receptive to nationalist sentiments. And yet, when it became apparent that Mossadegh was not as pliable as originally thought and Britain had gained a measure of legitimacy by going to the International Court of Justice, American sympathy for the Iranian cause waned. Western diplomats found 'Old Mossy' exasperating, thinking they had made some progress one day only to find themselves starting all over again the next.

Although some regarded his bouts of illness – the fits, the weeping, the collapses and retreats to his bed – as an act, the symptoms were real enough. He was a naturally passionate speaker and often wept as he delivered his speeches. Between Westerners and Iranians, responses to such episodes were markedly different: while the former were sceptical, the latter empathized with Mossadegh as a victim of powerful forces. Squatting on the mattress of his iron-framed bed as he received visitors and heard their submissions, the pyjama-clad prime minister would not compromise on the principle of nationalization. Nor, for that matter, would his people allow him to: Kashani once muttered darkly to Harriman that Mossadegh would go the way of Razmara if he backed down.

In September 1951 there were disturbing scenes in the *Majlis* – personal threats, the throwing of briefcases, talk of shooting a government minister – all over the question of oil. In October the sallow-faced premier teetered down the steps of a plane at New York's Idlewild Airport, the 'symbol of Iran's surging nationalism', as the *New York Times* put it. The purpose of his visit was to address the United Nations, where he made a strong impression among the delegates; the British submission of the oil dispute was postponed. Returning to Iran six weeks later, he was greeted by an enthusiastic crowd and nearly fainted at his reception. Arrays of flowers lined his route to the city and poetry was broadcast over loudspeakers. A chorus sang an oil anthem, written to celebrate nationalization. Acting premier Bagher Kazemi declared, 'You are the anti-imperialist hero.'[13]

Three weeks after the departure of the last British personnel from Abadan, Winston Churchill returned to office as prime minister. It was ironic that the man who had helped to rescue Anglo-Iranian some forty years before should now reappear like an avenging angel, but his resolve to uphold British interests was undimmed. Anthony Eden, who had been an undersecretary at the Foreign Office during the 1933 negotiations, was Churchill's foreign secretary. 'A further prolonged period of dilly-dally will be disastrous,' Eden declared.[14]

The Royal Navy's interception of an Italian oil tanker, the *Rose Mary*, which was carrying Iranian crude oil, evinced a new resolve to fight back. And, while an occasional American oilman like Alton Jones of Cities Service might breeze into Tehran with promises of technical help, the oil majors kept a united front and supported an embargo against Iran.

In July 1952 Mossadegh's request to be appointed minister of war and thus gain control of the army was rejected by the shah, triggering another crisis; Mossadegh promptly resigned as prime minister. Under pressure from Whitehall, the shah appointed Ahmad Qavan as prime minister in his place. An attempt to reopen talks with Anglo-Iranian failed, however, and Mossadegh was brought back to office on a wave of popular protest within a week. It was a hard lesson for the politicians and diplomats in London: they had again witnessed the power of the crowd to determine events in Iran, and seen the failure of another civilian prime minister.

Most of those who travelled to Tehran that summer were either impressed by Mossadegh's blinkered determination or shocked at how far he was prepared to go. Another attempt to resolve the dispute was made in August 1952 when a new initiative, known as the Truman–Churchill proposals, was put to him. Management and control of the Iranian industry would remain with the Iranian government and Anglo-Iranian would negotiate an arrangement for the distribution and

Mohammad Mossadegh in hospital after arriving in the United States, October 1951.

marketing of the oil. Claims for compensation would be submitted to the International Court of Justice. It was the nearest thing to a full recognition of nationalization that had so far been made.

The initiative was greeted with another denunciation of the company. Mossadegh's counterproposals included claims for compensation for the loss of oil revenues during Britain's blockade of oil exports and for £49 million apparently set aside at the time of the Supplemental Agreement. This went beyond what Truman and Churchill were prepared to countenance, and their plan duly foundered. Neither of them could have been greatly surprised and, in fact, the outcome served Churchill's purpose well.

There was a growing sense that the time had come for direct action: if Mossadegh were removed, then surely the problem would go away. The Joint Intelligence Committee in London was already discussing the prospect of finding an acceptable successor to Mossadegh, even if it meant overthrowing him. The idea of a coup appears to have come from the highest political circles and yet British decision-makers hesitated to act without the cooperation, or at least the tacit consent, of the Americans. That day was getting closer with each failed attempt to settle the matter – the Truman administration was simply running out of options for a peaceful solution to the dispute.

Relations between London and Tehran continued their sorry decline. Mossadegh broke off diplomatic relations in October 1952, the British chargé d'affaires was withdrawn and the British intelligence station in Tehran was relocated to Cyprus. The lack of a diplomatic presence (and spies) inside the country left a large gap in the intelligence reaching London and enhanced an overall feeling of detachment. There were plenty of new distractions in the Middle East to keep both diplomats and agents occupied in the meantime, such as the removal of King Farouk in Egypt and the rise of Colonel Gamel Nasser as the voice of Arab nationalism. Britain's interests were threatened across the board. In September the Buraimi Crisis erupted, pitching Britain against Saudi Arabia and making Britain even more enemies across the region. The November election in the United States brought Eisenhower to office and a different focus to American foreign policy. Combatting the threat of global communism was more pronounced; sympathy with nationalist causes less so.

All the same, President Eisenhower pursued a diplomatic line at first. In February 1953 another offer was made to Mossadegh, this time that Anglo-Iranian should return to Iran as part of an international consortium. Mossadegh rejected it, reminding his audience that what Anglo-Iranian had done in the past was 'sheer looting, not business'.[15] In April a popular police chief was assassinated, adding to the air of unrest in the country. It would take the combined efforts of the Dulles brothers – Allen Dulles, director of the CIA, and John Foster Dulles, U.S. Secretary of State – to persuade Eisenhower to support a coup.

The ensuing drama of the Iranian coup can be briefly told. The Americans took the lead in Operation Ajax (or Boot, as the British knew it) with the British playing a supporting role. The idea was to replace Mossadegh with a prominent figure favourable to British and American interests. General Fazlollah Zahedi seemed to be the right candidate, despite having been pro-Nazi and kidnapped by the British during the Second World War. In a climate of disturbance and protest against the National Front, the shah would be encouraged to appoint Zahedi as prime minister.

A CIA agent, Kermit Roosevelt (the grandson of President Theodore Roosevelt), was dispatched to Tehran with a brief to activate the mob and bribe key figures in the army. The shah was informed of the planned coup and his twin sister, the formidable Princess Ashraf, was persuaded to leave France for Tehran in order to stiffen her brother's resolve.

The line between success and failure in these situations is often finely drawn. The first attempt at a coup in August failed, largely because an army leader loyal to Mossadegh avoided arrest and turned the tables on the plotters. The shah fled abroad in fear of his life. During his absence, a second attempt was made. With British support, the CIA undermined Mossadegh's government by bribing influential figures, planting false reports in newspapers and sparking violence in the streets. By the end of the operation, some 300 people had died during the fighting in Tehran.

Much to his own surprise, the shah was invited to return to Iran and appoint Zahedi to replace Mossadegh as prime minister. The weary Mossadegh was put on trial, convicted and sentenced to three years' imprisonment. He was then confined to house arrest for the rest of his days, and died in 1967.

PERHAPS SIR WILLIAM FRASER had been right after all. He had resisted all demands from his enemies and attempts by supposed allies to surrender to Mossadegh, eventually conceding the merits of a 50–50 split too late in the day to make any difference to the outcome. Now that Mossadegh had gone and the prospect of returning to Iran arose, Fraser could afford himself a quiet smile as he contemplated events from his office high in Britannic House, Anglo-Iranian's headquarters in London. He saw a new scenario unfolding, and one that did not displease him too greatly.

Any thoughts of turning the clock back to the pre-Mossadegh days were misplaced. In Western oil circles, a return to Iran was now predicated on the idea of having a consortium of oil companies, of which Anglo-Iranian would be one. Any suggestion that the company might resume its former role was a non-starter in political terms, since such a move was bound to reignite the flames of nationalism and undermine the new regime's bid to distance itself from the past. While those in the Anglo-Iranian boardroom might still have a sentimental attachment to the past, it was apparent that those days were well and truly over.

The company had become increasingly marginalized as the dispute with Mossadegh's government went on, and any hope of restoring the status quo had been eroded by a series of negotiating gambits. Inexorably, Anglo-Iranian's position had shifted from being the only oil company in Iran to being part of an international consortium and then, as some Foreign Office officials saw it, to having no place in Iran at all. But with Mossadegh removed from the scene, it was time to resurrect the consortium idea. Moreover, after their leading role in the coup, there was a strong feeling among the Americans that they should take a large share of the spoils. This was not immediately accepted, and it was only after pressure from Herbert Hoover Jnr, the u.s. special envoy to Iran, that the idea progressed.

In December 1953, at the invitation of Fraser, representatives of the oil majors – CFP, Jersey Standard, Royal Dutch Shell, SoCal, Socony, Gulf Oil and the Texas Company – gathered in London to discuss the arrangements for a consortium to operate in Iran. At that stage Fraser was still taking the line that Anglo-Iranian would return to Iran as the primary oil company – talk about a consortium was purely hypothetical. Over the following weeks, however, his position was whittled down to a 40 per cent share of joint venture, which the Anglo-Iranian board accepted with some reluctance. The American oil companies would also have a 40 per cent share in the venture, with the remainder going to Royal Dutch Shell (14 per cent) and CFP (6 per cent). Nine smaller u.s. companies would join the consortium in 1955.

It was not such a disaster for Anglo-Iranian. Indeed, for a company that had seemed a lost cause in Iran, this was a remarkable comeback. There would be more battles along the way, such as the question of the compensation to be paid to the company for the loss of its 60 per cent share, but the company's return to Iran was assured, albeit in a reduced form. Fraser opened the next set of discussions with high expectations, seeking the sum of £280 million from the other companies. The board eventually settled for £214 million. Under a separate agreement with the Iranian government, the company was to receive compensation of £25 million for its losses.

A new Iranian concession was signed in September 1954 for the same geographical area as before with a 50–50 profit-sharing arrangement lasting for 25 years, with provision for three five-year extensions and a reduction of the concession area to about half its original size by the end of the third extension. The consortium entered Iran a month later under the overall supervision of the state-controlled NIOC, which retained ownership of the oilfields; a number of operating companies worked the oilfields on its behalf. Anglo-Iranian specialists were employed, together with American, British, Dutch and French employees, while the local workforce was re-engaged en masse. Naturally, none of this was to Fraser's liking, but it did strike a practical balance between foreign participation and overall national control at the same time as giving Iran a greater share of the oil revenues.

Historians have suggested that this outcome was actually the making of Anglo-Iranian (from 1954 known as British Petroleum (BP)). The company had dominated Iranian oil affairs for decades and its complacency had now been shaken. Forced to consider a future without Iranian oil, the company looked to expand its operations, making Iran one among many such oil ventures around the globe, rather than being the only one.

When all is said and done, however, it would be wrong to conclude that Fraser and his company had won an outright victory. Mossadegh's actions reverberated across the Middle East by putting an end to Britain's domination of Iran and giving nationalism a massive boost – the cat was out of the bag as far as the West was concerned. From now on, nationalization would not go away and, although the oil majors would make a point of demonizing Mossadegh as an inglorious failure, it was apparent that their supremacy had been dented, if only in perception; and there could be no going back. In the firmament of petroleum history, Mossadegh was a shooting star, brightly imprinted on the popular mind, falling to earth. It is small wonder that he remains a national hero in his country to this day.

ABOUT 65 KILOMETRES (40 MILES) northeast of Shiraz, near the confluence of two rivers on the spur of a little mountain, are the ruins of Persepolis, the ancient capital of Persia. It was here in October 1971 that Shah Mohammad Pahlavi presided over festivities to mark the anniversary of the founding of the Persian Empire 2,500 years before. Heads of state came from all over the globe, many of them deputizing for their leaders who were unwilling to attend: Georges Pompidou feared the event would be too grand for the president of France and jokingly remarked that he might be asked to act as head waiter. British diplomats advised against their queen attending because of fears over security and the company she might have to keep; in the event, Prince Philip and Princess Anne went in her place.[16]

Built in 1971 to commemorate the 2,500th anniversary of the Persian Empire, this monument in Tehran is today known as the Azadi ('Freedom') Tower.

The assorted guests were accommodated in a luxurious tented city that took its inspiration from the Field of Cloth of Gold, the famous venue of a meeting between King Francis I and King Henry VIII in 1520. More than 160 chefs were flown in from Paris with a ton of golden imperial caviar provided at the banquet that followed. The Iraqis, who were blamed for recent terrorist incidents in the country, were not present – the shah, when asked if anyone from Iraq had been invited, replied 'not to my knowledge' before realizing the irony of his reply.[17]

Far more disturbing was the condition of the countryside and its people, as evidenced by the drought and famine that affected the land. But the mass of pinched faces and ragged figures would not be seen here, for such spectacles were kept away from the braided and glittering pomp. Indeed, the only thing the organizers were unable to exclude was the desert wind, which blew up during a *son et lumière* show on the first evening and left the audience shivering under the night sky. As the celebrations were broadcast across the world through newspapers and televisions, many Iranians held them in contempt. No matter how much was spent, how much the icon of royalty was projected at home and abroad, the hearts and minds of the Iranian people were not so easily swayed.

As he looked across the banquet table at the assembled guests, the shah saw things in a different light. Here was a more confident, experienced and knowing monarch than the timid figure who had succeeded his father in 1941. He was proud of his achievements and determined to pursue his dream of greatness. There was an element of desperation in his plans, though, which were heedlessly formulated on predictions of an ever-increasing oil wealth – a great tide of money that ebbed out of the nation's coffers more quickly than it flowed in.

For the Americans, dealing with the shah was counterintuitive: as the main suppliers of Iran's military hardware, they wanted to sell more, but such was the shah's profligacy that they had to impose an annual review on *his* purchases. Those who thought this approach might clip the shah's wings were misguided. The shah had an independent – some might say stubborn – mind. And he was certainly nobody's fool, always well prepared for meetings and grilling complacent officials. He was a persistent negotiator who was difficult to refuse, especially when he interpreted anything short of a blank 'no' as a resounding 'yes'. All in all, it had become apparent that the shah intended to forge his own path in the Middle East.

During the 1960s Iran's military expenditure had swelled to between 23 and 33 per cent of the overall budget. In 1969 the shah fixed a five-year plan without being sure that the country would have the oil revenues to pay for it. Whereas earlier presidents had baulked at the shah's inflated demands, President Richard Nixon was more amenable – actually, he was wont to sidestep his advisers in order to give the shah what he wanted. There was more to it, however, since Washington had good strategic reasons for supporting the shah. Iran was the answer to the vexed question of how to counter communist expansion and fill an impending power vacuum in the Gulf. The Strait of Hormuz, where the Gulf narrows to a choke-point little wider than 32 kilometres (20 miles), was the sole outlet for oil exports from the region at that time. Iran, with its strong military forces, seemed an obvious candidate to protect it.

The Americans certainly thought so. In 1969 Nixon set about reducing troop numbers and training indigenous forces in Vietnam, a policy that was known as 'Vietnamization'. As part of an overall strategy against communism, the Nixon Doctrine extended the idea to the world at large and aimed to support allies while encouraging them to take measures for their own defence. The withdrawal of British military forces from the Gulf at the end of 1971 gave Washington an opportunity to apply the doctrine: the shah's regime was to be encouraged and supported in its new role of policeman of the Gulf, with Saudi Arabia playing second fiddle.

It was an idea that appealed to the shah's sense of history and ambition – and in his eyes it would surely lead to something even grander. On the eve of the British leaving the Gulf, Iranian troops forcibly occupied the Tunb Islands claimed by the Arab sheikh of Ras al-Khaimah. The fact that neither the United States nor Great Britain took any meaningful steps to persuade the shah to back down was a clear indication of the role they had in mind for him; but the action soured Iran's relations with the newly created United Arab Emirates, which still pursues Ras al-Khaimah's claim to the Tunbs, and Sharjah's claim to Abu Musa, to this day.

And so we leave the shah at the end of 1971 to consider events elsewhere. This was the shah's reign at its apogee with the future of his imperial domain awaiting the judgement of history. The wealth generated from oil enabled him to project an image of royalty far beyond his borders. Invested with visions of grandeur, and obsessed with building a new empire in the Middle East, the self-appointed king of kings sought to maximize his country's income from oil and then spend it on military expansion.

As he preened over the past and dreamt of glories yet to come, surely the plain truth of Persepolis had escaped him: for its crumbling ruins spoke of *former* greatness rather than continuity, his tented city a monument to the follies that oil wealth can bring.

IRAQ

FOUR

...E OIL GAME, 1903–28

O IL WAS PART OF daily life for many living in Iraq, or Mesopotamia as it was then known. European travellers in the nineteenth century were well acquainted with the 'Eternal Fires' around Kirkuk where gas associated with crude oil came to the surface, caught light and burned, seemingly without the flames ever going out. Cottage industries, where local people gathered oil from pits on the surface and refined it in a variety of strange contraptions, were a feature of the landscape. In certain parts, oil seemed to flow from every crack and crevice of the land.

With its geology inextricably linked to the Zagros Mountains and located in the Goldilocks Zone of the ancient Tethys Sea, the region is abundant in oil and gas reservoirs. And so, although losing out to Iran as the cradle of the modern petroleum industry in the Middle East, Mesopotamia emerged as an intriguing prospect for oilmen and politicians alike as the twentieth century dawned.

The Ottoman Empire – the ageing, creaking sick man of Europe – encompassed Mesopotamia. The empire was renowned for its bureaucracy and the need to lubricate officials. This made bidding processes a lengthy and expensive business in the corridors of the imperial capital, Constantinople (today's Istanbul). An investor's fortunes often rose and fell with those of his supporting power: sometimes the Germans were in the ascendant, at other times the British. In the meantime the sultan, Abdulhammid II, acquired land in the most promising petroleum areas by prolific use of the *tapous*, a legal document that local officials used to transfer land titles into the *Liste Civile*, his private account.

The key to Germany's early success lay in its political influence in the Ottoman Porte (as the government in Constantinople was known) and in its engineering prowess, especially in the matter of building railways. The grand design of *Drang nach Osten*, the German drive to the East, was to build an economic empire that would rival that of Britain in its scope and power. This was more than simply a war of words with the Anglo-Saxons or a feint towards the seat of their imperial power in India. It was a rivalry that found practical expression in the construction of a railway line from Berlin to Baghdad.

As was the tradition, railway concessions included a strip of territory running either side of the line for the exploitation of any mineral resources that might be found. The reports of European travellers about the mineral and petroleum prospects of Mesopotamia were well known in the corridors of Berlin, and the idea of finding and exploiting oil was a boon to the railway project, since any oil that might be extracted would clearly improve its profitability. Over the years various reports came in confirming the region's oil promise. For example, in 1903 Dr Paul Rohrabacher from a German technical commission reported that Mesopotamia's oil was likely to prove more plentiful than Russian oil, which at that time was the dominant centre of the industry.

In the same year the Anatolian Railway Company, controlled by Deutsche Bank, obtained a railway concession from the Ottoman government. These concessions included preferential rights for subsurface minerals and oil, initially for 20 kilometres (12.5 miles) and then for 40 kilometres (25 miles) on either side of a proposed line running through the *vilayets* of Mosul and Baghdad and terminating in Basra. The next year the company obtained a one-year option to investigate the oil prospects of the region and sent an expedition to Mesopotamia; but despite their geologists carrying out surveys, they failed to present a final report. The Ottoman government deemed the German concession as defunct and opened up the bidding process, such as it was, to a wider range of interested parties.

This was fertile territory for a businessman such as Calouste Gulbenkian. The son of an oil trader from Armenia, Gulbenkian had learned his trade in the bazaars of Constantinople and the oil markets of Baku, then part of Russia and the centre of the oil industry outside the United States. His skills combined the academic with the practical; although he held an engineering degree from King's College, London, he was well schooled in *bazaarlik, the practices of the bazaar, and the* Byzantine ways of Ottoman bureaucracy. He published a book and several articles about the future of petroleum, one of which, in the *Revue des deux mondes* in 1892, came to the notice of the Turkish minister of mines, who invited Gulbenkian to put together a report on the oil resources of the Ottoman Empire.

Gulbenkian was a small man with an unprepossessing appearance and yet, having established himself in the highest business circles of Constantinople and London, he was in a good position to advise leading British businessmen on the situation in Mesopotamia. They included Henri Deterding and Marcus Samuel, respectively of the Royal Dutch Petroleum Company and the Shell Transport and Trading Company, which combined in 1907 to become Royal Dutch Shell (commonly known as 'Shell'). By dint of hard work and good fortune, Gulbenkian returned to Constantinople as managing director of Shell's office and became the main player in the company's bid to obtain an oil concession from the Ottoman sultan.

If the Shell board were expecting to receive the support of the British government in their efforts, however, they were to be disappointed. The Foreign Office preferred a bid being prepared by the D'Arcy group, the same group that was so heavily involved in Iran. Such was the antagonism of William D'Arcy towards Shell that there was no prospect of the two groups joining forces. In official eyes, too, Shell was essentially a Dutch-run company whose interests were not squarely in the British sphere: they were, in essence, considered foreigners who should not be entrusted with Britain's interest in Mesopotamia's oil. Even so, Royal Dutch Shell still had a part to play in the wider realm of British oil interest, since its Far East network was worth protecting. Thus, while Whitehall favoured D'Arcy, and subsequently Anglo-Persian over Shell, it did not rule out supporting the latter in other parts of the globe.

Meanwhile, the D'Arcy group was beavering away in Constantinople, having entered negotiations with the Ottomans a few years before. Here the group's 29-year-old business manager, Herbert Nichols, navigated the swirling pools of oriental practice, bribing one official here, another there, gradually advancing the group's case for an oil concession through a host of foreign agents, intermediaries and spies. Together with his network of informers, Nichols had his own fixer, Hallis Bey, a 'wirepuller and scoundrel'.[1] Until 1908, that is, when the Young Turk Revolution forced out the old power brokers and Hallis Bey disappeared, leaving Nichols to pick up the pieces and start all over again. Such were the peaks and troughs of oil negotiations in the city.

Calouste Gulbenkian, *c.* 1900.

By April 1908 Nichols was on the verge of another breakthrough, having seen his bid progress to the final stages; all that was required was the sultan's signature to formalize the deal. Then another upheaval removed the sultan and brought his younger brother to power, and all oil rights from the *Liste Civile* were transferred to the Treasury. Nichols was back to square one. Like the fictional town described in Gabriel Gárcia Márquez's *One Hundred Years of Solitude*:

> It was as if God had decided to put to the test every capacity for surprise and was keeping the inhabitants in a permanent alternation between excitement and disappointment, doubt and revelation, to such an extreme that no one knew for certain where the limits of reality lay.[2]

New bidders appeared on the scene, including an American group led by Admiral Colby Chester and backed by the New York Chamber of Commerce. They proposed a railway scheme with adjoining mineral rights in Anatolia and signed a preliminary agreement with the minister of public works, depositing 20,000 Turkish lira in a Constantinople bank.

The German influence was growing again, supported by certain influential figures of the Young Turk movement: Enver Pasha, the former military attaché to Berlin, Talaat Pasha, the minister of the interior, and Djavid Bey, the minister of finance. With this resurgence, British and American influence slipped away.

IN LONDON, AWAY FROM the swirl of contention and intrigue, it was possible to discern two separate groupings. One was an alliance of oil and banking interests. The National Bank of Turkey had been created in 1909 as a vehicle for British investment and influence in the Ottoman Empire, and the possibility of gaining an oil concession was a good opportunity to make its mark. In 1911, under the guiding hand of Gulbenkian, the National Bank, Deutsche Bank and Royal Dutch Shell came together as partners in a new company, the Turkish Petroleum Company (TPC). The other grouping was, Anglo-Persian, which had inherited the D'Arcy negotiations, but made little headway since then. Anglo-Persian had one great advantage over TPC: while TPC had the makings of a claim through Deutsche

Bank's Anatolian railway and mineral survey rights, Anglo-Persian retained the confidence of the British Foreign Office.

On 16 February 1913 the former Ottoman grand vizier, Hakki Pasha, arrived in London for talks over Mesopotamia and there was some hope that he might also bring proposals to end the deadlock over its oil. While other knotty problems such as the Baghdad railway, navigation rights along the Tigris and Euphrates and spheres of influence in the Gulf were up for discussion, the future of Mesopotamian oil remained undecided. For the British government, oil was a top priority – as already noted, the decision to convert naval ships from coal to oil had generated great interest in Whitehall finding new sources of oil for the Fleet.

Hakki Pasha indicated that his government would consider granting an oil concession to a company with shareholders, which ruled out a single country gaining exclusive rights. Whitehall and Berlin were already cooperating over the Baghdad railway and, with the cost of developing an oil concession likely to be high, it made sense to join forces in the matter of oil. There was an understanding that the vehicle for a concession should be TPC, in which the Germans had a 25 per cent share, but the talks still dragged on. Each had their own priority: the D'Arcy group demanded a controlling share; the Foreign Office was reluctant to include Royal Dutch Shell because of its 'foreign' element; and everyone agreed that Gulbenkian was to be sidelined.

The Turkish government was growing impatient and, with rumours of rival bids in Constantinople and of American geologists exploring Palestine, it was imperative that the matter be settled without any more delay. Alwyn Parker, the Foreign Office expert in Turkish and Persian affairs, worked tirelessly to bring the parties to an agreement and, after some last-minute haggling, the parties swallowed their differences. On 19 March 1914, Parker brokered the final deal: Anglo-Persian and Royal Dutch Shell gained shares in TPC of 50 and 25 per cent respectively, from which they each gave Gulbenkian a 2.5 per cent beneficial interest; despite being a reduced shareholding, this would make him a very rich man indeed and earn him the monicker of 'Mister Five Percent'. German honour was satisfied through Deutsche Bank's 25 per cent share in the company, which it retained.

Under this agreement, known as the Foreign Office Agreement, TPC was to make a single, British-led bid for the elusive Mesopotamian

People crossing the River Tigris in Baghdad on a bridge made of boats, 1911.

concession. With <u>strong diplomatic support from the British</u> and <u>German governments,</u> the company was well placed to succeed. Indeed, it appeared to have done so on <u>28 June 1914</u> when the Turkish grand vizier, Said Halim Pasha, informed the German ambassador, Hans von Wangenheim that:

> The Ministry of Finance being substituted for the Civil List with respect to petroleum resources discovered, and to be discovered, in the *vilayets* of Mosul and Baghdad, consents to lease these to the Turkish Petroleum Company, and reserves to itself the right to determine hereafter its participation, as well as the general conditions of the contract.[3]

But if this document was meant to be an oil concession, it was meagrely dressed. <u>While agreeing to lease the territory for oil exploration and development, the Turks had left the terms and shares in the concession open.</u> It was less a <u>formal agreement than an unforceable pledge</u> – in future years there would be no lack of contenders willing to argue that.

Any arguments about the validity of the concession were soon academic, however. By a dreadful coincidence, on the very day that the grand vizier signed his letter, Archduke Franz Ferdinand of Austria was assassinated in Sarajevo, setting in motion the train of events that culminated in the First World War. And so, as war raged across the countries of Europe, the-ill fated letter was filed away for another day.

WHAT HAD THE AMERICANS been up to in Palestine? In January 1914 a strange meeting occurred in the desert to the east of Beersheba. Following a night of storms, three British horsemen rode into a camp that had been set up the previous evening by a group of strangers – two American civilians and their Arab assistants – on a patch of meagre scrubland between low-lying hills. Among the British party was a certain T. E. Lawrence, who would later find fame as Lawrence of Arabia. The Americans pretended to be tourists, the British curious passers-by. In fact, the Americans were Socony agents looking for oil in the wilderness of Palestine, and their visitors already knew as much, having been alerted to their presence the day before.[4]

This was no chance encounter in the desert, then. Socony was trying a different tack to the British and Germans. Having established an office in Constantinople, the company obtained exploration options from a group of Jewish businessmen in Palestine, away from the limelight. Socony was more than an opportunistic American company looking for new sources of oil: it was one of 42 offshoots that had emerged from the dismemberment of a single company, Standard Oil, following anti-trust proceedings in the U.S. courts. Socony had a strong interest in foreign exploration, and by November 1913 its geologists and mining engineers had explored part of Anatolia, were at work in Palestine and were yet to visit Thrace.

Palestine was considered the best of Socony's prospects. From earliest times, there had been reports of gas and oil seepages, and lumps of bitumen along the shores of the Dead Sea, which the Romans had named *Lacus Asphaltites*. Even if the Socony survey party was not the most proficient, and the prospect they identified at Kornub would prove to be of no commercial value, the mere fact that an American company had entered the arena would be of great importance when it came to settling the claims of the great powers towards Ottoman lands after the First World War. With this in mind, far-sighted Socony executives approved drilling operations at Kornub despite a pessimistic forecast of oil being found there in commercial quantities; it was politics more than geology that brought the Americans there.

As Lawrence's desert encounter demonstrated, Socony's activities struck a raw nerve with the British authorities. Equally, the ensuing diplomatic tussle spurred Socony executives to purchase a 25-year concession and extend their interests in Palestine. The company invested considerable resources in the project, spending some $250,000 in the process (about $30 million today), building a 32-kilometre (20-mile) road and setting up a camp in the desert as a prelude to sinking an oil well. Then the war intervened. The Ottoman authorities requisitioned Socony's shipment of trucks, and the British diverted the company's pipes and drilling equipment to Egypt, where they were impounded.

In the long run this was not a complete disaster since the company could claim to have established a presence in the Middle East without drilling any footage. On paper its credentials looked convincing: the company had obtained concessions for seven plots in Palestine and another sixty were in various stages of negotiation at the time war broke out.

THE WAR BROUGHT OPPORTUNITIES as well as threats. One of the first things Britain did was seize Deutsche Bank's 25 per cent holding in TPC and transfer it to the British Custodian of Enemy Property, thus ending Germany's association with Middle Eastern oil for many years to come. The most immediate risk to British interests in the Middle East was to the Anglo-Persian oilfields and facilities in southwest Persia. On 5 November 1914 Great Britain declared war on Turkey and dispatched a British-led Indian Expeditionary Force to secure them.

The main objective at that stage was to secure the Abadan refinery; otherwise Britain's war aims were dictated by military and geopolitical needs. The expeditionary force captured Basra and then rapidly advanced along the River Tigris before heading for Baghdad, spurred on by a perception that Ottoman forces were weak and could be easily defeated. This illusion was put to the sword at Kut-al-Amara, where the Ottoman army besieged General Townsend's men for four months, resulting in the surrender of 13,000 troops. In the spring of 1917 the campaign regained its momentum under the command of General Maude, whose army advanced up the river to Baghdad, entering Kirkuk in May; and there matters rested for a while.

Meanwhile a new scenario was emerging, one where the traditional suppliers of oil to Western Europe – the United States and Mexico – would no longer be able to meet its demands. Whitehall, troubled by its dependence on U.S. oil and rattled by Germany's initial successes with its U-boat attacks on transatlantic shipping, was actively seeking to secure sources of oil for the future. Persia was clearly identified as a strategic interest through the government's shareholding

A Turkish porter delivering Socony kerosene in crates, *c.* 1920.

in the Anglo-Persian Oil Company. Now, as the shape of post-war Mesopotamia fell to be considered, questions about its prospective oil resources could not be disregarded.

The debate was gaining momentum. Geologists already suspected that the oil belt of the Zagros Mountains extended into Iraq. During the war, the Germans were extracting oil from Qaiyara, even distilling some of it into fuel. In 1917 G. W. Halse, a geologist working in the Bakhtiari lands, was summoned to Baghdad and ordered to carry out an oil survey of central Iraq. Often travelling beyond the front lines in a Ford motor car and accompanied by a detachment of cavalry or armoured cars, Halse covered more than 1,600 kilometres (1,000 miles) and reported on several occurrences of petroleum: a lake of pitch (a form of bitumen), oil springs and primitive workings. His report was so encouraging that Arnold Wilson, then deputy civil commissioner in Baghdad, telegraphed the Foreign Office: 'It cannot be doubted that oil will be struck.'[5]

Oil was not an original war aim; it was first mentioned as such by the de Bunsen Committee, an interdepartmental body set up in 1915 to discuss Britain's future position in the Ottoman Middle East. Belatedly, it then made an appearance as one of the desired outcomes of the war, and securing the possible sources of oil was considered a secondary war aim. But, as the evidence mounted up, the case for occupying the areas of petroleum interest strengthened.

Admiral Slade was already aware of the potential of the Persian oil-fields and was convinced that Mesopotamia held similar promise. On 29 July 1918 he produced a memorandum entitled 'Petroleum Situation in the British Empire', in which he recommended, among other things, that British companies gain control over the future oil-producing territories and over the processes of refining and distributing the finished product. Geological reports had led him to believe that the region of Mosul had 'the largest undeveloped resources at present known in the world . . . There must be no foreign interests.'[6]

The idea of acquiring Mesopotamian oil, and Mosul in particular, was yet to be grasped in equal measure. The foreign secretary, Arthur Balfour, was unimpressed with Slade's memorandum – despite enthusiasm about it in some quarters, there were murmurings that Slade might not be entirely disinterested in the matter, himself being on the board of Anglo-Persian. Others in the army and the India Office still clung to the imperial notion that Mesopotamia was important as a strategic gateway to India, rather than for its oil, and that securing present and future railway routes and not Mosul was the ultimate prize.

For all that, the creation of the Petroleum Executive in 1917 to coordinate oil policy had sharpened the government's focus, and the Admiralty strongly supported Slade's report. Those such as Lord Curzon argued that occupying Mosul was necessary to undermine any French claim to the *vilayet*. Sir Maurice Hankey, the secretary of the War Cabinet in London, was smitten by the oil argument and urged the prime minister, Lloyd George, to take action in order to secure the 'valuable' oil wells of Mesopotamia.[7] Balfour came down in favour of extending British control there, and the War Cabinet recommended that all the oil-bearing lands should be occupied before the end of hostilities. Striking north towards the prospective oilfields of Mosul now became, in Hankey's words, a 'first-class war aim'.[8] Since the British army had already occupied Baghdad and the south, this effectively meant an advance on Mosul.

The decision to advance farther up the River Tigris was initially a military decision in the hands of the commanding officer in Mesopotamia, General William Marshall. Once the Turks had signed an armistice at Mudros on 30 October, Marshall marched his troops post-haste to Mosul in order to force the surrender of its garrison. His forces entered the city on 15 November, more than two weeks after the official armistice, and cleared the *vilayet* of Turkish troops. Britain now controlled the promising oil provinces and was in a strong bargaining position when it came to dividing up the spoils of war.

Things were not so clear-cut on the diplomatic front, however. Sir Henry McMahon, high commissioner for Egypt and the Sudan, had exchanged letters with Sharif Hussein of Mecca supporting Arab independence. But the French diplomat François Georges-Picot and British adviser Sir Mark Sykes agreed to split Mesopotamia, famously drawing a line on the map from the 'e' in Acre to the 'k' in Kirkuk. The Mosul *vilayet* was designated to the French and appeared to give them a substantial share of any future oilfields there.

In the face of French opposition, the former agreement faltered and the latter prevailed. The aristocratic Sykes was a member of the de Bunsen Committee and therefore, in a sense, the picture was complete – the war aims had been settled and territory apportioned – although Sykes, for all his enthusiasm and breadth of interests, lacked a deep understanding of the real issues that lay beneath the lines drawn on maps.

Raising the Union Jack over Turkish headquarters in Kirkuk, October 1918. A decade later, the area would be at the centre of Iraq's oil industry.

The oil companies, too, were increasingly attracted to Mesopotamia. Shell already had an interest in the region's oil through its shareholding in TPC. The war had cut off the company from its oil supplies in Romania and the Caucasus, and from markets in Russia and Europe, forcing it to bring oil from distant oilfields in the Dutch East Indies. The Standard oil companies redeployed their Baltic fleets to the Far East, creating more pressure there for Shell and Burmah Oil, which in turn drew those companies closer to Anglo-Persian. Shell also looked for new sources of oil, in Venezuela and Mexico for example, and sought allies in its drive for new markets, among them the French. The more the oilmen looked at it, the more Mesopotamian oil seemed a sure-fire prospect for a post-war, petroleum-fuelled world.

IN APRIL 1920, IN the seaside town of San Remo in Italy, as heavy clouds massed on the horizon and thunder rolled around the bay, the colonial powers came together for a conference about the future of the Middle East. But this was not simply a discussion about political boundaries and responsibilities, for the leaders also aimed to shape the future of oil development in the region. As it happened, the final agreements reached at the conference were remembered as much for what they left out as for what they kept in.

Before the war the French government preferred to allow the private sector, primarily the Rothschilds (major shareholders in Shell), to take up the challenge of finding sources of oil. The French oil industry, which Calouste Gulbenkian dubbed a 'monopolistic association of grocers', was disorganized.[9] The wartime spectacle of soldiers being transported to the front line in Parisian taxis instead of trains demonstrated in dramatic terms how important oil was to the military effort and, ultimately, to the outcome of the First World War.

As with the British, there was a recognition that, although the Allied victory was fuelled by American oil, the Atlantic shipping route was vulnerable to submarine attack. Realizing that they needed a more secure source of oil, the French government made a deal giving Shell favourable access to the French market in return for their support for a bid to obtain Germany's forfeited share of oil interests in Romania and Mesopotamia.

Even though commercial oil had still not been found in Mesopotamia, politicians on both sides of the Channel were thinking of the time when it would be. French aspirations over Syria were strong, and the Quai d'Orsay (French Foreign Ministry) supported claims for a Greater Syria extending from the Turkish mountains to the Egyptian border. On a more practical level, the French prime minister, Georges Clemenceau, held a strong hand by threatening to use his country's control over Syria to block the export of oil along the shortest pipeline route to the Mediterranean. Whitehall now wished to clear away the obstacles to future oil development in the area.

There was a problem, however. British troops were in Mosul, which was due to the French under the Sykes-Picot Agreement. The matter was apparently resolved at a meeting on 1 December 1918, when Lloyd George persuaded Clemenceau to transfer the remainder of the Mosul *vilayet* to the British sphere of influence. In return the French gained Britain's support for their mandate in Syria and a share of any oil discovered in Mosul. It was a strange decision for the French to make. Mosul was, after all, within their agreed sphere of influence and historians have puzzled over Clemenceau's decision to abandon the Mosul *vilayet*, which promised much in terms of oil, so cheaply.

The answer is that he did not abandon it, exactly, since there was little to abandon. The territory south of the Lower Zab, precisely where the main oil-bearing land was believed to lie, was already under British control; and it appeared that the British-led Turkish Petroleum Company already had the right to operate in the French-controlled part. While it is not entirely accurate to say that Clemenceau had nothing to give away in Mosul apart from a few goat pastures, this interpretation of events is closer to the truth than some accounts have suggested. From now on, the French would pursue their interest in Mesopotamian oil through a share in TPC.

And so we return to the San Remo conference. At the close of business on 24 April, League of Nations mandates for Syria and Mesopotamia were announced, and subsequently assigned to France and Britain respectively, giving them control over those territories until they were ready for independence. A British mandate for Palestine was also agreed, incorporating the 1917 Balfour Declaration which favoured a national home for the Jewish people in the territory. This decision would affect oil operations in a way unimagined but, for the time being, there was another decision that would have a more immediate impact on oil development in the Middle East.

Among those waiting in the wings was Sir John Cadman who, as head of Whitehall's Petroleum Executive during the war, had grappled at first hand with the predicament of keeping Britain supplied with oil. By a separate oil agreement, Cadman and the French diplomat Philippe Berthelot settled the future arrangements for oil exploration in Mesopotamia. Britain and France would operate through TPC, the French acquiring Deutsche Bank's 25 per cent share in the company, while the British kept control of its management; pipelines would carry oil through the French-controlled territories. In time, the French government would assign its share in TPC to a new company, Compagnie Française des Pétroles (CFP), which was established three years later under the chairmanship of Ernest Mercier.

The Americans did not take kindly to the news, since in their eyes the colonial grab of Mesopotamia's oil was a betrayal of the principles of open diplomacy and the self-determination of peoples that President Woodrow Wilson had outlined in his famous Fourteen Points. In November 1920 U.S. Secretary of State Bainbridge Colby protested to the British foreign secretary Lord Curzon:

This [U.S.] government finds difficulty in reconciling the special arrangement . . . set forth in the so-called San Remo Oil Agreement with your statement that the petroleum resources of Mesopotamia, and freedom of action in regard thereto, will be secured to the future Arab State, as yet unorganized.[10]

He had a point. The Anglo-French carve-up seemed to contradict Article 8 of the oil agreement, which pledged the indigenous government (as and when it appeared) a 20 per cent share in TPC. In fact, as Colby suspected, the TPC shareholders had no intention of honouring this promise. Five years later they gave the Iraqi government the right to 20 per cent of any *future* share issue in lieu of its right to an immediate shareholding; there was never any intention of actually issuing them.

There was another puzzling aspect to it all. When American geologists had tried to access the Middle East, they met a brick wall of imperial officialdom. British officers attended the Socony office in Jerusalem and demanded to see maps of the company's concessions: by now it claimed to have 64 concessions in Judaea. American oil companies were also refused permission to send geological survey parties into Mesopotamia.

The stock British answer was that measures were necessary because the Iraqis needed time to make their own decisions about the future economic development of their country, as well as preventing a 'rush of speculators'.[11] The Americans could hardly object to this rationale, since it echoed the sentiments of President Wilson, who had promised to save the world for democracy. All the same, they saw through the facade and recognized these as superficial excuses designed to prevent them from exploring the region.

The Americans were certainly direct in their approach. They wanted equal access to Middle Eastern oil without strings, and it was already apparent that Washington was wedded to the 'Open Door' principle and would support them. Earlier in the year Congress had passed the Mineral Leasing Act, which denied U.S. drilling rights to firms from those countries that did not allow reciprocal access. Now a more direct approach was required. In May 1921 U.S. Secretary of Commerce Herbert Hoover told a group of U.S. oil company executives that he would back their efforts to enter Mesopotamia.

Among the group was Walter Teagle, chairman of Jersey Standard. He presented an imposing figure, tall with an encyclopaedic knowledge of the oil business. His company was another one of the proverbial dragon's teeth – an offshoot of the giant Standard Oil Company that had sprung up as a powerful company in its own right. We have already seen how the company was pressing for oil rights in Persia. It was now one of the largest oil companies in existence, and the forerunner of Exxon. In these circumstances Teagle was the obvious choice to lead the U.S. consortium. In many ways his part was skillfully performed, especially in the way he enlisted the diplomatic support of the U.S. Department of State in order to avoid any anti-trust difficulties. But exactly how feasible was the Open Door when Britain and France were so well embedded in the Middle East? Teagle was about to find out.

On the plus side, there were signs of a thaw in Anglo-American relations on the question of oil. Representing the TPC partners, Sir John Cadman visited the United States and conceded that in principle there was no objection to American participation in the Middle East. The British also dropped their objections to a Socony survey in Palestine. As far as Mesopotamia was concerned, the agreed vehicle for Anglo-American oil exploration was to be TPC, with the Americans taking a share in the company together with British, French and Dutch interests. The devil was in the details, however, and it would take another six years before a formal agreement was hammered out.

One problem was how to create an international cartel without compromising the free-market principles of the Open Door; the two concepts seemed diametrically opposed. Another was Anglo-Persian's demand for adequate compensation for losing part of its 50 per cent shareholding in TPC to the Americans. And finally, there was Gulbenkian, who insisted that his share of the profits should be paid in cash rather than crude oil for the eminently sensible reason that he had no facilities to refine and distribute petroleum.

The Mosul question was one more complication.[12] Despite the post-war agreement between Clemenceau and Lloyd George, the future of the former Ottoman *vilayet* was now to be decided by the League of Nations. As if the oil scenario were not confused enough, Admiral Colby Chester, the veteran concession hunter of pre-war fame, reappeared on the scene. He now gained rights to build a railroad in Anatolia and exploit oilfields alongside the line, including any found in Mosul. The Turks no doubt considered that Chester's interest would attract U.S. support for their claim to the *vilayet*. In the end it all blew

Walter Teagle (third left) leaving a meeting, Washington, DC, 8 May 1923.

over when Chester was unable to get the necessary funding, and the Turks cancelled the concession on the grounds of non-performance.

The episode came as a timely reminder to the British to work with the Americans, if only to prevent them from siding with the Turks over Mosul. The developing TPC talks gave them some hope. In 1923, by which time the British Mandate was active and the country was officially known as Iraq (instead of Mesopotamia), it was agreed that TPC should seek a new oil concession from the Iraqi government, though another two years passed before this was achieved. The delay brought a 'mushroom growth' of speculators to Baghdad, as Gulbenkian tersely observed.[13]

At last, on 14 March 1925, the Turkish Petroleum Convention was signed and doubts about TPC's right to be in Iraq were laid to rest. The 75-year concession was to provide Iraq with royalties of £400,000 (£22 million today) per annum and a tax revenue of 4 shillings in gold for each ton of crude oil. In a nod to the Open Door, a plots system was enacted: TPC would select up to 24 plots of 20 square kilometres (8 sq. miles) each for testing and exploitation, while the Iraqi government would offer 24 similar plots for lease by public auction. Article 5 of the convention also required the company to start work on an oil pipeline from Iraq to the Mediterranean coast as soon as it was commercially viable. In 1926 the League of Nations decided the Mosul question in Britain's favour, with the *vilayet* being awarded to Iraq and Turkey gaining a 10 per cent share of Baghdad's royalty payments for 25 years.

Meanwhile in Iraq, British, French and American geologists had been clambering over rocks and writing their reports. Thanks to their surveys, TPC was able to start a number of wells during the spring of 1927 at Pulkhana, Injana and Khashm al-Ahmar. It was the well at Baba Gurgur, near the oil and gas seepages known as the Eternal Fires, that would prove to be the most challenging of all. At 3 am on 14 October 1927, when the well had reached a depth of 460 metres (more than 1,500 ft), gas and oil suddenly gushed out, rising high above the derrick and spraying out across the barren land. This was an unfolding disaster, for soon a river of oil was flowing westwards along a wadi. The flow was stemmed by building a series of dams that saved the downstream towns and villages from the deluge. Ten days later, after workers had failed to reach the derrick through the spraying oil, an aero engine was used to slant the gusher to one side, allowing them to reach the control valve and stem the flow. By then, more than a million barrels of oil had spilled into the desert.

For the people of Kirkuk, there was more to come. In the late summer of 1928 a party of eleven German geophysicists from Messrs Siesmos GmbH arrived to undertake a series of seismic surveys for the company. The procedure brought detonations, which alarmed the local population, but as it turned out, the surveys produced mixed results.

The official opening of the No. 1 well at Pulkhana, 5 April 1927.

Within three years of the drama at Baba Gurgur, though, the outline of the Kirkuk oilfield was delineated and a single, supergiant oilfield up to 100 kilometres (62 miles) long and 4 kilometres (2.5 miles) wide was revealed. It raised a quandary for IPC: the plots system might allow other companies to drill around the field, drain it dry and flood the market with oil. Perhaps this was alarmist talk, but it was reason enough for the company to consider getting rid of the plots altogether.

Before that could be done, there was the matter of American participation to be formally settled. On 31 July 1928 representatives of the oil companies and Gulbenkian met at a hotel in Ostend in order to sign a formal partnership document. This fixed the future shareholdings in TPC as follows: 23.75 per cent each to Anglo-Persian, Royal Dutch Shell, CFP and the Near East Development Corporation (NEDC) representing Jersey Standard and Socony, and 5 per cent to Gulbenkian.[14] Anglo-Persian would receive an additional 10 per cent royalty in order to account for the reduction of its stake in TPC, and the French would pay Gulbenkian for his share of crude oil.

The agreement for joint working went far beyond the boundaries of Iraq by defining the area of the company's interest across the Middle East. A red line was drawn on a map enclosing Arabia, the Levant and Turkey, and excluding Egypt, Iran, Kuwait and the Farasan Islands. Gulbenkian claimed the credit for impulsively drawing the line at an earlier meeting based on his recollection of the pre-war boundaries of the Ottoman Empire; it was an improbable claim, but the document nonetheless went down in history as the Red Line Agreement.

There was another aspect to it all. As a sop to indigenous interests, the agreement allowed the Iraqi government to appoint a director to the TPC board. As it was, the first such director, Muzahim al-Pachachi, had taken up his appointment a few months before the agreement was signed, but it was largely a nominal appointment and carried little weight. The company dominated the country's oil industry and yet there would be no effective Iraqi participation in its affairs as the partners tended to make the important decisions at group meetings, away from meetings of the board.

In 1929 TPC became the Iraq Petroleum Company (IPC), which would hold a virtual monopoly of Iraqi oil for more than forty years. The IPC companies extended their reach through the Mosul Petroleum Company and the Basra Petroleum Company so that, by July 1938, it held concessions for the whole country except the Khanaqin oilfield, which was held by a subsidiary of the Anglo-Iranian Oil Company.

It was a done deal: Britain's interests in the Middle East were now inextricably linked with Iraqi oil.

League of Nations: Founded On 01/10/1920, and is Known as the first worldwide intergovernmental organisation, whose principal mission was to maintain world peace. It ceased operations on 04/20/1946, when it failed to stop WW II. While it was founded by Woodrow Wilson, the LN didn't included the U.S. It's also the predecessor to the United Nations.

FIVE

BIRDS OF ILL OMEN, 1928–45

I N THESE YEARS, THE pace and direction of oil development were determined not in Riyadh, Tehran or Baghdad, but in the board-rooms of London, New York, Paris and . . . an ancient castle in the Scottish Highlands. For all their power and influence, there was a feeling of frustration among the chairmen (they were not called 'tycoons' until much later) of the big three, the largest oil companies of the time: Royal Dutch Shell, Anglo-Persian and Jersey Standard.[1]

In 1928, as they looked down from the high Georgian windows of Achnacarry Castle, Messrs Deterding, Cadman and Teagle saw a world awash with oil. Large discoveries in Texas and Oklahoma had brought huge increases in oil production. As well as cheap oil from Russia, oil was flowing from Romania, Iran, the East Indies and Venezuela. In 1928 the oil kings met and drew up the Pool Agreement, otherwise named the 'As Is' Agreement. This attempted to limit oil production by fixing market share according to their respective shares in the world market at that time: the arrangements should remain 'as is'. Ultimately it failed: the Great Depression and the number of independent oil companies made it impossible to control the price of oil as the oil kings intended.

For similar reasons, they tried to delay the export of oil from the Kirkuk oilfield. Believing their companies had more than enough crude already, they were in no particular hurry to build a pipeline to the Mediterranean coast. If it was built, there would be more oil on the market and prices would fall even more. But they failed to win over their IPC partners, Gulbenkian and the French, who wanted pumping to start as soon as possible. And CFP had a good card to play: if IPC failed to build a pipeline to export Kirkuk's oil, there was a good chance it would lose the Iraq concession. Put like that, there really was only one option, and the issue soon changed from *whether* to build a pipeline to *where* to build it.

When it came to choosing a route for the pipeline, the French preferred a route that went through their mandated territories of Syria and Lebanon, the 'northern route'. The British on the other hand wanted the pipeline to run through the territories they controlled – Transjordan and Palestine – the 'southern route'.

The shorter northern route would need only four pumping stations to maintain the flow of oil along the line, whereas the southern one needed five. On purely economic grounds, the French argument was compelling but, in reality, the disagreement with the British was more about the former wanting to control the flow of oil and the latter wanting to avoid that outcome at all costs. In the ambition of the king of Iraq, Faisal I, to see a railway built from Baghdad to Haifa, the British had a bargaining chip. The arguments went on, leading CFP chairman Ernest Mercier to describe the negotiations as 'mere comedies'.[2]

In the end, it was Walter Teagle who broke the impasse. In April 1930, the French representative Horace Finaly approached Teagle and warned against Jersey Standard taking an 'unfriendly attitude' towards France. The implication was clear: there would be sanctions against the Americans if they did not swing behind the French in the pipeline business.[3]

Teagle was quick to respond to the whiff of blackmail. France, he firmly reminded Finaly, could not look to the oil majors for support if she harassed them at home. On Teagle's suggestion, the pipeline route was split in two, creating a Y-shaped configuration. Two parallel pipelines would run from Kirkuk to the Iraqi border and then separate at Haditha, one taking a southern route and the other taking a northern route. There would be more arguments to follow but that, essentially, was how the final configuration of the pipelines emerged.

The pipeline system was only part of it; there was also the plots system, which Cadman was anxious to discard. In early 1931, when TPC and the Iraqi government were on the verge of a new agreement, a last-minute hitch brought Cadman, now IPC chairman, and John Skliros, the IPC general manager, on a plane to Baghdad.

In those days the city was a swirling mass of humanity, a profusion of religions and races. The daily grind was epitomized by the crowds, camel drivers and men on donkeys competing with a few rickety motor cars on the ancient streets. The River Tigris carried its staple trades through the centre, witnessed by the heavily laden coracles and variety of other craft flitting across the brown water. In winter, the roads into town were choked as dust turned to mud in the rain; in summer, their surfaces cracked open to reveal all manner of pits and potholes.

King Faisal ruled Iraq. He was a man of contradictions: being of royal lineage, the second son of the king of Hejaz in western Arabia, he was nevertheless an outsider in Iraq; the figurehead of the Arab Revolt, he found himself outmanoeuvred in the post-war division of the region between Britain and France; a British protégé, he had struggled to find his rightful place, and was removed from the Syrian throne by the French and installed in Baghdad after a rigged referendum. Now, ten years later, he presided over a chaotic state of affairs in Iraq where conflicting interests – tribal leaders, clerics and landowners – vied for political influence.

Even an experienced Middle East hand like Cadman found it difficult to make sense of the situation that confronted him when he arrived in the capital. The government was chaotic and cabinet ministers were threatening to commit 'suicide'.[4] Faisal complained that his people resented IPC's disregard of Iraqi affairs. Prime Minister Nuri as-Said was more specific, accusing the company of dragging its feet in order to delay as long as possible the sale of Iraqi oil on the world's markets.

Both Cadman and Nuri were, to a large extent, playing to the gallery. Whatever their differences, Baghdad and IPC were bound together in a symbiotic relationship based on oil. The Iraqi government relied on oil revenues and IPC needed to control the oil pumped out of Kirkuk. Therefore, despite an undercurrent of popular mistrust, the relationship between the government and the company prevailed.

On 24 March 1931 they reached an agreement. The oil-rich areas in the Baghdad and Mosul *vilayets* east of the River Tigris went to IPC. The detested plots system was abolished. The new agreement left an Anglo-Italian group, British Oil Development Ltd (BOD), to obtain a separate concession for the less-promising territory west of the Tigris; this they gained a year later. Despite discovering some oil, and gaining German and Italian investment, the venture failed and was bought up by the IPC shareholders. In 1941 the reconfigured company was named the Mosul Petroleum Company, and operated

King Faisal I at his palace in Baghdad, 6 October 1932.

the concession as a member of the IPC group. Oil was subsequently
discovered in commercial quantities at Ain Zalah and Butmah.

For now, with the Great Depression looming, the new pipelines
would not come on stream for some time, and production from the
Kirkuk field would remain static until then. Activity declined, with
the amount of drilling undertaken by the company falling by half.
Another argument broke out between the IPC partners, with Shell

representatives urging a further delay in the pipeline project, which the French resisted.

Newspapers were full of gloom and doom, and there was much scepticism that the Mediterranean pipelines would ever see the light of day – except that the shareholders were, as Skliros put it, 'caught in the pipeline trap' and unable to extricate themselves.[5] The pipelines were duly built and by 1934 IPC was loading shipments of crude oil, the first from the northern line in July and then from the southern line in October. The company formally inaugurated the pipelines in a series of ceremonies held the following January. Since King Faisal I had died two years before, it was his eldest son and successor, King Ghazi, who officiated over the ceremonials. Over the next two weeks, eighty or so guests and officials were flown to functions in Damascus, Tripoli, Haifa and Amman in a variety of aircraft. The British ambassador piloted his own plane and other guests arrived in a train fitted with sleeping and restaurant cars.

The pipelines were considered an engineering marvel of their time and, for the first few years, were highly effective, coping with a production from the Kirkuk field that increased fourfold between 1934 and 1938. The oil in the southern pipeline travelled at a moderate walking pace, about 2 miles per hour, and took up to eleven days to travel from Kirkuk to Haifa.

During the arguments over the pipeline route, the French had voiced doubts about the security of the southern pipeline. These they repeated as the project went on, with the French saying that the working gangs were vulnerable to bedouin attack, just as the British said exactly the same about the northern line. Much as these concerns might have been dismissed as scaremongering at the time, they were also indicative of a deeper Anglo-French rivalry in the region.

In fact their fears materialized during the so-called Arab Revolt of 1936–9 with a series of attacks on the southern pipeline. In some cases, the oil ignited and could be seen burning from miles away. The incidents were dealt with by stopping the flow of oil upstream and repairing the punctured tube. Then the British formed the Special Night Squads under the leadership of Captain Orde Wingate, who who targeted the Arabs in their villages; attacks on the pipeline declined. Recognizing that a hostile Arab population might create a dangerous fifth column in Palestine in time of war, the British eventually softened their approach towards the Arabs vis-à-vis the Jews, a policy that would see a substitution of roles: after the war, Jewish groups took against the British and resorted to violence against them.

For now, the oil would still flow: the pipelines were the only method of exporting Iraqi oil to the West. The French argued for a doubling of pipeline capacity while the Americans wanted to build a new pipeline to the Persian Gulf in order to supply their Far Eastern markets. Acting as peacemaker, Skliros suggested that the shareholders give the French additional supplies from the Kirkuk oilfield. As the debate became more entrenched, the French announced their own plan to build a pipeline. Less a practical idea than a means to pressure the IPC shareholders into making a decision, it did the trick. They agreed to build new Mediterranean pipelines, but, as it transpired, the plan was shelved when the Second World War broke out in September 1939.

THE ITALIAN LEADER BENITO Mussolini claimed he would turn the Mediterranean into an 'Italian lake'.[6] His words mimicked the old saying about the Persian Gulf being a British lake, but in fact were a throwback to an earlier time, to the Roman notion of *Mare Nostrum*. In the remote parts of Arabia, such grandiose ideas were of little consequence. Here the conflict was known as a *Nasrani* war, a great battle of the Christians and their devilish machines being thrashed out on the far side of the world.

At first, it seemed to be so, for the impact of the war was only felt indirectly. But, as the months passed, the Mediterranean became increasingly unsafe. Oil shipments from Iraq were curtailed and, within nine months, the situation had changed dramatically: Paris had fallen, Mussolini's Italy had joined the war on Hitler's side and the Vichy French under General Henri Dentz controlled Syria and Lebanon. The latter were now collaborating with the Germans, presenting a direct threat to British oil interests in the region and, potentially, to the Suez Canal. In these circumstances, IPC had no choice but to stop pumping oil along the northern line to Tripoli.

The Italians duly made their entrance. The Comando Aeronautica dell'Egeo (Aegean Air Force Command) began a series of air raids on the Haifa refinery from its Dodecanese air bases. On 15 July 1940 five Italian aircraft attacked the refinery and dropped more than fifty bombs, with about half hitting the target area. They set ablaze three

Laying the Kirkuk to Haifa pipeline, 1934.

oil tanks and a power station, and knocked out the town's electricity supply. The raid was considered a success, and all the aircraft returned to base, their aircrews filled with a 'lot of joy'.[7] Over the next two years, Italian, Vichy and German aircraft carried out a total of 27 air raids on the refinery.

The Italians advanced from Libya towards Egypt, and the Vichy French in the Levant remained a source of concern. British generals considered the defence of the Suez Canal as their main priority; but since oil was vital to the war effort on both sides, Kirkuk oil had to be denied to the enemy. On 1 November 1940 a secret report advised that plans to destroy the oilfields and pipelines should be 'perfected' without telling Baghdad.[8] At this moment, John Skliros, the managing director of IPC, pointed out that if the Iraqi government heard about the plans there would be repercussions.

As the arguments ran on, events took an alarming turn. The Iraqi cabinet was split between rival pro-British and pro-German factions, and broke off diplomatic relations with Germany without declaring war; it also maintained relations with Rome even after Italy had joined the war. Baghdad was a hotbed of intrigue, with the Italian legation and the grand mufti of Jerusalem, a renowned supporter of the Nazi cause, at its centre. And now, at the beginning of April 1941, a military coup saw the Anglophobe Rashid Ali al-Gaylani being installed as 'chief of the national defence government'. The infant king, the regent and the former pro-British prime minister, Nuri as-Said, fled to Jordan along with a number of other prominent Iraqi politicians.

The new Iraqi government took control of the oilfields, leaving the wells and infrastructure intact. At the main camp in Kirkuk, expatriate women and children were evacuated leaving behind a core of key IPC staff, who supervised basic operations to make petrol and operate the mechanical and motor transport workshops; oil production almost came to a halt. The remainder of the staff were rounded up and detained in a local schoolhouse. Here the captives managed to keep up with the news using concealed radio sets. Indian cooks and assistants still worked at the camp, and their wives helped to smuggle in food packages to the men through the school fence.

Many Iraqis faced a conflict of loyalties. These were men who had worked for the British-led IPC for many years and yet were patriots to a man. Some were 'steadfast in their loyalty' to the company while others backed the winners – whoever they might be.[9] Quite what this meant for the Rashid Ali rebellion was difficult to discern since, despite the momentous nature of the revolt, indecision prevailed. It seemed that many Iraqis were biding their time, waiting for the outcome in order to emerge on the winning side.

There was worse to come. With Rashid Ali's permission, British troops had arrived at Basra but, rather than being posted to Egypt or Palestine, they remained in Iraq. Under the Anglo-Iraqi Treaty of 1930, Britain had the right to maintain two airbases and transport military forces and supplies through Iraq at all times. When Rashid Ali refused permission to land any more troops, the British disregarded him. The Iraqi army converged on the RAF base at Habbaniyah and came up against decrepit British aeroplanes and a beleaguered garrison. At this juncture, Rashid Ali's appeal to Adolf Hitler for armed support appeared to bear fruit. On 14 May British officials saw a 'strange' German aircraft at the Kirkuk aerodrome.[10] It was later confirmed that the Vichy French authorities were allowing German forces to travel through Syria on their way to Iraq.

LATE IN THE AFTERNOON, as the sun's rays slanted down on the domes and minarets of Istanbul, a plane with German markings flew in from the west. This bird of ill omen carried no lesser person than Franz von Papen, the German ambassador to Turkey and the man whom Adolf Hitler expected to open up the Middle East. In answer to Rashid Ali's call for help, an advance party led by the former German ambassador to Iraq, Franz Grobba, had arrived in Baghdad with gold and a promise to set up the German oil company, Kontinentale, once the British had departed from the oilfields.

In the event, Germany's attempt to intervene in Iraq was a half-hearted affair. All in all, five bombers, twelve fighters (to add to the two already in the country), three transport planes and an assortment of mechanics and pilots came to assist the Iraqis; twelve fighters of the Italian Air Force were based in Mosul under German command. It was all too little, too late.

The arrival of British troops from Palestine helped to drive the Iraqis back towards Baghdad, despite a few sporadic attacks from the German aircraft. On 30 May a British forward unit reached the outskirts and received a message that two Iraqi officers wished to parley on the Iron Bridge leading into the city. At 4 am the following morning, the meeting took place and a truce was signed, effectively ending the Anglo-Iraqi war. Rashid Ali and his entourage, the pro-Axis ministers and the grand mufti of Jerusalem fled to Iran, and the German mission, too, had departed. The British army occupied all the important points in the country, including the oilfields. The regent of Iraq, Abd al-Ilah, was reinstated and a new government took office under Nuri as-Said. In the following weeks British, Australian and Free French forces invaded Syria and overcame the Vichy forces. The Allies now gained air superiority and enemy attacks on the Haifa oil terminal declined. Adolf Hitler's focus was elsewhere and, when the invasion of Russia was launched, the direct German threat to Iraq diminished even more.

Back at Kirkuk, the military still needed oil, so IPC looked to restoring some output from the oilfield. The company built a 10-centimetre (4-in.) pipeline from Kirkuk to Mosul to keep the

Loading passengers and cargo onto an RAF Vickers Valentia at H4 pumping station on the IPC oil pipeline. H4 was used as a base for military operations against the Rashid Ali regime.

army supplied with fuel, and pumped oil to Tripoli for the Royal Navy. Other work included mounting fuel supply tanks on military vehicles, installing lorry and rail-loading facilities, erecting kerbside pumps and oil storage facilities, and generally providing advice and assistance for the war effort.

In view of the German advances in Russia, British generals drew up plans to protect the oilfields from aerial bombardment and attack by paratroopers. The Rashid Ali experience had unsettled their confidence in the loyalty of local troops, and there was a proposal to disarm the Iraqi army should the Germans again come within range of Kirkuk. This was no fantasy: in June 1942 the Wehrmacht arrived at El Alamein, only 112 kilometres (70 miles) from Alexandria, and by August their troops were at Stalingrad and in reach of the Baku oilfields.

It was time to get serious about denying the Kirkuk oilfield to the enemy. Skliros again opposed the idea, stressing the futility of plugging the oil wells when the Germans could easily drill new ones to a depth of 914 metres (3,000 ft) in a short time. The generals heeded his warning – partly – and the Royal Engineers reprieved six wells. The wisdom of this decision was soon apparent when the German threat again subsided; the Allies made advances in North Africa and the Wehrmacht surrendered at Stalingrad. Oil production from the Kirkuk field revived and reached 4.62 million tons in 1945, although IPC was forced to cut back on its other activities. Drilling would be suspended for the duration of the war and for two years afterwards in order to give the company a chance to get back on its feet.

Meanwhile, among the IPC shareholders, the war had been a depressing story of strife, dissent and recrimination. In July 1940

The regent Abd al-Ilah in the foreground with the prime minister, Nuri as-Said, behind at the opening of the Iraq Parliament in November 1942.

Britain declared that French companies and persons residing in Occupied France were 'enemy aliens' – a definition that included Calouste Gulbenkian, much to his chagrin. They lost access to Iraqi oil for a time, with Gulbenkian's enemy status being lifted in 1943 and CFP's two years later.

All this was of small concern to most Iraqis, since few – if any – would have been aware of such squabbles. There was a general unease in the country after the war, however. They had seen their country fought over by the Western powers for its oil, and emerged from the war as a people under occupation. British troops did not depart until October 1947, by which time the voices of Arab nationalism were stirring. The 'ungrateful volcano', as Churchill once called Iraq, was set to erupt again.[11]

SIX

PUMPING DUST,
1945–71

I N 1918 A YOUNG Arab officer emerged from the dust of war riding beside Faisal and Lawrence of Arabia on their way to Damascus. This was Nuri as-Said, one of the more remarkable politicians to emerge from the upheavals of the war in the Middle East. Upon arriving in the city, the thirty-year-old Iraqi stayed on in a civilian capacity, serving under Faisal during the latter's brief sojourn as king of Syria.

After his return to Iraq, Nuri held several influential positions before becoming prime minister for the first time in 1930. He was the consummate survivor – sixteen years later, he was forming his tenth government – and served fourteen terms as prime minister altogether. His politics were defined by his support of the king and his pro-British leanings. The parliamentary system was unstable, but there was always the military to restore control. The fact that martial law was used seventeen times between 1931 and 1958 confirmed the democratic failings. It was said that power changed hands within an elite of some forty leading families.

The parties of opposition, when not forced underground, occasionally made an impact. The communists made little progress in parliamentary elections against vested interests and tribal sheikhs, and elections were often rigged. The connection between the British and Iraqi governments remained close; it was inevitable that political activists should have the British government as much as the Iraqi in their sights, and IPC a target for their discontent.

There was a dangerous complacency about the British presence in Iraq. It was said that before the First World War no one dared to leave Baghdad's South Gate after dark for fear of bandits. Now it was relatively safe. Many Iraqis who used to walk about with one hand on their heads to ward off *djinns* no longer did so. Was it too much to credit the British for these changes? They had, after all, brutally suppressed the 1920 revolt, helped to discover its oil and were its protector and guarantor of its future. Central to the relationship between Britain and Iraq was the 1930 treaty that permitted the former to maintain two military bases in the country and required the Iraqi government to employ British-approved advisers. But it was also said that in the countryside nothing really changed: the *fellahin* went hungry as the landlords and sheikhs lived off the fat of the land.

[margin note: an Egyptian peasant]

In May 1946 IPC began building two new 40-centimetre (16-in.) pipelines in order to increase production from the Kirkuk oilfield in anticipation of a growing post-war demand for oil. But, as the southern pipeline advanced towards Palestine, its future looked increasingly uncertain. The old 30-centimetre (12-in.) pipelines had occasionally been attacked and, although the war had seen a lull in activity, there was a series of explosions on the southern pipeline and installations once the war was over; these were the work of Jewish groups.

In March 1947 saboteurs dynamited the oil tanks at Haifa, starting a fire that destroyed part of the waterfront and burned for 24 hours, casting a thick pall of smoke that rose high in the air, destroying eight oil tanks and seriously damaging six.

The future of Palestine was a pressing issue. Having been mandated to Britain, the territory was now to be partitioned into Arab and Jewish states by virtue of UN Resolution 181 of November 1947. The British announced their intention to withdraw their military forces from the territory by 15 May 1948. That date hung like a guillotine over IPC operations as repeated attacks on the southern pipeline made it increasingly likely that they would withdraw from the territory.

Back in Baghdad, news of an Anglo-Iraqi Treaty in January 1948 triggered an outbreak of civil unrest that became known as Al-Wathba (The Leap). The result was chaos: the regent Abd al-Ilah repudiated the treaty and Prime Minister Salih Jabr resigned. A new government was formed, but the disturbances continued. A disappointing result for the opposition parties in the subsequent elections perpetuated the problem; the ruling elite retained their hold on power while high prices and food shortages hit the poor. A strike by IPC workers at the Haditha pumping station was a prelude to the industrial troubles to come.

The blade fell on IPC's southern pipeline when the independent state of Israel was declared, and the Iraqi government prohibited the company from pumping oil to Haifa, which rendered any further work on the new pipeline futile. IPC abandoned construction on the southern route altogether, and stopped pumping oil through the existing 30-centimetre (12-in.) section. On 15 May, as a result of the Israeli declaration, the Arabs invaded; thus began the first Arab-Israeli war. IPC turned to completing the new northern section to Tripoli.

After the Arab defeat in the war with Israel, and with Nuri back in charge, Iraq calmed down again. But short of money and driven by populist sentiment, Baghdad wanted more money for its oil. In March 1949 Nuri demanded royalties to match those received by Kuwait and Saudi Arabia.

This was hardly a radical notion but, by the time the negotiations were complete, the balance in the petroleum world had shifted once more. Britain's devaluation of sterling seemed to leave Iraq further behind and then, when it appeared that an agreement had been reached, news of Saudi Arabia's 50–50 profit-sharing agreement with Aramco broke; it set a precedent that could not be ignored. Spurred on by Mossadegh's termination of the Anglo-Iranian concession, Nuri publicly committed himself to getting a 50–50 deal for Iraq. He repudiated the draft agreement and, after much posturing on the Iraqi side and intransigence on the British, a deal was hammered out in February 1952. What Baghdad wanted – a fairer income base based on 'posted prices' – appeared to have been achieved.

The deal stopped the nationalization movement in its tracks. The Iranian experience stood out as a warning beacon of the perils of going it alone. But, although the 50–50 agreement went some way towards meeting Iraqi demands, the promise of more wealth did not bring contentment. A general strike in the Zubair oilfield near Basra in 1951 was followed two years later with a strike by Basra Petroleum (BPC) workers for higher pay and better working conditions. The company made a number of concessions to workers' demands. Consultation committees were set up for management

[handwritten margin note: refusal to change one's views or to agree about something.]

and workers to discuss welfare, safety and technical issues, but not pay. Training schemes were introduced and water wells were drilled. With hindsight, one can see that the problems of Iraq ran far deeper than industrial relations policy could reach; but, for the time being, the illusion prevailed that the troubles of the industry were curable by such means.

Oil workers on an Iraqi drilling rig, 1955.

BY NOW WORK HAD started on an even larger 80-centimetre (32-in.) pipeline from Kirkuk to a new loading terminal at Banias on the Syrian coast. This pipeline was unofficially dubbed 'The Third River', an 893-kilometre (555-mile) stream of oil to compare – figuratively – with the two great waterways of that country, the Tigris and Euphrates.[1] On 18 November 1952 there was an inauguration ceremony at Kirkuk at which the seventeen-year-old king of Iraq, Faisal II, symbolically opened a valve to start the flow of oil to the sea.

In London, senior oil executives and government officials marked the occasion with drinks and canapés in the grand ballroom of Grosvenor House. For a company determined not to make the same mistakes as Anglo-Iranian, this seemed a good start: the new pipeline increased revenues, and the 50–50 agreement ensured a fourfold increase in share of profits due to the Iraqi government. Despite this success, memories of the Abadan scuttle would still have been fresh in the minds of the assembled guests.

It was undeniable that the Iraqi oil industry was growing fast. In the north, the Mosul Petroleum Company was pumping oil from Ain Zalah and Butmah oilfields to the Kirkuk pipeline complex. The Kirkuk oilfield operated by IPC was expanding and part of the supergiant field of Rumaila had just been discovered. In the south, the Basra Petroleum Company was building a pipeline from the recently opened Zubair oilfield in southern Iraq to a tanker terminal at Fao on the Gulf.

But the Middle East was growing restless and events elsewhere would have a knock-on effect in Iraq. The turning point came with the Suez Crisis, triggered by Egyptian President Nasser's nationalization of the canal on 26 July 1956. It was a provocation that the British and French would not ignore and, on the contrived pretext of keeping warring Egyptians and Israelis apart, they sent a joint task force to the area. In November, however, as warships of the Anglo-French task force lay off the Egyptian coast, truckloads of Syrian troops were trundling into the desert, heading for three IPC pumping stations on the northern and Kirkuk–Haditha sections of the Mediterranean pipelines.

The pumping stations were remote settlements about 100 miles apart. As the name implies, their function was to pump the company's oil through its pipelines to the sea. Their situation and purpose were a tempting target for the Syrians at a time when anti-Western feelings were running high. All the same, IPC had no inkling of the danger before the Syrian army arrived and blew up three stations, leaving the staff to make their way overland to Homs and then back to the West. It was not until March 1957 that IPC was able to pump crude oil to Banias again. Meanwhile, the loss of oil shipments to Europe was made up by exports from the United States.

These incidents persuaded the oil companies to review their shipping routes. It was apparent that pipelines were vulnerable to attack and to political pressure, and that the Suez Canal might be used to blackmail the West in the years to come. One solution was to use the sea route around the Cape which, although longer, could make use of newly developed supertankers and thus avoid the drawbacks of the Suez Canal.

The withdrawal of British and French troops from Suez was a devastating blow for their prestige in the region, and was an immense boost for Arab nationalism. It brought 'disbelief and consternation' in Iraq, and put the Hashemite regime in great danger.[2] Perhaps, if he had been dealt a better hand, Nuri might have survived. But frustration with the 'most feared' man in Iraq was rising following another clampdown on civil liberties and the signing of the Baghdad Pact, a pro-Western alliance of countries designed to resist Soviet aggression; and now the Suez debacle added fuel to the fire.[3]

There were other issues, too. At a time when the oil wealth should have been applied to the benefit of the whole population, there were glaring disparities. The creation of the Iraq Development Board promised to divert oil money towards public infrastructure projects such dam construction and road building. When viewed in isolation, these were all well and good, but in the wider context of Iraqi society they left much to be desired. Social problems were not tackled, and problems of poverty were not addressed.

The creation of the United Arab Republic of Egypt and Syria under Nasser's leadership in February 1958 was an ominous warning for the Hashemite monarchy. By May Nuri was out of office again, having been appointed president of the Arab League, but his ability to bounce back made him a marked man nevertheless. There had been many coups and plots in the past and perhaps Nuri might have thought himself indestructible, having survived each time: he once said, 'the man has not been born who can assassinate me'.[4] Like a game of Russian roulette, though, there was always a chance

UK motorists queuing for rationed petrol after the Suez Crisis in 1956.

that one bullet would eventually reach its target and put an end to Nuri's days.

And then it happened. In July, a worsening situation in the Lebanon brought the U.S. Sixth Fleet to Beirut, and a plot to assassinate King Hussein of Jordan triggered a request for military assistance from his cousin, King Faisal II. Units of the Iraqi army were ordered to proceed to Amman in order to support the beleaguered king; but the troops never got beyond Baghdad.

At dawn on the 14th a brigade led by Abdul Salam Arif, passing through Baghdad on the pretext of travelling to Amman, seized the radio station. There followed a second brigade, held in reserve, which entered the city and occupied key locations. Faisal, his uncle and members of his family were murdered. A mob searched the streets of Baghdad for Nuri as-Said. Hearing the sound of gunfire, Nuri escaped across the River Tigris, but the next day he was caught by the mob and murdered. With this also came the passing of the old order in Iraq; the oilfields remained intact, but their future remained uncertain.

THE NEW LEADER OF Iraq was Brigadier Abdul al-Karim Qasim, who had commanded the rebels' reserve brigade during the coup. Western leaders held their collective breath as they waited to see which way he would turn. Qasim headed the Free Officers' group in Iraq and typified a new generation of army officer who was motivated by a resentment of the elitism that was rife in Iraqi politics. In contrast to Nasser, who was the son of a village postmaster, Qasim came from a relatively well-to-do middle-class family living in a town on the outskirts of Baghdad. With a Sunni father and a Shi'ite mother, he preferred to call himself a nationalist rather than a pan-Arabist in the mould of Nasser. Largely unknown before the coup, he lacked the Egyptian leader's polish, having a nervous habit of winking at press conferences as if he were sharing a joke with his audience. In fact, he was deadly serious: he was a newcomer to the scene, but no one could possibly argue that this tall, khaki-clad and ascetic figure was a political dilettante.

No doubt IPC chairman Geoffrey Herridge was somewhat relieved when his plane touched down at Baghdad in August 1958. Reports had confirmed that IPC personnel were still in place and the oilfields were functioning normally. Qasim appeared conciliatory, and did not press full nationalization, probably accepting that Iraq lacked the necessary technical resources to go it alone. His demands were not impossible. Upon the start of talks, the Iraqi leader made it clear that he expected IPC to surrender most of its non-producing acreage, but Herridge was cautious; he was wary of setting precedent for other Arab oil-producing nations to follow. Herridge offered to give up 54 per cent against Qasim's demand for 60 per cent, and rejected an Iraqi demand for a 20 per cent shareholding in the company – a demand that went back to the San Remo Oil Agreement of 1920. The talks dragged on.

Meanwhile, the political situation was far from mended. Within the Free Officers there was a division between those such as Arif and the Ba'athists who wanted to unite with Egypt and others like Qasim who were staunch nationalists. There were the communists, too. Though not a communist himself, Qasim increasingly relied on the communist party to support his regime. The failings of this policy were soon exposed as the communists became increasingly powerful. On the oilfields, armed groups of the People's Resistance Force roamed the camps in trucks, chanting slogans, setting up roadblocks and searching IPC personnel and vehicles. Feelings were running high among the workers, and managers had to adopt a softly-softly approach, treading a thin line between appeasement and being reported to the police. An uprising in Mosul and its brutal repression brought the spectre of show trials. In the feverish atmosphere that prevailed, the IPC general manager in Mosul was denounced as 'Mr Poison', denounced as a spy and asked to leave the country and his counterpart in Basra was also withdrawn as a precautionary move.[5]

Recognizing that things had gone too far, Qasim sought to restore the balance. He began to purge the communists from the army, retiring officers with known communist sympathies. The oppression of the Turkomans (the original inhabitants of Kirkuk) was eased, encouraging many exiles to return home for the first anniversary of the revolution. On 14 July 1959, as the festivities got under way, disaster struck: the communists had planned a rally but feelings boiled over and the Kurds attacked the Turkomans, resulting in thirty deaths. In the aftermath, Qasim stepped up his campaign against the communists and the People's Resistance Force was disbanded.

Relations between IPC and the Iraqi government continued their downward path. Qasim was caught between his people's rising expectations, a shrill, anti-Western press and the unblinking stare of IPC. His failure to strike the winning blow was bound to reflect on his personal standing and give sustenance to his enemies. Added to that, a combination of factors did little to improve his disposition. He survived an assassination attempt by disaffected officers who included a certain Saddam Hussein, and there was an ongoing dispute with the IPC group over freight charges for oil shipped from Basra. What could he do? In a corner, he decided to go on the offensive.

In March 1961, when IPC agreed to relinquish 75 per cent of its territory, plus 15 per cent in nine years' time, Qasim promptly increased his demand to 90 per cent. Although IPC subsequently yielded, it still refused to give way on Qasim's demand for a 20 per cent share of the company. A month later, at the close of yet another fruitless meeting, Qasim told IPC negotiators that the company could not search for any new oilfields, and reinforced his demand with a threat of military force. Meanwhile, as disturbances broke out in Kurdistan, Qasim found in IPC a convenient whipping boy for his troubles.

The *coup de grâce* came on 12 December when Law No. 80 was enacted. This expropriated the undeveloped parts of the IPC group's concession areas without compensation. For example, while the group retained the Kirkuk oilfield, it lost the supergiant North Rumaila field, discovered but as yet undeveloped; the company was allowed to participate in developing the latter field, but only on terms set by the government. IPC was effectively pegged back to their producing fields and prohibited from finding any new sources of oil.

In the short term, the new law confirmed Qasim's anti-Western credentials but, in the longer term, it consigned the Iraqi oil industry to a decade of petroleum torpor. IPC had no incentive to invest in the country's oil development, and building new pipelines, developing new oilfields and investing in new equipment were out of the question. For the next ten years, oil production from Iraq rose by a modest 37 per cent, compared with 277 per cent for Iran and 267 per cent for Saudi Arabia. Although the oil majors could easily make up the loss of Iraqi oil from other sources in the Gulf, the same did not apply to the Iraqi government and its oil revenues; the simple truth was that Iraq's need for oil was greater than the oil majors' need to extract it.

The IPC partners made noises and threatened other companies with legal action should they be minded to take up concessions in the expropriated areas but, ultimately, they decided to wait out events. Qasim's position looked increasingly shaky, and moves were afoot to remove him anyway. Much as Qasim himself suspected, the Americans were stirring up trouble in Kurdistan. U.S. President John F. Kennedy looked on with rising concern as Qasim challenged American influence in the region and renewed old claims to Kuwait, and the CIA had been at work destabilizing the regime for some months. Setting up a base in Kuwait, communicating with Qasim's opponents and arming the Kurds, the agency even set up the euphemistically named Health Alteration Committee, which counted among its achievements the infamous gift of a poisoned handkerchief sent to Qasim – all to no avail.

In the event, it fell to a group of army officers to stage a coup. On 8 February 1963, after gun battles in Baghdad, Qasim was captured and executed. Abdul Salam Arif, the former associate of Qasim, became president of Iraq.

Momentarily it looked as if the new government might settle its differences with IPC. The new oil minister, Abdul Aziz al-Wattari, a

General Qasim greets a cheering crowd in Baghdad following the suppression of a
Kurdish revolt in March 1959.

petroleum engineer with a doctorate from Colorado State University, proposed that the company should be allowed to return to the North Rumaila oilfield. It was certainly a tempting prospect, but the IPC shareholders wanted the company's rights restored. The oil majors could 'swallow' oil from elsewhere to make up their supplies in the meantime.[6] Executive director Lester Murphy arrived in Baghdad for talks at the head of a low-key IPC delegation, known as the Murphy Mission. Al-Wattari wanted to increase oil production, and IPC wanted Law No. 80 revoked. Since no Iraqi politician in his right mind could possibly agree to this demand, the talks broke down at the end of April.

IN NOVEMBER 1963 THE wheel turned again, and another coup brought a new government into power. An old plan from the Qasim era was revived to create a national oil company to explore and develop the territory regained by Iraq under Law No. 80. Three months later the Iraq National Oil Company (INOC) was born. In spite of the new company developing slowly, its mere existence was highly significant. Even the most cynical IPC managers could not deny that it was the next step, albeit symbolic, towards full nationalization.

IPC still had a few more years to go, though it was getting more difficult to foresee what the Iraqi government might do. This was most apparent in the summer of 1965 when the company had another chance to settle its differences with Baghdad. By now the IPC shareholders were no longer on the warpath: lawyers considered the company's claim against Law No. 80 weak, and the creation of INOC had opened the door to foreign rivals; the French were keen to do a deal. And so the shelved discussion of two years before – the Al-Wattari plan no less – was revived. Iraq would restore 750 square miles of the area expropriated under Law No. 80 and IPC would return to the North Rumaila field in a joint venture with INOC.

It was a debacle, however. Al-Wattari was shouted down when he presented the document to the Iraqi cabinet in July and six ministers resigned. There were other distractions in the meantime – a dispute with the Syrians over pipeline transit rights, for example – but the Six-Day War of June 1967 was the real game changer. This radicalized Arab opinion against the West and set the oil-producing countries on a new trajectory. As we shall see in a later chapter, the Arab producers imposed an oil embargo against certain Western countries with mixed results.

In August, a new government took further measures against IPC, passing Law No. 97 which excluded the company from the North Rumaila oilfield and gave INOC a monopoly over the confiscated territory. Law No. 123 reorganized INOC and put it under direct political control; Adib al-Jadir, one of the leading opponents of the Al-Wattari agreement, and a new management replaced the technocrats in INOC, giving the state-controlled company a distinctly left-wing outlook.

A new dimension opened up. A deal with ERAP/Elf enabled the French to explore and make a discovery of oil, though its quality was poor and relations with INOC were strained. An Iraqi–Soviet agreement saw Russian advisers helping to develop the Rumaila field, one of several deals with foreign companies that reduced Iraq's dependency on the IPC group.

On 17 July 1968 a Ba'athist coup brought the ailing Ahmad Hassan al-Bakr to power, replacing Abdul Rahman Arif as president. A number of senior INOC managers, including Adib al-Jadir, departed amid allegations of corruption, possibly linked to the ERAP/Elf deal. Saddam Hussein, a kinsman of al-Bakr and vice-chairman of the Revolutionary Command Council, was tasked to nationalize IPC and its associated companies in Iraq. The son of a shepherd from a small village near Tikrit in northern Iraq, Saddam had been in the political background since taking part in the failed assassination plot against General Qasim in 1959. Now he was elevated to one of the highest offices in the land, while those 'nice . . . Sandhurst-trained colonels' with whom IPC executives had done business in the past were gone, mostly executed, exiled or imprisoned.[7]

There was no beauty in oil; it was a commodity to be possessed, controlled and used as a weapon. The IPC rump still dominated Iraq's oil industry and could not be ignored, particularly when the group stubbornly refused to increase oil production. Three years later and the dispute was building to a climax as both sides faced each other with proverbial daggers drawn. The country's vice president, Salih Mahdi Ammash, declared that his country was ready for 'any battle with the company that was necessary'.[8]

Almost twenty years had passed since Nuri was at the height of his powers and the young King Faisal II was awkwardly turning the valve to let the oil flow along the new Banias pipeline. And now, as Iraqis listened to Saddam Hussein speaking on Baghdad Radio, those who remembered those days must have thought them a world away from the passion and sway of the strong man's roar.

.

ARABIA
AND
THE GULF

SEVEN

THE PLENTY QUARTER, 1920–44

HE CROSSED THE NARROW strait between Bahrain and the Arabian mainland, chasing a bedouin rumour. Here, on a shore that few Westerners had visited before, he found a landscape that was remarkable for its dullness: low sandy hills that separated a hazy, shallow green sea from burnished salt pans running behind the shore. Ahead, the palm-decked oasis and cultivations of Qatif stood out as a glint of green amid the dreary hinterland. Crescent-shaped dunes creeping towards the date plantations threatened to swallow the oasis whole, leaving wells abandoned in their wake, their crumbling stone well-shafts poking through the sands like the chimneys of an abandoned village.

The year was 1920 and Harold Dickson had come in search of oil. An English political officer in Bahrain, he was following up reports of an oil seepage. Dressed in the ill-fitting Arab garb he liked to wear for his excursions, he mounted a camel and set off with a bedouin guide and donkey in tow, taking the short causeway to Tarut Island. Paying his respects to the local governor, Sheikh Jasim, his real motive was to inspect a relic of the erstwhile Turkish occupation: a copy of an old report that might give substance to the rumour of an oil seepage behind Qatif. The local *mutasarrif* had sent the original report to Constantinople some years before.

Having exchanged *salaams* with the governor and read the report, Dickson crossed back to the mainland, travelling inland for 9 kilometres (6 miles) to look for the seepage amid the dunes; but he found no sign of it. Thinking that the rumours might have located the seepage in the wrong place, he abandoned his search. He turned his little party

[handwritten margin notes:]
Administrative authority of Sanjaks who were appointed by the sultan of the Ottoman Empire directly

Sanjaks were administrative divisions of the Ottoman Empire akin to districts.

Common greeting in many Arabic-speaking & Muslim countries

The fort at Tarut, 1924.

around, headed for a low hill called Jebel Dhahran, and boarded his boat on the shore for the return journey to Bahrain.

Some years on, after further attempts to find oil had come to nothing, Dickson was still unrepentant about the rumoured seepage, claiming that 'it was covered by a gigantic sand dune, one of the very many to be found, continuously on the move, west of Qatif palm-belt'.[1] Later geologists would dismiss the possibility of an oil seepage in that vicinity, but in those early days rumours spread quickly and probably came to the notice of Ibn Saud, then emir of the Nejd and Al Hasa.

If the emir heard this rumour, he could hardly have ignored it, yet he was preoccupied with other things. Being a hypochondriac, Abdul Aziz ibn Saud (Ibn Saud) had several doctors to advise him, including ones from abroad. In 1921 Sir Percy Cox, the British high commissioner in Iraq, received disturbing reports that American missionary doctors in Riyadh were stirring up anti-British feelings. On Sir Percy's suggestion, Ibn Saud accepted the offer of a British doctor to replace them. Dr Alex Mann was about to retire from the British High Commission in Baghdad when he received orders to travel to Riyadh. It soon became apparent that he was a poor choice of medical adviser to Ibn Saud, at least for the British who had hoped he would be a moderating influence. Mann began advising Ibn Saud on more than purely medical issues, leading the emir to believe that he was well connected, and to appoint him as his London agent.

There was an element of quiet plotting in this, for Ibn Saud hoped that Mann would wangle things behind the backs of British officials. He asked Mann to find a company to explore for minerals and oil in the eastern province of Al Hasa. Mann duly met Edmund Davis, a director of Eastern and General Syndicates Limited (E&GS), whom he knew through London's Jewish community. At first glance, a concession held little interest for the company because Arabia was so remote, and E&GS had no track record of oil exploration. But the company was in the business of dealing in oil concessions, buying them up in order to sell them on, making a profit in the process.

Major Frank Holmes, a British-New Zealander who was a partner in E&GS, took up the challenge. Formerly commissioned in the British army during the First World War and variously described as mining engineer turned driller of water wells and concession hunter, Holmes claimed to have a 'nose' for finding oil – in these early days few prospectors possessed any other expertise in petroleum. In the course of his travels as a quartermaster with the army in the Middle East and East Africa, he had learned Arabic and heard stories of an oil seepage on Bahrain Island.[2] After a brief stint in Aden, he returned to Bahrain, making friends among the local Arab community.

Most of all, Holmes was a concession hunter. In the autumn of 1922 he travelled with Mann to Riyadh and obtained in principle an oil concession from Ibn Saud. He then travelled to Basra to get a final agreement drawn up in Arabic. Returning on the steamer *Barjola*, he encountered amid a crowded deck the writer Ameen Rihani, who was also heading for Arabia. The affable Holmes disingenuously remarked that he was travelling for his health: like the yarn he would later spin to Harold Dickson about searching for a rare butterfly, it was a flimsy ruse. As it turned out, all three of them ended up in the same place, at Uqair on the Hasa coast, where a military-style camp had been set up for a meeting between Ibn Saud and Sir Percy Cox. It was December, and early morning fog and seasonal damp frequented the dreary venue.

On one side of the camp white tents had been set up for the British delegation. On the other side were Ibn Saud's two large tents, one of which was a *majlis* guarded by armed black guards at its entrance. It was here that the Saudi delegation sat and waited for the British to arrive. One evening a messenger delivered the mail from Riyadh, which was opened in Ibn Saud's presence – the important letters were opened by the emir himself. One such letter brought a change in his mood:

'It is from home, from our people,' he said. 'And they complain of distance and absence.' Still there was no sign of the British. 'Allah sift the English!' a tribesman declared as another cup of coffee was downed.[3]

The following evening, the tooting of a horn in the harbour and the movement of a speck of light towards the quay signalled the arrival of the British delegation. Ibn Saud with horses and assorted retainers went down to meet them. Soon they were making their way back to the camp with their guests, the slaves' red robes in the moonlight being the most striking feature of a muddled throng. The leading actors took up their places under the glare of arc lights: in the centre, the imposing Ibn Saud, to his left the immaculate Sir Percy Cox and to his right, a hook-nosed and bleary-eyed Fahad Beg al-Hadhal, a tribal chieftain. In the evening the British would dress for dinner and enjoy all the comforts: tables laid with white linen, fine crockery, cutlery, glassware, whisky and cigars, all courtesy of Ibn Saud.

The conference had been arranged to settle the vexed question of frontiers. After five days of intense negotiation, those issues were resolved by the creation of Neutral Zones along the Hasa borders with Kuwait and Iraq. Then the question of Holmes's oil concession for Al Hasa fell to be considered. All along, no doubt to Cox's irritation, Holmes had been lingering in another tent waiting for Cox and Ibn Saud to emerge.

This was typical Holmes. Dismissed by British officials as a 'rover in the world of oil', he had the unnerving habit of popping up in awkward locations, slipping under the net of imperial control in the Gulf.[4] He was the prime mover of the oil business in Bahrain, Arabia and Kuwait, scuttling about long before the oil majors took a serious interest – no wonder that the Arabs would later dub him 'Abu Naft', the Father of Oil. Perhaps revelling in his vexatious reputation, he stood out at Uqair among the delegates and their retainers, more resembling a displaced tourist than a businessman with serious intent: he was accustomed to carrying a large white umbrella with a green lining, and wearing a French colonial-style white helmet with a green gauze veil draped over his face. He had also brought with him at least fifty cases of presents for the emir.

As far as the oil concession was concerned, Ibn Saud felt obliged to seek Cox's approval, since he received an annual stipend of £60,000 (£3 million today) from the British government. At last, when the discussions could proceed, Ibn Saud produced a map prepared by Holmes showing a proposed oil concession for eastern Arabia marked in blue pencil. Much to Cox's annoyance the area included Qatar, suggesting that it belonged to Ibn Saud. Annoyed at this barefaced attempt to bluff him, Sir Percy took hold of a red pen and, like an angry schoolmaster, crossed out Holmes's line and redrew the frontier with a line firmly drawn across the base of the Qatar Peninsula.

Ibn Saud had more serious business at hand. His ambition to extend his rule across the Arabian Peninsula depended to a large degree on a radical religious group known as the Ikhwan. They belonged to the Wahhabi tradition of Islam, taking a strict interpretation of the Quran. They also made an efficient fighting force, and Ibn Saud was concerned about losing control of them. Upon his return to his capital, Riyadh, he addressed an audience in his capacity as imam, holding a great *durbah* after *Jumaah* prayers. It was a large gathering with about 300 Ikhwan present in the hall:

> 'Understand this, I say, I am placed by God to rule over you, and I shall punish most severely any breach or disregard of my own orders as well as those of my emirs.' As he spoke towering above the heads of all, Ibn Saud drew his sword and brandished it over his head, greatly overawing those present. He ceased his peroration with the words, 'I have nothing more to tell you.' He then immediately rose and went out.[5]

It was a reaffirmation of his authority and a powerful warning to the Ikhwan in the crowd, one that left them 'dumbfounded' and fearful for their lives.

It was not until May 1923 that Ibn Saud returned to the subject of oil, albeit in a rather more defiant frame of mind. The British had stopped his stipend and he no longer felt obliged to seek Sir Percy's advice, or that of any other British official for that matter. The Hasa oil concession remained unresolved, and the British authorities were holding out for Anglo-Persian to make an approach. When nothing was forthcoming, Ibn Saud went ahead and granted Holmes a two-year concession, taking advice from no one beyond his own advisers and Ameen Rihani.

Between 20 April and 1 July 1924, as instructed by Holmes, geologist Arnold Heim carried out a survey of Kuwait, eastern Arabia and Bahrain, travelling on foot, camel and donkey. The desert conditions

Major Frank Holmes and his wife in Kuwait, 1924.

[handwritten margin note: A nomadic Arab of the desert]

were made more difficult by a rising temperature that rendered field-
work almost impossible towards the end of the trip. Bedouin attack
was a constant worry in certain parts, and one excursion nearly
resulted in the death of two local guides from thirst and exhaustion.
Significant seepages were found at Bohara in Kuwait and asphalt
pits at Ain al-Qar on Bahrain, and evidence of submarine seepages
were noted from tar deposits washed up on the shore. The result was
inconclusive, however; there were no clear signs of exploitable oil.
Heim concluded that Kuwait was a country of 'some possibility, but
not of high promise', and drilling on Bahrain and the Arabian coast
would be 'a pure gamble'.[6]

The Anglo-Persian geologist George Martin Lees did not think
Bahrain was worth drilling and indeed he was reported as saying he
would 'drink any commercial oil found in Bahrain'.[7] Emanating from
a man like Lees, who was usually open-minded and believed in obser-
vation and deduction, this was a puzzling remark. In fact he only made
it after carefully summing up the evidence for and against finding
commercial oil on Bahrain. He certainly kept his options open when
it came to Qatar, observing that drilling there would be justified if
operations on Bahrain proved successful. Even so, his remark did reflect
a general consensus about the area, which was that, in the words of one
pipe-smoking Shell executive, 'there is no oil in Arabia.'[8]

With hindsight, it seems extraordinary that this view should have prevailed. Hugo de Böckh, the leading Anglo-Persian geologist, dismissed Arabia as an oil prospect because it lacked the favourable 'lagoonal' context that had been identified on the other side of the Gulf; it was a theory that served him well in Persia, but not here. But, in any event, the two main oil companies in the region were fully occupied elsewhere so there was no pressing need to investigate the Arabian aspect. Following its astounding oil strike at Baba Gurgur, IPC was fully focused on developing Iraq while Anglo-Persian was similarly engaged in Iran. And so, five years after Holmes had gained the Hasa concession, no drilling had started anywhere in the Gulf or on the Arabian mainland.

It was a long way from the West, and the vastly different language, culture and customs of the Arabs made the region seem even more daunting. Communications were not easy in an age when the quickest way to send a message from Riyadh to Baghdad was by camel and boat to Bahrain and then telegraph onwards. Yet it was here, on this palm-decked island, that a Westerner might reasonably entertain an expectation of progress. Frank Holmes obtained a concession from the ruling sheikh to drill for water, and such was his success that the grateful ruler granted his company a licence to explore for oil. Holmes looked for a prospective buyer and, in January 1928, the Gulf Oil Corporation sent a geological party led by Ralph 'Dusty' Rhoades to investigate the possibilities.

Local conditions were basic but not impossible and Holmes went out of his way to reassure the visitors that Bahrain was as comfortable as New York, quoting his own ample girth as evidence that a person living on the island 'does not altogether fade way'.[9] Building on Holmes's extensive work, the party finished its survey in six weeks. 'It is concluded that a test well favourably located on the Bahrain anticline may reasonably be expected to encounter oil,' Rhoades reported.[10] Encountering oil was one thing, finding it in commercial quantities, however, was quite another.

Although Bahrain was a scene of activity, the real action now switched to San Francisco, New York and London. Gulf Oil was a member of the IPC group at that time, which meant that the Red Line Agreement prevented it from drilling on Bahrain Island without the consent of its partners. Since this was not forthcoming, the company was forced to assign its interest to Standard Oil of California (SoCal), another Standard Oil offshoot. Lacking supplies of oil for its overseas markets, SoCal had explored Latin America and Southeast Asia in the 1920s and was determined to find new sources across the globe. But there was a major obstacle to an American company wishing to operate in Bahrain.

For historical reasons, Britain was the guardian and gatekeeper of the Gulf, and exercised those roles with great diligence. Between 1913 and 1923 the rulers of Kuwait, Bahrain, Qatar, the Trucial States, and Muscat and Oman had all signed undertakings not to grant oil concessions except to companies approved by the British government. SoCal's interest in the Bahrain concession faced strong opposition from the Colonial Office and the India Office. But times were changing, and it was becoming increasingly difficult for the British to exclude the Americans from the region. In the end, anxious to avoid the squabbles that had marred the negotiations over the Iraq concession, the Foreign Office softened its approach. The Americans were allowed to overcome the objections of the British by registering a new company, the Bahrain Petroleum Company (Bapco), in the British dominion of Canada, with a guaranteed number of British employees. In 1930, for the sum of $50,000, the Bahrain concession was assigned to Bapco and drilling began at a desolate site near Awali, on a hill known as Jebel Dukhan. It was less than 3 miles from the Ain al-Qar asphalt pits that Pilgrim and Heim had once inspected.

Towards the end of May 1932 the No. 1 well passed a depth of 610 metres (2,000 ft). Sir Arnold Wilson, now the managing director of Anglo-Persian, was confidently predicting that Bapco would abandon it; but he was in for a shock a couple of days later when the well struck oil. A sense of quiet satisfaction prevailed among the drillers. 'The well came in like a lamb,' wrote the site manager, Ed Skinner. 'It was driller's dream.'[11] The Political Resident broke the news to London in rather more prosaic terms: 'The Bahrain Oil Company have struck oil and the well is making over 70 tons a day.'[12]

There was an obvious connection to be made here: if there was oil on Bahrain, then surely there was oil to be found on the Arabian Peninsula, too. As they stood on Jebel Dukhan in the clear light of early morning and gazed across the shallow stretch of water that separated Bahrain from the mainland, the American drillers could see the low outline of the Dhahran hills in the province of Al Hasa. To the trained eye, those humps in the distance were an obvious oil prospect, but all the drillers could do for the moment was to look and dream wistfully of a time when oil derricks would rise out of the desert haze.

One spell had been broken, and another cast in its place.

IN JANUARY 1929 U.S. millionaire Charles Crane, his son John and missionary Rev. Henry A. Bilkerd set off from Basra at dawn by car, heading for Riyadh by way of Kuwait, hoping to meet Ibn Saud in his capital. Crane was a veteran of Middle Eastern politics, having been appointed to the King-Crane Commission (1919–22) to survey Arab opinion on the question of self-determination.

As their car trailed dust over the 137-kilometre (85-mile) drive to Kuwait, they made a fateful decision by choosing to disregard warnings about tribal raiders in the area. Another 10 miles on, at the village of Zubair, some shepherds yelled at them that it was dangerous, but they continued their journey. Every now and then Bilkerd would stand up in the open-top car and peer about, though he could see no trouble. After some 96 kilometres (60 miles), men suddenly sprang up from behind rocks and opened fire, peppering the car and killing Bilkerd. Although RAF planes subsequently flew from their base in Transjordan to bomb the perpetrators, the pilots returned with all their bombs intact, having seen no one.

This was one of the last brutal atrocities committed by the Ikhwan, the radical religious group that had once been supported by Ibn Saud and had now turned against him. Two months later, at the battle of Sabilla, Ibn Saud with British military assistance defeated the group and order was restored, reopening the door to oil exploration. Since the E&GS concession had effectively been abandoned and Holmes was persona non grata in Riyadh for failing to keep up with the payments due under it, the king turned to Charles Crane for help. After the exchange of gifts – two white horses for Crane and a box of dates for Ibn Saud – the American agreed to find an engineer to conduct a survey of Al Hasa. In Karl Twitchell he found such a man: mining engineer, live wire and admirer of the Arab way of life.

In January 1932, at the end of his survey, Twitchell out of curiosity crossed to Bahrain. The Political Agent observed that he stayed for three or four days and travelled 'everywhere on the island', including a visit to Awali.[13] To the workers on the site, he was an odd sight, an

Casoc geologists Art Brown and Robert Miller examining aerial photographs in the desert as Saudi soldiers stand by, November 1934.

American striding about in full *Nedji* robes and headgear, and they speculated that he might be a spy. When Twitchell asked Ed Skinner if he thought there was any oil in Arabia, Skinner replied that Twitchell ought to find a skilled oil geologist to undertake a survey.

Twitchell had in fact found encouraging signs of oil: asphalt seeps in the vicinity of Qatif. On his return to Riyadh, however, he advised Ibn Saud to await the outcome of the Bahrain No. 1 well before inviting bids for a concession for Al Hasa. And so, when Bahrain No. 1 well came on stream a few months later, all eyes were on Ibn Saud. As Ibn Saud's British adviser, Harry St John Philby, hawked the possibility of an oil concession around London that summer, two oil companies took an interest: Anglo-Persian, acting through IPC, and SoCal. In the negotiations that followed in Jeddah, IPC's bidding was lukewarm while SoCal showed a greater determination, and it was this that won the day. That said, the negotiations were long and tedious, with Philby playing both sides, and it was never a done deal until the moment when Ibn Saud was prodded from a fitful slumber to sign the final agreement. For a sixty-year concession, the Americans made a down payment of £35,000 (£2.3 million today) in gold, which, on account of a U.S. embargo, had to be obtained on London's black market. Annual rental payments of £5,000 (£328,000) followed.

The American oilman had one big advantage over his British counterpart. He lacked the imperial baggage of his transatlantic cousin; in Ibn Saud's eyes, he had not yet lost his New World shine. Later, there would be talk of the Saudis achieving their manifest density in the same way the early pioneers had done in the American West, but ultimately Ibn Saud was a pragmatist – and the Americans were willing to pay.

All credit to the oil company that would persist with Arabia when others fell away. SoCal formed the California Arabian Standard Oil Company (Casoc) to explore and develop the concession. In 1936 the Texas Oil Company took a half share in the company. By early 1938, having drilled several shallow wells around Dammam and spent $15 million with no commercial oil to show for it, SoCal was seriously considering withdrawing from Al Hasa.

At the same time Casoc geologists were exploring the great sand desert known as the Rub al-Khali, or Empty Quarter, which covers 583 square kilometres (225,000 square miles) and is larger than France. Their presence raised several troubling questions. They needed to know, for example, where the geographical boundaries of their concession area lay. In those days, the boundaries of Qatar, the Trucial States, Oman and the Aden Protectorates were uncertain. The British, who protected their interests, took the view that the southeastern border of Saudi Arabia had been defined by the Anglo-Ottoman convention of 1913, which Ibn Saud did not accept. As diplomats argued and suggested various frontiers, the Saudis gained ground with each new line that was drawn on the map.

Until the matter was settled, Casoc geologists had to be especially cautious when travelling around the fuzzy edges of their territory, and were always accompanied by armed Saudi guards. The Casoc expedition that set off for the Liwa Oasis in February 1938 was the first motorized party to penetrate the southern sands. There was a second attempt to explore the Empty Quarter in the following season when a survey team mapped the northern reaches of the desert. While many of the settled tribes and nomadic bedouin acquiesced in their intrusions, others remained sullenly hostile.

The search for oil went on. Although the first well drilled at Dammam had some success, it was not enough to justify a full commercial operation. Hopes were fading when geologist Max Steinke insisted that the seventh well should be drilled to a greater depth than the others. The plan worked: in March 1938 oil was struck in an older rock formation that came to be known as the Arab Zone. By the third day the well had achieved a flow rate of 3,690 barrels of oil, not a major output when compared with IPC's wells in Iraq, but highly significant as the first commercial oil strike on the Arabian Peninsula. Saudi Arabia was an oil-producing nation.

In May 1939 Ibn Saud travelled to Ras Tanura in order to open a new oil terminal there. Where once his caravan would have been a line of lumbering camels trailing dust, it was now a dark column of black cars riding the simple desert roads and tracks. Their arrival was a scene of wild celebration. The king's red-robed guards stood on the running boards of the leading car, each wearing a long sword in a black scabbard, a dagger, a pistol, a magazine rifle slung over their shoulders and two bandoliers crossing their chests. White-robed bodyguards in open-top trucks followed, all yelling, hollering and waving their rifles. Tents were set up near the Casoc camp, and cauldrons of rice and mutton were cooked and served on large copper trays. The feasting began after evening prayers and was followed by traditional dancing as lines of retainers performed shuffling, monotonous steps to the beat of a great drum, with a single dancer occasionally stepping forward to fire his rifle in the air.

When the valve was duly opened and oil began to flow into a tanker, the *D. G. Schofield*, waiting offshore, it was not only a great occasion, but it would be remembered many years later as the moment that the kingdom of Saudi Arabia made its first tentative steps into the modern world. In July 1939 SoCal won a sixty-year concession over a larger area, paying Ibn Saud $1,156,400 for the concession and $165,000 yearly rental. At one point the Japanese had entered the discussions, but their efforts were in vain: the American domination of Saudi Arabian oil was now almost complete. IPC gained a concession for Western Arabia, but abandoned it after a brief survey in difficult conditions.

The Second World War interrupted the Americans' progress. As we have seen, the Italians had been bombing Haifa. On 18 October 1940 they attempted something more ambitious. Four of their bombers took off from the island of Rhodes loaded with fuel and straining to gain height as they headed southeast. Their mission was to fly to the island of Bahrain and drop their bombs on the oil refinery at Manama. After a hazardous flight across sea, mountain, desert and gulf they arrived in the early hours of the morning to find the refinery illuminated like a 'Texas oil town'.[14] Three planes dropped about eighty small bombs on Bahrain and the fourth plane, which had lost its way earlier in the flight, fixed on Dhahran and dropped fifty bombs there. They all reached the safety of Eritrea just before their fuel tanks ran dry, having made an epic 4,000-kilometre (2,500-mile) journey.

All – except the Italians – agreed that there was no serious damage and most bombs had failed to explode or fallen harmlessly away from the oil installations. Italian news stations saw it differently, proclaiming 'Bahrain has been destroyed!'[15] In truth, the raid unsettled the Allies considerably. A blackout imposed in the capital of Manama was almost impossible to enforce during Ramadan when local people stayed up to eat their evening meal. The British army drew up plans to disable the oil wells and installations in Iraq and Qatar. The Americans, who had not yet entered the war, drew up similar plans for their Dammam oilfield, and for their staff to escape across the Rub al-Khali to Aden in the event of a German invasion from North Africa. There was talk in the Manama *suq* that the dastardly British had staged the air raid in order to bring the United States into the war on their side. By the time the Americans entered the conflict, Casoc had evacuated all but essential staff from Al Hasa, leaving a core of workers – the famous 'Hundred Men' – behind.[16] As the war went on, the company would use Italian prisoners of war captured in Eritrea to meet a shortage of local labour; such were the fortunes of war.

EIGHT

BIG AND LITTLE WHEELS, 1924–44

A MONG THE FEW WESTERNERS frequenting this desert world was William Richard Williamson, an Englishman who became a significant figure in the pre-oil affairs of Kuwait, the lower Gulf and Oman. At the age of thirteen he had run away to sea and, after many adventures in America and the East, he came to settle in Iraq in the 1890s. A colourful character, he once rode a penny-farthing bicycle through the Zubair *suq*, careering through an astonished crowd and causing pandemonium. 'The Jinn of the Big and Little Wheel' they called him, hurling sticks and stones in his direction until he found refuge in the house of a friendly merchant.[1]

Having gone native, Williamson converted to Islam and took the name Abdullah Fadhil, making the holy pilgrimage to Mecca and thus earning the moniker of 'Haji'. He adopted the dress and customs of a town Arab but, when doing business with Westerners, he would put on a navy-blue suit with double-breasted jacket while retaining his headdress, in those days an eccentric fusion of East and West. The local sheikhs liked and respected him, seeking his advice about matters unrelated to oil, such as illnesses affecting camels and horses.

Now, in 1924, in his fifties and with sons needing a good education, Williamson was looking for an occupation more reliable than trading in horses, camels and cargo. Sir Arnold Wilson knew him as a spy during the war years and, seeking an interpreter, guide and negotiator to carry out business with the sheikhs, appointed him as an inspector of Gulf agencies for Anglo-Persian. Among other things, Williamson was required to counter the company's unpopularity in Kuwait and use backdoor methods to out-manoeuvre Major Frank Holmes, lavishing gifts and throwing lunches for local notables, smoothing the way for the real business of the day.

Although Holmes would play the more prominent role in Kuwait, he and Williamson were of a similar disposition – both independent with an apparent empathy for the Arab point of view. No doubt Holmes felt more at home socializing with the British and Williamson with the Arab, but that was not the cause of their rivalry. Haji became so suspicious of Holmes in Kuwait that he looked nervously over his shoulder for an assassin trailing in his wake – an imaginative fiction, perhaps, but Williamson did grow increasingly bitter about his rival's machinations. British officials, too, were watchful of Holmes, for there were times when his unseen hand seemed to be everywhere. If a sheikh was holding out for more generous terms, surely Homes had put him up to it; and if Holmes visited a certain locality, the British wanted to know why.

Kuwait had long been a part of the imperial equation. It was considered vital to Britain's interests, being at the head of the Gulf and guarding access to southern Iraq and the overland route to Europe. The scent of oil should have brought a new dynamic into play, but progress was sluggish: Anglo-Persian executives had enough on their plate and remained tentative about Kuwait.

After commissioning a survey, the company's disposition did not improve when the geologists' report indicated that the chances of finding commercial oil were slim. Meanwhile, Holmes had gained an option for the Saudi–Kuwaiti Neutral Zone for his company E&GS and, as he had in Bahrain, began drilling water wells in Kuwait. One of his water wells revealed traces of oil, and in 1927 E&GS sold its interests to Gulf Oil. But progress was slow throughout the 1920s: the ruler, Sheikh Ahmad al-Jabir Al Sabah, had shown no great desire to grant an oil concession for Kuwait since he was still smarting from the British agreement with Ibn Saud at Uqair to cede part of his territory to Saudi Arabia.

The notorius red line, drawn to demarcate IPC's area of operations in the Middle East, took a strange turn when it approached Kuwait. It skirted around the sheikhdom, leaving a kink on the map in order to preserve Britain's interests there. In 1928, when Holmes landed on the Kuwaiti shore, he was acting for Gulf Oil, much to the chagrin of British officials who insisted that there should be a nationality clause, restricting any oil concession to a British-controlled company. Holmes's first offer to Sheikh Ahmad was rejected, but he was not deterred: like a latter-day diviner, Holmes sensed that Kuwait had plenty of oil.

In April 1932, Whitehall dropped the nationality requirement and, a month later, Anglo-Persian was ready to make a new bid. The company applied for a licence to prospect for oil but this too was refused. By now, oil had been struck on Bahrain and Sheikh Ahmad was convinced he could get better terms.

At this point, Archibald Chisholm, known to the Arabs as 'The Tall One', made an appearance on behalf of Anglo-Persian. Over the next year there ensued a friendly rivalry with Holmes to win the sheikh's favour. Holmes's local intrigues were met in equal fashion by Haji Williamson, and feasts and largesse abounded as each attempted to win the ear of one Arab notable or another.

In due course Anglo-Persian and Gulf Oil joined forces to set up the Kuwait Oil Company (KOC) in equal shares. As a result, Holmes and Chisholm now found themselves working together – both on the side of the angels, as the Political Resident would have it. In early 1934 the appearance of a dark horse in the form of a British company, Traders Ltd, threatened to derail the negotiations. The Americans suspected an Anglo-Persian plot to double-cross them, since Traders was a consortium of British businessmen who were determined to block American participation in Kuwait.

When it came to it, Sheikh Ahmad ruled out their bid and on 23 December awarded a 75-year concession to KOC. This outcome was a

Sheikh Ahmad al-Jabir Al Sabah of Kuwait (centre) at the Bahra No. 1 well in 1936.

considerable achievement on the sheikh's part, since he had managed to secure an American commercial presence in his sheikhdom without alienating the British, his protectors. And, although he did not receive as much as he would have liked, by the standards of the time it was a considerable sum all the same: a signature payment of £35,700 (£2.3 million today), an annual rental fee of £7,150 (£469,000) until oil was found and then £18,800 per annum and a royalty of three rupees per ton of oil extracted. Holmes was appointed the sheikh's representative to the company in London.

In 1936, after geological surveys, the first well was drilled at Bahra and ended in a dry hole. A seismic survey followed, leading to another well being drilled near the location of an oil seepage at Burgan, a site that Holmes had visited back in 1931. Oil was struck in February 1938 at a depth of 1,120 metres (3,675 ft), revealing the Burgan oilfield, which turned out to be the largest oil accumulation in a sandstone reservoir in the world. Kuwait's future was assured but, as it happened, not exactly in the way imagined.

THE NAMES OF MANY Gulf states are familiar in the world today, though this was not the case a hundred years ago when they were little known in the West. In Qatar the ruling family was the house of Al Thani, whose roots stretched back into the Arabian past. Following the departure of the last Ottoman forces from Doha in 1915, Britain had bestowed a degree of legitimacy on their hegemony by signing a treaty with the ruler and head of the family, Sheikh Abdullah bin Qasim. He pledged not to cede any territory or enter into any agreements with foreign governments without British permission; in return they guaranteed to protect his sheikhdom from attack by sea. As Percy Cox's intervention at Uqair in 1922 demonstrated, the British would not brook any interference from Ibn Saud in Qatari affairs.

Certainly the Political Agent in Bahrain would have been watching closely when Major Holmes made a foray into the sheikhdom in 1925. Holmes made a favourable impression on Sheikh Abdullah (apparently he was able to identify the pedigree of the sheikh's dogs, which in the latter's mind was a sure sign that his visitor would find oil), yet he was unable to make headway in Qatar, despite gifts and entreaties. Anglo-Persian took little interest in the sheikhdom, sending George Martin Lees and Haji Williamson on a cursory survey in 1926, and a few years passed before anything much happened. In the meantime, the wealth of the Al Thani suffered with the dwindling fortunes of the pearl industry, which was in terminal decline. Six years on, the oil strike on Bahrain changed everything as company officials scrambled to sign up Sheikh Abdullah without delay. Several envoys made the sea voyage across the Gulf from Abadan, including Charles Mylles and Archibald Chisholm of Anglo-Persian, both of whom found the sheikh to be a formidable negotiator.

Haji Williamson came too, blending in rather more effectively than his colleagues, being dressed in Arab robes and speaking the language fluently. In January 1933 he accompanied two geologists as their guide, interpreter and camp boss. At times the expedition resembled a jamboree: using an Admiralty map of the coastline, the party set out by car with the geologists in the front seats and two bedouin guards in the rear singing camel songs at a tempo that varied according to the car's speed. Williamson followed them in a truck with all the equipment, camp gear, labour and remaining guards. They drew up their own map of the concession area, and visited one of the most promising features, Jebel Dukhan. This was an anticline on the western side of the peninsula with relatively steep dips and similar rocks to those found in Bahrain. In their report, the geologists observed that there was a 'fair chance' of finding a profitable oilfield there.[2]

Exploration licences were granted, but reaching a final concessionary agreement proved awkward. The Al Thani had close trading links with Kuwait, and Sheikh Abdullah was kept informed about the progress of negotiations there, no doubt hoping to achieve parity or even better terms from Anglo-Persian. In March 1935, when a settlement seemed tantalizingly close, the ruler insisted that certain political issues be resolved, in particular retaining his jurisdiction over his Muslim subjects and the security of his realm. Since the 1916 treaty only provided British protection from maritime aggression, it made sense to seek a cast-iron guarantee of protection on the landward side. At this moment, the Political Resident in the Gulf, Lt-Col Trenchard Fowle, intervened and agreed to give the sheikh the assurances he sought.

At last, when it came to settling the payments to be made under the concession, the sheikh presented his most dramatic scene:

He started to tremble and his sons wept. [His adviser] not to be out of the fashion made rather an ineffectual pretence at weeping. The sheikh in his agitation shouted hysterically that he was a man dying of thirst to whom I had given a bowl of water, but just as he was about to drink I snatched the bowl away and left him to die in agony.[3]

On 17 May 1935 Sheikh Abdullah put his pen to a concession agreement for a period of 75 years in return for a signature payment of 400,000 rupees (£2 million today) and a rental of 150,000 rupees (£756,000) per annum, which was to double within five years, and royalties of 2 Indian rupees (£9.79) per ton of crude oil shipped. In order to meet its obligations under the Red Line Agreement, Anglo-Persian transferred the concession to an IPC associate company, Petroleum Development (Qatar) Ltd (PDQ), which later became the Qatar Petroleum Company (QPC).

After a number of surveys, the company began drilling at Jebel Dukhan and in January 1940 struck oil, not as expected in the Cretaceous limestone formation found in Bahrain, but in the same Jurassic formation where Casoc had found oil on the Arabian mainland. PDQ christened this oil-bearing rock formation the Zekrit formation after a small harbour on the western coast of the peninsula; it was customary to name rock formations after nearby geographical features. But in Dammam, Casoc geologists had called the same formation the Arab Zone, and this is the name that is familiar to us today. It describes one of the most prolific regional oil reservoirs in the Middle East.

On 14 January the Political Agent wrote to Sheikh Abdullah to congratulate him on the discovery of oil in Qatar. He 'earnestly hoped that future drilling will prove that Qatar possesses a valuable oil field', while regretting that operations would be delayed by the war. 'I pray to God to materialise our hopes which will lead to mutual benefits,' the sheikh replied. 'I also pray to God to grant a speedy victory to the Democratic Powers so that the situation may return to normal.'[4] Indeed, the oilfield turned out to be a lucrative one, but almost ten years would pass before any oil was exported from Dukhan.

ABDUL RAZZAK, THE BRITISH representative in Sharjah, was always on the lookout for strangers, but it is unlikely that he had seen any like the two Westerners who suddenly appeared in the sheikhdom one day in October 1936. The presence of a single-engined executive aeroplane at Sharjah airport brought the inquisitive Razzak swiftly to the scene in order to probe its passengers, an English speculator named Francis W. Rickett and his American companion, a man described as 'Smith', who was Ben Smith, a Wall Street financier. According to Rickett's account, the plane had been forced to land because of engine trouble.[5]

Razzak had received orders to detain the two visitors. How much he knew of Rickett's background is uncertain, but the British authorities had good reason to be wary. The previous year, acting on behalf of Standard-Vacuum, Rickett had pulled off an astonishing coup by obtaining a 75-year oil concession from Haile Selassie, the emperor of Ethiopia. Although the episode was subsequently fictionalized in Evelyn Waugh's novel *Scoop*, it was certainly not a piece of fiction. When news of the deal broke there was an outcry on both sides of the Atlantic, and the concession was abandoned a few days later. Perhaps fearing a repeat in the Persian Gulf, British officials were on their guard.

Now in Sharjah, Rickett showed no apparent interest in oil. Nevertheless, since the air route through the Persian Gulf was closed to private aviators, his presence, whether intentional or not, was most irregular. He told Razzak that his companion, Smith, was an 'American savage' interested only in gold mines. In an attempt to draw them out, Razzak told a tale about gold and presented Rickett with two small gold coins. This prompted Rickett to speak of the magnificent gold mines of Ibn Saud and ask if there was any place with black sand where pieces of gold might be found. Although Razzak's replies were generally non-committal, he did turn down Rickett's request for a motor car saying that travel was too dangerous on account of smallpox in the area; thus the two men stayed at the airport fort. When the ruler visited the fort that evening, Razzak made sure that Rickett and the sheikh were kept apart. Afterwards, Rickett offered the services of an American geologist to look for gold, but Razzak did not pass on the offer to the ruling sheikh.

The aeroplane was briefly impounded, and then released when Rickett complained of a duodenal ulcer that required treatment in London. After the two men had departed, no doubt bemused by their reception, a flurry of messages went between the Foreign and India Offices and travel restrictions were placed on Rickett in relation to any future visits to the Gulf. As far as is known, Rickett was never heard of again in Sharjah, although he was involved in oil ventures across the globe, including places such as Mosul and Mexico.

At the time of Rickett's visit, Sharjah was one of seven sheikhdoms in an area known as the Trucial Coast (today's UAE). It was so called after a series of nineteenth-century truces between Britain and the littoral sheikhs, and was still under British protection. By undertakings given in 1922, the ruling sheikhs could not grant oil concessions without the agreement of the British authorities. The senior British representative in the Gulf was the Political Resident. He was based in Bushire until 1947, then in Bahrain, and had to sanction any agreement that the sheikhs might wish to make. Since he was likely to favour a British oil company, the opportunities for the sheikhs to grant concessions to other foreign companies were remote. There was always a local political officer to deal with any approaches that slipped through the bureaucratic net by issuing a stiff reprimand to a recalcitrant sheikh and, as a last resort, the Residency Agent such as Abdul Razzak to muddy the waters.

On the face of it, Anglo-Persian was the obvious choice to take up oil concessions on the Trucial Coast, but the Red Line Agreement prevented the company from acting alone. Therefore, although Anglo-Persian made the first moves, it was the IPC group that took up the concessions through an associated company, Petroleum Concessions Limited (PCL). The problem of finding local representatives to negotiate with the sheikhs was solved by appointing both Frank Holmes and Haji Williamson to act on the company's behalf. Holmes was now a poacher turned gamekeeper, acting for the company rather than in competition with it, but the mistrust between him and Williamson still endured.

It was a recipe for disaster. The Political Resident gloomily predicted that Holmes would bring 'the usual atmosphere of confusion and intrigue which he creates wherever he goes'.[6] After local plots against him, Haji Williamson was denied a visa to return to the Trucial Coast. He retired to his family in Iraq, though he retained the respect of the oil companies and many sheikhs. Holmes himself proved dilatory and was relieved through ill health, having failed to secure the sheikhdoms apart from Dubai. It lay with IPC stalwarts Basil Lermitte and Stephen Longrigg to finish the task of signing up the rulers.

Meanwhile geologists Jock Williamson and David Glynn-Jones had visited the Al Ain/Buraimi Oasis where they carried out a brief survey. Back in Abu Dhabi, they loaded their vehicles onto a dhow

An Englishman gone
native: Haji Williamson
in Arab dress in Qatar, 1935.

and sailed along the coast to Jebel Dhana and Khawr al-Udaid, but
the impassable desert prevented any further exploration of the interior. In 1938 Williamson ventured inland to the Al Ain/Buraimi Oasis,
although tribal difficulties prevented him carrying out a detailed
survey; geological information about the area remained sparse.

There was brighter news from the coast. After considerable difficulties, the last pieces of the concessionary map were falling into place.
By early 1939, as a result of efforts by Messrs Lermitte and Longrigg,
agreements had been made with most of the sheikhs, including the
recalcitrant ruler of Abu Dhabi, Sheikh Shakhbut bin Sultan Al Nahyan,
who granted a 75-year concession to Petroleum Development (Trucial
Coast) Ltd (PDTC), an IPC associate created to operate the concession.

Yet the physical difficulties of oil exploration in the deserts and
on the dunes, and a glut of oil in the global market, delayed progress
along the Trucial Coast. The clock ticked slowly as the sheikhs looked
on, hearing of oil strikes in Bahrain, Saudi Arabia, Kuwait and Qatar,
and wondering if ever it would be their turn.

THE 1902/3 SEASON SAW a burgeoning interest in the geology of
Oman. Anxious to protect their interests in India, the British wanted
to identify any sources of coal for the Royal Navy in the area and prevent them from falling into Russian or French hands. Two geologists

143

were dispatched and were able to recover samples, though curious tribesmen took an interest in their activities and dispatched several ill-aimed bullets in their direction. The coal, however, was not of the desired quality. Two years later the geologist Guy Pilgrim briefly visited Oman during the 1904/5 season as part of his survey of the region. Although he preferred Iran as an oil prospect, he also described the geology of Oman and drew its first geological map.

Since he did most of his survey work alone and had no modern aids to assist him, it was hardly surprising that Pilgrim should have found no direct evidence of oil in Oman. Aside from Bahrain, there were few reports of seepages and no verifiable signs of oil on the Arabian Peninsula as a whole. Occasionally there were rumours of oil, one of which originated in the Omani desert, a few miles inland from Duqm. Today you can still see the likely source of that rumour, a freshwater spring fringed by ribbons of black algae. It is an optical illusion that could easily be mistaken for an oil seepage from a distance. In the early 1920s this innocent trickle might well have sparked the rumour of an oil seepage that reached Anglo-Persian's head office in Abadan.

Actually, it was the name of Frank Holmes that galvanized Anglo-Persian into action. In early 1925 Holmes visited the sultan of Muscat and Oman, Said bin Taimur, in order to enquire about obtaining an exploration licence for his company, ES&G. In a pre-emptive move, Anglo-Persian obtained a two-year licence through its exploration arm, D'Arcy Exploration, to prospect for oil in Oman. The wording of the agreement was ominous, stating that certain parts of the territory were 'not at present safe for its operations', a reference to the unsettled interior.[7]

In November 1925 a survey party gathered in Muscat. It included the geologists George Lees and K. Washington Gray, with 'Haji' Williamson as their guide. The party visited the mountain country on camels, arriving at Yanqul on the western side of the Hajar range. On account of tribal unrest they were unable to visit one of the most interesting geological areas, the Dhahira plain. Lees did manage to note from a distance several hogback anticlines, possible indicators of oil, breaking the contours of the plain. They moved down the coast, landing near Nafun to investigate the reported oil seepage, but they were unable to locate it and retreated after being 'greeted by a hail of stones'.[8]

Lees correctly predicted the difficulties that lay ahead: 'Systematic exploration of the Arabian Peninsula, or indeed its fringes, is greatly hampered by formidable natural barriers and by the still more serious obstacles caused by the independent spirit of its inhabitants.'[9] The waters of the Persian Gulf presented a less daunting prospect, and in 1927 an Anglo-Persian party of geologists surveyed its coast and islands, again with Haji Williamson as their guide.

In 1937 IPC had another attempt at Oman, obtaining concessions for Oman and Dhofar through its associate company, Petroleum Development (Oman and Dhofar) Ltd (PDO). The following year, company geologists Henry Hotchkiss and Lester Thomson travelled to Buraimi with the blessing of the sultan. The leading sheikh of the village appeared to welcome them with open arms, but he was plotting to ambush them, seeing their arrival as a God-given opportunity for a 'first-class hold-up'.[10] The geologists emerged unscathed from the ambush and managed to report on the geology. But then, as with other parts of the region, oil exploration was put on hold with the advent of the Second World War.

A SINGLE COUNTRY TODAY, Yemen used to be three separate political entities. There was Yemen proper, an ancient country once under Turkish rule that became independent on the collapse of the Ottoman Empire in 1918 and was then ruled by a succession of imams. The second element was the colony of Aden, established by the British in 1837 as a coaling station for the London to India route via Suez. Aden would also become an important military base until Britain withdrew in 1967. The third element was the southeastern hinterland known as the Aden Protectorate, a conglomeration of small emirates. This area was loosely known as the Hadhramaut to the geologists who first explored there: the Hadhramaut itself is a deep and wide wadi carved through the land, curving southwards to meet the Arabian Sea.

The first geological report of the territory was delivered in the 1840s by Dr Henry Carter, based on observations from the survey ship HMS *Palinurus* and from various landings along the southwestern coast of Arabia. But the region was seldom visited and, like the rest of the peninsula, was considered a poor oil prospect in the first decades of the twentieth century. In 1921, however, rumours of oil seepages in Yemen

The port of Mukalla, which was a base for the first geological surveys of southwestern Arabia.

led British officials to report that there was evidence of petroleum at many points in the interior of the country.

Among those who believed that the region was worth investigating was the Quaiti Sultan of Mukalla and Ash Shihr on the southern coast. In 1918 the geologists Beeby Thompson and John Ball reported on the sultanate's coal and oil prospects and, the following year, Dr Little of the Geological Survey of Egypt described the stratigraphic and palaeontological features of the area. Shell even discussed a concession for Ash Shihr, only for their partners in the (then) Turkish Petroleum Company to rule it out.

Attitudes changed in 1932 when Bapco struck oil on Bahrain Island and SoCal acquired the oil concession for eastern Arabia a year later. At that juncture IPC took an interest in Yemen as part of an overall strategy to forestall u.s. oil companies by girdling the Arabian fringes with its own concessions. In 1936 IPC obtained an exploration permit for the Aden Protectorates. In 1937 an IPC party working in neighbouring Saudi Arabia obtained the Imam's permission to investigate the geology to the north of Hodeida, but the results were unpromising. In 1938 geologists R. W. Pike and H. R. Wofford conducted aerial surveys for the company, taking in some structural mapping of the Hadhramaut and also around Mukalla; but otherwise the tribes were restless, and the geologists kept away.

NINE

CHASING THE ARAB ZONE, 1944–71

EVERYTHING WAS SEEN THROUGH Western eyes. As President Roosevelt remarked to Lord Halifax, the British ambassador in Washington in 1944: 'Persian oil is yours. We share the oil of Iraq and Kuwait. As for Saudi Arabian oil, it's ours.'[1] It was an interesting remark, revealing as much about the state of play in the Middle East as about Western attitudes to oil, the presumption being that the region's oil resources were there to be carved up between a bankrupt Britain and a resurgent America. It was quite a turnaround from the previous war, when the colonial powers jockeyed for oil rights, and the Americans were left out in the cold.

The Second World War changed many things. There were fuel scares: at one point New York was down to two days' supply of fuel oil, Boston two and a half, Providence to three. In two months, the u.s. Fifth Fleet consumed 630 million gallons of fuel oil and an armoured battalion moving 160 kilometres (100 miles) required 17,000 gallons of gasoline. A single bombing mission of 1,000 planes over Germany consumed twelve times more fuel than had been consumed during the whole of the First World War. The petroleum system creaked under the strain of supplying the Allies with oil: six of the seven billion barrels of oil required to fuel their war effort came from u.s. sources. At one point, it looked as if the country might run out of oil.

In the past Washington had allowed American oil companies open season in the Middle East, taking the view that competition should prevail and government interference should be kept to a minimum. On the other hand, with the apparent depletion of domestic reserves, it was imperative that new sources of crude oil should be found beyond the borders of the United States, and that the u.s. government should take the lead. With this in mind, President Roosevelt authorized the establishment of the Petroleum Reserves Corporation under the presidency of Harold Ickes. When geologist Everette Lee DeGolyer visited the Middle East on behalf of the corporation in 1943–4 and reported favourably on its oil potential, the answer seemed clear to the Americans: the future lay in the Middle East.

Yet circumstances were against them. Great Britain controlled 81 per cent of the region's oil production at that time compared with the Americans' 14 per cent, with a similar imbalance in refining capacity. Ickes's first step was to negotiate a complete buy-out of the Saudi concession, but he met strong opposition from business groups and within government itself. When this failed, Ickes proposed a government-owned pipeline from eastern Arabia to the Mediterranean and the oil lobby denounced this too. Washington then changed tack, with Secretary of State Cordell Hull being tasked to coordinate oil policy with Great Britain. The result was the Anglo-American Oil Agreement of 8 August 1944.

The oil agreement was never ratified, though it formed the basis for transatlantic cooperation over the next few years, and Washington drew a line against closer links. Although the United States conceded Britain's military primacy in the Gulf, this did not extend to economic collaboration, and it was on this basis that further talks were held in Washington in October 1947. Despite a subsequent British claim that these talks had secured American support for their position, the pronouncements were in fact non-committal, full of aspirations about the integrity and independence of indigenous states but lacking any common agreement over joint policies.

As DeGolyer predicted, a new petroleum order was emerging. IPC struggled to get its oilfields into full production after the war, yet the Saudi Arabian oil industry was booming: by 1948 its output was six times greater than Iraq's. Looking on from the sidelines, the two American partners in IPC were unhappy with their lot. Jersey Standard (later Exxon) and Socony-Vacuum (Mobil) already had access to Iraqi oil and the promise of oil in the Gulf states, but this seemed small change when compared with the great possibilities that beckoned in Saudi Arabia. Casoc's discoveries had outstripped others in the region and the company, now known as the Arabian American Oil Company (Aramco), was set for a lucrative future.

Tempting as it was to join such a venture, one major obstacle stood in their way: the Red Line Agreement. Now approaching its twentieth anniversary, the joint-working arrangement had been a straitjacket on the companies concerned. Attempts by certain partners in the 1930s to make separate deals in Bahrain and Al Hasa had failed. The Americans came up with an imaginative legal device to confound their opponents, arguing that declaring the French and Gulbenkian enemy aliens during the war had created a 'supervening illegality' that nullified the Red Line Agreement.[2] The French still fought tooth and nail to preserve their rights under the agreement since it provided them with a much-needed source of crude oil. Gulbenkian, too, resisted any changes. Eventually in 1948, after much debate, horse trading and legal proceedings, the IPC partners agreed to release the two American firms from their obligations so they could join Aramco. The Red Line Agreement would still operate for existing agreements, but for future ventures it was dead.

New discoveries in Saudi Arabia vindicated the Americans' decision. A promising anticline was discovered at Wadi Sabha, but not drilled until after the war. This turned out to be the first of many such successes in the area and revealed the full extent of the onshore oilfield of Ghawar, the 'elephant of elephants', which would prove to be the largest oilfield in the world.[3] Geologists such as Max Steinke developed new techniques that included structural drilling, the sinking of relatively shallow wells in order to determine the rock structures hidden beneath the surface terrain. Across the peninsula, as geologists and geophysicists traversed its deserts and mountains, the notion developed that the oil-producing rock formation that produced the largest and most prolific of these discoveries, the Arab Zone, might be found elsewhere. For some geologists, particularly those in IPC, finding the Arab Zone became something of an obsession.

As more knowledge about the regional geology of Saudi Arabia was acquired, it was possible to make some educated guesses about the whereabouts of oil reservoirs. One of those making predictions was geologist Dick Kerr, a geophysicist and pioneer in the aerial mapping of the Arabian Peninsula. Before the war, he drew a red arrow on a map of the northern Gulf and wrote: 'Possible high area offshore.'[4] The location was just beyond a spit of land known as Safaniya, which, according to one translation, means the 'place where navigators meet', possibly an ancient meeting place for mariners. A few years later this was revealed as the location of the largest offshore oilfield in the world.

IN DECEMBER 1944 IBN Saud and his retinue set out to engage with the outside world. They travelled overland to Jeddah, whence they boarded the destroyer USS *Murphy* and sailed for the Great Bitter Lake, part of the Suez Canal, to meet with U.S. President Franklin D. Roosevelt aboard the heavy cruiser USS *Quincy*. With the account of Colonel Thomas Eddy, a U.S. special adviser who was present at the meeting of the two heads of state, we have a colourful picture of 249 American sailors and 48 Arabs steaming cheerfully towards their rendezvous, the Arabs having brought a flock of sheep on board to be slaughtered for their evening meals. They refused cabins, preferring to sleep on the deck.

Today, the start of the special relationship between the United States and Saudi Arabia is often attributed to the subsequent meeting between Ibn Saud, the desert sheikh, and Roosevelt, the long-serving president. Beyond the pleasantries, there was a genuine warmth between them. Within a month, the State Department was drawing up a scheme of financial assistance for the Saudis to receive a supply programme worth $10 million ($138 million today) plus an extra $5 million for the current year and an export–import loan of $5 million. A further loan would go towards a radio station, thus freeing Aramco from its dependence on the British firm of Cable and Wireless. Ibn Saud would receive the sum of $300,000 into his private bank account, and his own aeroplane, a DC3. Finally, the U.S. government would build an airbase at Dhahran.

From now on the Americans would have a firm foothold in a former bastion of British influence, although Roosevelt would not live long enough to see this through, dying of a brain haemorrhage two months after meeting Ibn Saud. In 1946 the American diplomatic mission in Jeddah was given full embassy status, and the final agreement for the Dhahran airbase was signed five years later. The quid quo pro, never publicly admitted, was American access to Arabian oil: U.S. foreign policy in future would be closely aligned with Saudi Arabia as a force of stability in the region. Riyadh's increasingly proactive role among the oil-producing countries, and Washington's support for Israel, would bring challenges to their newfound alliance, nonetheless.

It was a curious affair. At the main oil camp in Dhahran, a sun-baked version of an American township had sprouted in the desert. The camp had tarmacked roads, picket fences, air-conditioned fly-proof houses, in fact all the conveniences of modern living. A visitor would be suitably impressed perhaps; yet the contrasts ran deep. The

King Ibn Saud with President Roosevelt aboard uss *Quincy*, February 1945.

geologists and drillers who had to mix with the local population went out of their way to blend in, growing beards and adopting the local style of dress by wearing the *ghutra* and *thobe*.

Apart from the to-ing and fro-ing of Arab labourers from the towns and villages of Al Hasa, there was little contact between the camp dwellers and their neighbours, however. Those towns comprised the same mud-walled buildings that had been crumbling for centuries, the same date palm plantations that had been cultivated and fought over since before the time of the Prophet. Meanwhile, oil was pumped into tankers off Ras Tanura and, from 1950, through a 1,710-kilometre (1,063-mile) pipeline known as the Trans-Arabian pipeline (Tapline) to Sidon on the Mediterranean shore.

As this unfamiliar new world was being unwrapped around them, the Saudis carried on their traditional ways, seeing no pressing need to change. Even as survey parties motored into the desert, armed with seismographs, gravity meters and water rigs, slave caravans were still making the long journey from the Buraimi Oasis to Riyadh: slavery was tolerated in Saudi Arabia well into the twentieth century. Saudi society was cocooned against the intrusion. Westerners were tolerated, though they found Saudi society opaque, a vague pattern of shapes and shadows glimpsed from a distance. An unbeliever – no matter how cultured, well mannered or wealthy – remained an outsider. Harry Philby found himself caught between the two worlds, having gained full admittance to the inner circle by converting to Islam, but remaining an infidel to the Ikhwan and 'obstinate and tiresome' to the British.[5]

As the 1950s hove into view, the Saudi government was still rudimentary. Based on Sharia law and a strict interpretation of the Quran, Wahhabi teaching underpinned the Saudi state, which was controlled by the religious body known as the *ulema*. These Muslim clergy were devoted to the Wahhabi faith, which had derived from the teachings of Muhammad ibn Abd al-Wahhab and emerged from the Nejd with the Saudi conquests of the eighteenth and nineteenth centuries. Ibn Saud may have brought a measure of stability to a country once notorious for its tribal infighting, but the *ulema* embedded the Wahhabi faith in society. When the *ulema* opposed the introduction of radio transmitters to the country on the ground that the Quran did not support their use, it took all Ibn Saud's powers of persuasion to convince the clerics that radio would be put to good use by spreading the word of God through broadcast readings of the Quran.

The House of Saud was nearly bankrupt. The new-found wealth had brought years of excess that had wreaked havoc with the national finances, a large part of which were used to support family members in a life of luxury. With an allowance of four wives at a time and money to boot, there were few constraints on procreation, and the royal family was growing at an alarming rate. Ibn Saud fathered 26 children by seven different wives and his eldest son would go on to have 74 children from 23 wives. Each wife and child could expect their share of the king's largesse and Ibn Saud never begrudged this; yet it made the job of balancing the books a delicate matter.

In January 1951 Aramco made its famous 50–50 agreement with Saudi Arabia, the first of its kind in the Middle East. An increase in oil production bringing money, jobs and investment to the kingdom was most welcome to the king. The Saudis also pressed Aramco for more money, with the result that the company was forced to explore the southern desert in order to decide which areas to relinquish. There was a high expectation that the Arab Zone might extend beneath the southern desert.

When the results of surveys around Abqaiq showed a likelihood of oil south of Dammam, and geologists also reported the possibility of gas and oil deposits around Jebel Hafit, near the Buraimi Oasis, an area ruled by the Sultan of Oman and the sheikh of Abu Dhabi. The territory in between was effectively a no man's land. When Aramco executives asked Ibn Saud how they should proceed in this politically sensitive area, his stock response was: 'You tell me the areas that interest you and I will tell you if it is mine and you can develop it.'[6]

Washington was in a cleft stick, caught between their support of Saudi Arabia and its interests in the Gulf states. U.S. foreign policy could not be weighted too heavily in favour of the former. As well as being in Saudi Arabia, U.S. oil companies were represented in the Gulf through the IPC group, Bapco and the Kuwait Oil Company. It was certainly not the administration's intention to supplant Britain in the region, since it was recognized that the British performed a valuable military role in the Gulf as a bulwark against the spread of communism. Hence there was a divergence between the administration and Aramco – more a difference in emphasis than outlook – that made Washington wary of taking sides.

With the independence of India and Pakistan in August 1947, the focus of British interest had shifted to the Gulf. A growing optimism about oil in the area meant that Whitehall's commitment to the sheikhs was assured, at least for the time being. But Britain's relations with Saudi Arabia had seen a dramatic change. The war years had seen a loss of influence to the Americans, and post-war currency crises and the cost of reconstruction had left Britain financially weak. The first test of its position came with the Buraimi Dispute, an argument between Saudi Arabia and Britain (acting on behalf of the rulers of Abu Dhabi and Oman) over the ownership of nine villages in southeastern Arabia known collectively as the Buraimi Oasis. Basing their territorial claim on the precedents of past conquest and the collection of tax in the area, the Saudis occupied one of the Buraimi villages in September 1952.

A standstill followed; the British blockaded the village and resorted to diplomacy. Washington took a neutral stance, urging arbitration. In September 1955 an arbitration tribunal was arranged, but the proceedings foundered when the British delegation withdrew after making allegations of bribery and interference against the Saudis. Six weeks later British-led troops expelled a Saudi contingent of police officers from the oasis after a short battle. That was not the end of it, for the dispute lingered on until 1974 when an agreement over oil rights and borders was apparently reached between Faisal, then king of Saudi Arabia, and Sheikh Zayed of Abu Dhabi by the Treaty of Jeddah.

The dispute contributed to a growing stress in transatlantic relations. A year later the Suez Crisis caused an even more painful rupture

An Aramco worker connecting
a drilling pipe, Saudi Arabia, 1948.

and confirmed the displacement of Britain and France by the United
States as the leading Western power in the region. The Eisenhower
Doctrine of January 1957 built on this turn of events by promising
U.S. support to any nation against tyranny. There was a limit to the
Americans' ambitions, though. The doctrine excluded the Gulf, where
the need for a significant British presence was recognized. Despite
a legacy of mistrust in Anglo-American relations, it was clear that
Washington had drawn a line in the sand as far as the Gulf was concerned. As events in Kuwait would later demonstrate, the Americans
were content for the British to retain and bolster their sphere of influence in that part of the region.

So far Aramco had enjoyed good relations with the Saudi government. Through its Arabian Research Division, the company assisted
Riyadh by conducting research and translating documents for the
Buraimi arbitration proceedings. After the death of Ibn Saud in 1953,
the accession of his eldest son, Saud, brought a different approach.
When the Saudis were expelled from the oasis, King Saud directed his
anger against Britain and a request was made to Aramco for military
hardware, which was declined. At this point the Saudis began dis-
tancing themselves from the company, and senior managers found it
increasingly difficult to read the government's mind.

The appointment of Abdullah Tariki as Saudi Arabia's first director of petroleum in 1960 marked a new phase. Being a passionate
believer in Arab nationalism, the 'Red Sheikh' assembled his own team

of experts in order to mount a challenge against Aramco. Among other things, he insisted that the company should become an integrated company, which meant branching out into the full range of petroleum activities – refining, transporting and marketing – as well as producing crude oil. In this way the government hoped to widen its revenue base. It was not a step that Aramco and its parent companies were prepared to take, and an impasse followed. A complete breakdown in relations was unlikely – Saudi Arabia was too dependent on its oil revenues and Aramco too dependent on oil for that to happen – but the disagreement did strike at the very core of Aramco's operations.

Tariki was an advocate of nationalization, though he fell from grace in 1962. By that time the nationalist call of Colonel Nasser had captured the public imagination across the Middle East; the oil industry provided a convenient target for Arab aspirations because it was a tangible sign of the control that Western nations exercised over the region. New and more strident voices were being heard as Saudi Arabia, once a traditional desert kingdom with little to offer the West, found itself propelled to the forefront of global affairs.

As groundbreaking as they were, the 50–50 agreements that followed Riyadh's lead were merely a prelude to a greater shift in the balance of power towards complete state ownership of oil industries. Across the Middle East, the nationalization bandwagon would soon gain a momentum all of its own.

OLD AERIAL PHOTOGRAPHS OF Doha bear little resemblance to the affluent metropolis of today, and the black-and-white grain of the images accentuates the sense of paucity that prevailed at the time. Like other Gulf sheikhdoms, the old wealth from pearls had died away, the new wealth from oil was yet to come. Sheikh Abdullah was a wise and in some ways enlightened ruler, deciding in the war years to build a hospital in Doha at a time when there were few such facilities in the Gulf; but he was old and ailing too. De facto power was exercised by his second son Hamad, assisted by Abdullah Darwish, who was his adviser in matters relating to the 'swelling of his wealth'.[7]

Darwish was from a family originating in Iran and a merchant in his own right. He was also Anglo-Iranian's agent in Qatar and a fixer for PDQ. The oil companies often relied on people with local knowledge to make the necessary contacts and smooth the way, and Darwish is an early example. Knowing the man who had the ruler's ear was an important part of negotiating with local potentates and then, when operations were up and running, in arranging labour and supplies. It was far removed from today's global networks of middlemen and lobbyists; business was less complicated in the days of Abdullah Darwish.

Ultimately, the vagaries of political life were his undoing. Having become the main adviser to the ruler, Darwish fell out of favour in the mid-1950s. By then Hamad had died and Abdullah had been succeeded by his eldest son, Ali, also an old man at the time of his succession. Sheikh Ali was a unifying influence and family tensions over the growing wealth were kept in check. It was only later, during the reign of Ahmad in the 1960s, that grumblings about the distribution of the oil money erupted into open dissent, resulting in his removal and replacement by Khalifa, whose family has ruled the emirate since 1972.

Yet now, in the 1940s, the main concern was the sluggish pace of oil development. No sooner had Sheikh Abdullah received news of the Dukhan discovery than the oil wells had been 'plugged and junked' in order to deny them to a possible Japanese invasion.[8] Naturally, Sheikh Abdullah appreciated that the British had more pressing concerns, but reports that the Americans were pumping oil from their Dammam and Bahraini wells unsettled him. In fact, PDQ had plugged their oil wells so effectively with cement and scrap metal that they were beyond repair, and new wells had to be drilled after the end of the war, a process that was time-consuming for the oilmen and frustrating for the ruler.

After the war, much as IPC had done with the Kirkuk oilfield in the late 1920s, PDQ carried out seismic surveys to delineate the Dukhan structure. More wells were drilled, and Umm Said on the eastern coast was identified as the site for a future marine oil terminal where tankers could be loaded with oil for export abroad. As operations developed, so the modern accoutrements of oil production began to appear, such as degassing stations, tank farms and pipelines. The first pipeline ran across the Qatar peninsula from Dukhan to Umm Said and a second, 60-centimetre (24-in.) pipeline, was built. On 2 February 1950, at a ceremony attended by the sheikh, the new pipeline was inaugurated. At last, Qatar had joined the ranks of the oil-producing nations.

Apart from the obvious signs of oil development, an outsider might still have considered Qatar a backwater at this time and, indeed, progress was slow. As with the other Gulf sheikhdoms there was much to be done to modernize a traditional society. Sheikh Ali was certainly alert to the 50–50 deals being made across the Middle East, and in 1952 negotiated his own agreement with the oil company. This led to a large rise in the country's oil revenues, from $1 million (£10 million today) to $23 million by 1954.

Even though Qatar was remote and protected, it was not wrapped in cotton wool. When Mossadegh nationalized the Iranian oil industry in 1951, PDQ had to increase oil production to make up for the shortfall from Iran and then, when Iranian oil exports recommenced in 1953, to cut it back again. Anyone thinking the sheikhdom might escape other aspects of the modern age was deluded. The oil company had its share of industrial problems, and Arab nationalism was an increasingly influential voice in the sheikhdom. A number of Egyptian teachers were working in the sheikhdom's new schools and sympathized with Colonel Nasser, spreading his nationalist message. In August 1956, in the febrile pre-Suez atmosphere, there was a demonstration of anti-British protestors who marched through Doha.

In the aftermath of Suez there were explosions in the oilfields, one setting light to the pipeline that carried crude oil from Dukhan to Umm Said, and the other blowing up an oil well in the Dukhan field. The company suspected sabotage: witnesses reported fire billowing through a small hole in the well assembly. 'No worm ate that hole through the metal except the two-legged variety,' observed one oilman.[9] Once the fire had been extinguished by the renowned American firefighter Paul 'Red' Adair, and the Suez Crisis had passed, Qatar resumed its steady progress towards modernization while demands for a greater share of the oil wealth grew among members of the ruling family.

At this point Qatar was in danger of being a one-trick pony as far as oil discoveries were concerned. Dukhan was the one and only oilfield in the sheikhdom and the onshore search for oil in other parts of the sheikhdom failed to uncover any new sources of hydrocarbons.

In 1957 the Qatar Petroleum Company (QPC), as the renamed PDQ was now known, drilled a test well that went far deeper than conventional drills. It had planned to drill to a depth of at least 4.5 kilometres (15,000 ft) and then use the equipment for deep tests on the Trucial Coast, in Oman and Iraq. The well actually went to a depth of around 4 kilometres (13,000 ft) and, while failing to find any deep oil-producing strata, it did locate gas in the Khuff formation, which Qatar Petroleum

Sheikh Ali bin Abdullah Al Thani (right) sitting with QPC General Manager
George Heseldin at Doha in 1955.

developed some twenty years later. As for the drilling rig, it was found
to be too cumbersome and was never used again.

Aside from that, after early setbacks, the search for offshore oil met
considerable success. The first offshore concession had been granted
to Superior Oil of California in 1949. Despite being a veteran of offshore drilling, Superior found conditions in the Gulf too arduous and
withdrew from the venture because of 'financial developments in the
company's U.S. operations'.[10] Shell took over in 1953 and experienced
its own set of difficulties, including the catastrophic sinking of a rig
with the loss of five Qatari lives; nevertheless the company persisted.
Its exploration programme restarted, and successful wells were drilled
at Idd al-Shargi (1960) and Maydam Majzam (1962). Oil exports from
these fields began in 1964.

Although the oil revenues came in, and the Dukhan field
remained a good source of oil, it became apparent that Qatar would
not retain its place among the major oil producers for long. Perhaps
the small emirate would have slipped back into obscurity had it not
been for the discovery of offshore gas in the enormous North Field
in 1972, which propelled a country of dwindling oil resources into
the top league of natural gas producers.

IN ABU DHABI THE oilmen were growing restive. Early drilling had brought disappointing results. As a consequence of the Buraimi Dispute, PDTC was forced to drill the Murban No. 1 well several miles from the best location. The well struck traces of light oil and gas at a depth of about 3 kilometres (9,800 ft), but drilling halted when an escape of gas from the Arab Zone killed two petroleum engineers. The well had to be plugged and abandoned. A post-mortem was carried out on the well, revealing traces of oil from a Cretaceous rock interval known as the Upper Thamama.

The disappointing findings from this well pushed exploration westwards towards the region where the productive Jurassic Arab Zone reservoirs might be found. PDTC resumed its drilling programme in the Abu Dhabi desert where two more seismic structures were discovered, Gezira and Shuweihat. Both were drilled and proved dry.

Quite naturally, Sheikh Shakhbut was anxious for a favourable outcome. In 1953 he had granted an offshore concession that went to Abu Dhabi Marine Areas Ltd (ADMA), an Anglo-French venture involving British Petroleum and Compagnie Française des Pétroles (later Total). The flamboyant explorer of oceans, Jacques Cousteau, and his research ship *Calypso* were hired to map the seabed and take geological samples. A full seismic survey followed and the first offshore test well site was selected.

In 1958, using a marine drilling platform, the *ADMA Enterprise*, oil was struck at a depth of about 2.7 kilometres (8,800 ft). Named after an overlying pearling bank known as Umm Shaif, the oilfield came on stream in 1962. It was an important discovery, revealing the potential of Cretaceous (as opposed to the Jurassic) carbonate reservoirs in the region. The Murban No. 3 well brought onshore success in 1960 and more discoveries followed, propelling Abu Dhabi into the top rank of global oil producers.

These events were a great clarifier. In the early 1960s PDTC relinquished much of the Trucial Coast area, but retained Abu Dhabi and changed its name to the Abu Dhabi Petroleum Company (ADPC). In 1965 the company signed a 50–50 oil-sharing agreement with Sheikh Shakhbut; ADMA agreed similar terms in 1966. Shakhbut's rule was fated, however, and in August he was succeeded by his younger brother, Zayed, whose accession allowed the brake to be taken off oil development.

And yet, as other oil-producing nations became increasingly assertive, Abu Dhabi took a moderate line towards nationalization, striking a balance between establishing state ownership and retaining the technical expertise of the oil companies. Once the seven sheikhdoms of the Trucial Coast had come together as the United Arab Emirates under the presidency of Sheikh Zayed, a state oil company was created that acquired a 60 per cent interest in the two oil companies, ADMA and ADPC, through the state-owned Abu Dhabi National Oil Company (ADNOC). And finally the Buraimi Dispute, which still cast a shadow over oil development in the area, was ostensibly settled by the Treaty of Jeddah. Saudi Arabia gained a stretch of coast around Khawr al-Udaid and the hydrocarbons from the Shaybah/Zararra oilfield in return for settling its boundary dispute with the UAE.

Zakum offshore oilfield, discovered in 1963, is today the biggest oilfield in Abu Dhabi and the third largest offshore field in the world. Back then many local people lived in 'arish (palm-frond) huts and there was little infrastructure. By 1971 there were roads, an international airport, telephones and the start of modern housing. The hub for offshore operations, Das Island, mushroomed into a small city, with a population of 7,000. The island is still an important centre today; it also houses a gas liquefaction plant that processes gas from the oilfields as well as from the vast Khuff gas reservoirs that lie under the Abu al-Bukhoosh and Umm Shaif oilfields. In contrast to the early days of oil exploration, a number of international oil companies now operate in the UAE, including Japanese, Korean and Chinese firms.

In Dubai, where the Continental Oil Company acquired a 50 per cent share in the concession, the Fateh ('Good Fortune') field was discovered in 1966. The difficulty of storing oil in shallow waters was solved by building and transporting large floating tanks, known as khazzans, and towing them to where the oil was produced offshore.

On 22 September 1969 the first tanker of oil was exported from Fateh Field, bringing the wealth that helped to lay the foundations for the world-famous city of the same name. In Sharjah, progress was less impressive. A protocol agreement with Iran over the disputed Abu Musa Island meant that when the Mubarak field was discovered in 1972, its oil would be shared with Iran. This oilfield was discovered about 34 kilometres (21 miles) east of the island by the Buttes Gas and Oil Company operating through Crescent Petroleum. Initially the field went on stream at high rates, and other wells tested even higher, though by 1985 production had fallen from a high of 60,000 barrels per day to one tenth of that amount. Sharjah's dispute with Iran over Abu Musa and Ras al-Khaimah's over the Tunbs were taken up by the United Arab Emirates after its formation in 1971. In respect of the Tunbs, the argument was more about the strategic location of the islands, which are near the entrance to the Gulf, than about their oil prospects – but it remains a contentious issue in the region today.

Oil exploration gave rise to several other disputes between the rulers over their maritime boundaries. Kuwait was bordered by Saudi Arabia and Iraq, and faced Iran. This led to arguments over maritime boundaries that would hinder oil exploration and development in the area for many years to come. A dispute between Saudi Arabia and Bahrain over the Fasht Bu Saafa oilfield was settled in 1958, with the former extracting the oil and agreeing to share the proceeds with the latter. Qatar and Abu Dhabi argued over Halul Island until two British experts determined that it belonged to the former and the Al Bunduq oilfield was to be shared between them. Sheikh Shakhbut refused to accept the decision, and his hostility towards the British is often traced to this moment. Dubai and Abu Dhabi quarrelled for many years over their maritime boundary, particularly when the Fateh field was discovered, until the quarrel was settled in 1968 after Shakhbut had been removed.

Equally contentious, if apparently resolved now, was the long-running dispute between Qatar and Bahrain over the Hawar Islands, which was exacerbated by the prospect of finding oil in the area. The British Political Agent ruled against Qatar and, when it came to delimiting the maritime boundaries in 1947, the UK government confirmed his decision. The dispute was eventually settled by international arbitration in 2001: Bahrain retained the Hawar Islands and Qatar kept Zubarah, part of the mainland to which the Bahrainis had laid claim.

THE SUCCESS OF ARAMCO's exploration of eastern Arabia sparked a renewed interest in the regional geology of southern Arabia in the post-war years. But IPC was heavily committed elsewhere in the Middle East and uninterested in Dhofar, the southernmost province of Oman. The operating company, Petroleum Development (Oman and Dhofar) Ltd,

Sheikh Zayed bin Sultan Al Nahyan, the future ruler of Abu Dhabi, with the
British Political Agent, Colonel Hugh Boustead, in 1962.

dropped 'Dhofar' from its title and withdrew. This allowed Sultan Said
to grant a concession to Wendell Phillips, who was a visiting American
archaeologist with little knowledge of the oil business. Phillips assigned
the concession to an American oil company, Dhofar-Cities Service
Petroleum Corporation, while retaining a 5 per cent interest. The company spudded in its first test well at Dauka in April 1955, followed by
three wells at Marmul from 1956 to 1958 that located oil. The early signs
were encouraging, but did not last; the oil flow declined on testing and
the oil was too heavy to exploit commercially. More disappointments
followed, as low oil prices and the problem of loading crude on the
coast during the monsoon season only added to the difficulties. In
1967, after an expenditure of $40–50 million and 29 wells sunk, the
Americans decided to relinquish the concession.

Sultan Said bin Taimur wished to progress matters in central Oman,
even though a delicate tribal situation constrained him. His title, sultan
of Muscat and Oman, reflected a dilemma at the heart of his rule. His
influence was strongest around Muscat and along the Batinah coast,
while the inland tribes tended to follow a religious leader, the imam. By
the Treaty of Sib in 1920, a truce had existed between the two groups,

but the sultan was reluctant to authorize survey parties to explore the interior for fear of offending tribal sensitivities. PDO decided to approach the main oil prospect, Jebel Fahud, from the south via Duqm Bay, which was suitable for a seaborne landing. Although the landing was successful, the sultan forbade any surveys from going north. The situation changed when the imam passed away in 1954 and his successor expelled the sheikhs of the Duru tribe from their homelands. This gave the sultan a pretext to send an armed force into the interior, taking the geologists with them.

The most interesting oil prospect, Jebel Fahud, was within the Duru lands, and the geologists reached the jebel in October 1954. It was judged suitable for drilling, but the subsequent well proved to be a dry hole: as with the Dauka well in Dhofar, the Arab Zone was absent. Meanwhile, the tribes tolerated the geologists as they scouted the mountains and wadis of their lands, and only occasionally fired a bullet in their general direction. Between 1956 and 1960 three more exploration wells were drilled, at Ghaba, Haima and Afar, and two seismic parties and a gravity party were at work without finding any indication of oil in commercial quantities. All this was very disheartening. The supply of crude oil exceeded demand, prices were still low and tribal instability an ever-present danger – all leading to a major rethink of the Omani concession. Three of the IPC partners decided to withdraw from Oman, leaving Shell (85 per cent) and Gulbenkian's firm Partex (15 per cent) as the two remaining partners in Petroleum Development Oman (PDO).

As the lead company, Shell took over the management of the company and instigated a review of the geological and seismic data. Discoveries had been made in the Cretaceous Thamama of Abu Dhabi, hinting at new oil-bearing formations that might exist in Oman. Hugh Wilson, Shell's regional exploration manager, closely studied the cores, cuttings and logs from the dry IPC wells. In 1962, as a result of his work, a new drilling programme was started that led to the discovery of oil and gas in the Yibal oilfield 48 kilometres (30 miles) southwest of Fahud. The Natih anticline, 32 kilometres (20 miles) northeast of Fahud, proved productive in 1963, followed by Fahud itself in 1964. A pipeline was laid from these oilfields for a distance of 275 kilometres (171 miles) to the coast at Mina al-Fahal, where a tank farm, moorings for sea-going tankers and a 20-megawatt power plant were built. The first export of Omani oil took place on

A seismic crew working in the Abu Dhabi desert, 1971.

27 July 1967, and the Government of Oman took a 60 per cent stake in PDO in 1974.

In the Hadhramaut, the search for oil went on. In the 1950s another IPC associate, Petroleum Concessions Ltd (PCL), had sent survey parties into the interior. In 1953 geologist Mike Morton established a geological base near the bedouin well at Thamud, and his colleague Ziad Beydoun led a series of geological surveys over the next six seasons, complemented by geophysical surveys. This was at a time when borders and therefore concessionary areas were ill-defined, which could lead to misunderstandings. The neighbouring Yemenis watched the geologists' progress closely, and broadcast details of their 'Nasrani invasion' on the radio in an attempt to inflame public opinion against them. There were also rumours of Aramco survey parties pressing farther south through the Rub al-Khali towards the Aden Protectorate.

In October 1955 Jim Ellis, a British officer leading a patrol of Arab levies, came upon an Aramco party camped in the sands. He claimed that the Americans were trespassing on British-protected territory and demanded that they leave. After a brief contretemps, the party deserted the camp and left its mobile rigs in place. The equipment remained there for many years and was a popular tourist attraction for visiting IPC geologists. An abandoned bulldozer from the camp later found its way to the Hadhramaut Valley for use in irrigation projects there.

IPC geologists laid the foundations for later exploration, though their search for oil in southwest Arabia was ultimately fruitless. In 1960 the company relinquished its concessionary areas. The continuing low price of crude oil on the market had made exploration of peripheral areas less attractive, and the IPC partners preferred to develop their interests in other Arab countries; the two American partners had already joined Aramco in Saudi Arabia and the IPC group was on the verge of finding onshore oil in Abu Dhabi.

Nevertheless, Yemen remained a tantalizing oil prospect and would fascinate geologists for many years to come. With the Trucial Coast and Oman producing oil, it became the final frontier of Arabian oil exploration. In 1961, amid much local excitement, American drillers of the Mecom group spudded in a wildcat well at Salif, a coastal town north of Hodeida, but it was dry. In 1964 Pan American (Amoco) drilled a number of holes in the Aden Protectorate that were also dry. As if it were not complicated enough, political difficulties and corporate confidentiality meant that for many years there was no single picture of the geology on both sides of the Hadhramaut–Yemeni border. It was not the first time that lines drawn on maps frustrated the search for oil, and it would not be the last.

One important matter had been settled, however. By now the myth of the Arab Zone – that the oil-rich rock formation somehow extended across the Arabian Peninsula – had been laid to rest. As it was, for both schools of thought, there were consolations. The Arab Zone proved to be a prolific oil reservoir in Saudi Arabia, Qatar and even the UAE (albeit mostly bearing sour gas there), while a host of new oil-bearing formations had been discovered, with more to come to light. To a lay person, they presented a roll call of bewildering names such as Thamama, Shuaiba and Wasia, but the petroleum geologist knew exactly what they were: the ultimate prize.

THE
MIDDLE EAST

TEN

VOICES IN THE DARK

I N THE MIDDLE EAST, celebrations of the oil age were few and far between. In some countries, at various times, the ritual burning of the effigy of an Englishman or Uncle Sam was counted as such, in others a rather more mundane procession of trucks with placards of oil production figures mounted on their sides. In Saudi Arabia celebrations were muted: perchance the polite applause of an appreciative crowd as a royal motorcade went by. It was different when national passion and oil coincided, as in the case of the Buraimi Dispute, when there were cardboard tanks and wild outpourings on the streets of Dammam. Elsewhere across the region, the message of oil tended to be wrapped in platitudes about progress, prosperity and wise leadership.

Among those few who wrote about the impact of oil was the desert explorer Wilfred Thesiger. Not himself an oilman, he was appalled at the inevitable changes that oil would bring to southern Arabia. In the course of his travels in the latter part of the 1940s, in which he criss-crossed the great desert known as the Rub al-Khali (the Empty Quarter) on camel, Thesiger spent much time in the company of his bedouin guides and escorts. While they still pursued a way of life that had remained unchanged for centuries, Thesiger saw the new oil wealth that was already intruding on the wider Arab world as a threat to their society.

News of the oil camps in distant Saudi Arabia and Qatar had already percolated back to the remote towns and villages of the region. Thesiger had seen how the bedouin's love of money might easily corrupt him, especially when there was an oil job in the offing. Whether it was simply sitting under a palm tree guarding an oil company store, driving a geologist around the desert or labouring at a well site, the rewards

The present arrangements have proved remarkably resilient in the face of rapid change. Only when the bond no longer accommodates the majority of the population do the cracks begin to show, as with the Arab Spring demonstrations in Bahrain, where the Shia population outnumbers the ruling Sunnis. If progressive change is not possible, then there is only one way for the government to go: repress the demonstrations and assert the status quo.

It was always so. The first oilmen, and the diplomats too, sought out the local rulers to make their agreements. Those such as Ibn Saud exercised their power across large swathes of oil-rich lands, while others governed small, ill-defined territories wracked by petty wars. As the oil wealth became a reality, so there was a growing need to define boundaries and agree who should be recognized as the rulers of the land. There were no democratic structures as such; any system of local engagement revolved around the *majlis* where local people could make submissions to their ruling sheikh.

The British were content to recognize these structures and, in some cases, build on them. In the case of Iraq, an attempt to foist a form of parliamentary democracy on the country came to a bloody end with the death of King Faisal II and his family in 1958. On the Trucial Coast, on the other hand, the union of seven sheikhdoms to form the United Arab Emirates (UAE) in 1971 was a relatively seamless transformation of tribal structure into modern government. The structure that was so predominant in the UAE was only part of the political make-up of a more developed country like Iraq but, whatever the situation, the British meddled at their peril.

Across Arabia, local people had a good awareness of the resources close at hand: water, dates, camels and goats were the staples of the desert life. Coffee and tobacco were among the few luxuries they enjoyed. Water was more important than oil, so much so that in the early days the bedouin had little idea of the use and importance of oil. Indeed, why should they? Everything they needed was garnered from their immediate environment, whether it was the dates that nourished them or the camels' milk that quenched their thirst. There were celebrations and feasts in honour of esteemed guests.

And there were bad times too; this was not an idyllic existence by any means. Communities were vulnerable to devastating locust storms when branches would be stripped bare by the invading horde; to disease and sickness, which they attempted to cure with local remedies;

to loss and bereavement as a result of bedouin raiding, which was still happening in parts of Arabia into the late 1940s. Their devotion to Islam encouraged a stoical view, seeing these events as being manifestations of God's will. These issues were not simply confined to the bedouin, though; they also resonated through the non-Arab tribes of Iran, especially the Bakhtiari tribes for whom the advent of oil was a two-edged sword.

And then came the geologists with their red faces and strange fixation with rocks, the motor cars and trucks with their evil-smelling fumes, and the oil wells with their incongruous derricks sprouting on the desert landscape. In some quarters, Westerners were seen as a potential threat. In the 1930s when American engineers first arrived in Saudi Arabia to drill for water, a Wahhabi preacher denounced them and accused the king, Ibn Saud, of 'selling the land, and his people, into bondage of unbelievers'.[2] When the preacher appeared before him, Ibn Saud heard his arguments and tried to persuade him to change his mind. When he did not, the king threatened to punish him, at which point the preacher backed down. A similar argument was made over the flying of aeroplanes above the desert and the introduction of radio transmitters to the kingdom.

In time these objections would fall away, yet oil companies still had to be sensitive to their local environment in order to avoid disturbing the patterns of life. Tapline, the trans-Arabian oil pipeline, dissected bedouin migration routes. Although most of the line was buried, its above-ground portions presented obstacles to bedouin with livestock, and life would have been difficult had Aramco not built ramps of sand at frequent intervals to allow them to pass over. Twenty years before, IPC had gained the right to extract water along the route of its pipeline through Palestine, in effect taking water from the local population without providing any compensation, although its geologists located many new sources of water along the route that were drilled for the benefit of local people. One unintended consequence was the gradual settlement of bedouin around areas where water wells had been drilled; no longer did they have to follow the rains.

THE COMING OF OIL had far-reaching consequences for the traditional societies. Where tasks had once been done by hand, they were now carried out by the machines driven by steam, oil and electricity.

These powered the vessels that carried people and goods across the sea, the vehicles that transported them across the land, and the equipment that ran the factories and irrigated the plantations. Prices in the towns soared and simple commodities that bedouin needed from the markets – pots and pans, water skins or saddlebags – could no longer be exchanged for a goat or bag of dates. The desert life became unsustainable, causing many tribespeople to abandon their customary haunts and settle in the towns or shanties on their outskirts until such time as the oil wealth was redistributed through government programmes and aid.

Young men began leaving their villages for well-paid jobs in the oilfields, staying away for two or three years before returning home with enough money to build modern houses to replace their traditional dwellings. They brought back knowledge of new techniques such as the use of cement for building. Those on the coast might use their newly acquired wealth to purchase a small boat with an outboard motor and fishing nets. Others stayed with the oil companies for longer, receiving an education and travelling abroad to complete their studies at the company's expense.

These were the first members of a new emerging class in the Middle East, the technical and managerial middle class that was to grow alongside the traditional merchants and artisans. It was not only the oil industry that brought education to the region; there was a strong tradition of religious education and oral history, too. In the 1950s an influx of Egyptian and Syrian teachers to the Gulf states fostered nationalist ideas. Increasing self-awareness brought a growing desire among Arabs to take control of their own resources – in this aspiration, they were seeking to achieve the old bedouin idea that natural resources were for the use of the people of the land. In Iran the nationalist movement went back to the time of the Tobacco Revolt and beyond.

Families found new ways to supplement their incomes as local economies began to grow. Abu Dhabi resident Mohamed Abd al-Muhairi described how his family's small business expanded with the coming of oil. His father supplied provisions and water to the most important sites in the sheikhdom, and had an exclusive concession to fish off the shores of three of its islands. He was able to export his surplus catch to Kuwait, Qatar and other neighbouring states. He also had contacts with merchants and notables and was therefore well placed to do business with incoming Western companies, such as BP.

From there, Mohamed went into business to supply the oil company's base at Das Island with rations and workers, then branched out into freight operations. Today the family is engaged in various trade and construction projects and Mohamed owns a group of private companies of his own. This story is typical of so many businesses in the Gulf region. In Dubai, which has a long tradition of merchant trading, a number of local families were among the first to receive trade licences from the government, thus laying the foundations of the massive construction, trading and commercial activities that characterize the city today.

In some ways their existence was blessed. The tribesmen who so recently had been tending their herds in the desert pastures now found themselves liberated from the land by an influx of foreign labourers. The golden cities of the Arabian coast were now rising up through the sweat and toil of Iranians, Baluchis and Pakistanis who crossed the narrow gulf, or Yemenis who had made their way overland to Saudi Arabia, many in search of wages to remit to their families back home. Westerners took the skilled jobs until such time as nationals could be trained up to take over from them; sadly the track record of these regionalization programmes has not been a resounding success.

Then there were those Arabs who had migrated from Iraq and the Levant countries to find more lucrative employment in the Gulf states. The example of Jordan is a case in point, where a country with very little oil benefited from the oil wealth elsewhere. During the 1970s and '80s up to 350,000 skilled Jordanians found employment in the Gulf. The money they remitted to their families helped to revive the local economy. On the other hand, the country was also hit by contractions in the oil industry, such as happened in the late 1980s, and today remains a relatively poor country with large foreign debts and few natural resources of its own.

Despite being outnumbered by expatriates in their own countries, citizens of the oil-rich Gulf states enjoyed a generous helping of public services, housing, welfare benefits and cash allowances. They came from different tribal groups, yet they had one thing in common: all had a vested interest in the oil boom and its attendant affluence. The drive to nationalize the industry solidified the state–oil connection, leading to the emergence of rentier states, where the government's main sources of revenue are derived from its natural

Kuwaiti merchants, 1952.

resources and rented to external clients. Once the industries were nationalized, the revenues were no longer controlled by private companies but by state companies, a fact that, taken with the impact of the Organization of Petroleum Exporting Countries (OPEC), saw a huge increase in money for the oil-producing states. The governing structures were preserved as the state became the main allocator of wealth and welfare.

On the whole there is little appetite in the Arabian petroleum states for radical political reform while the oil revenues keep flowing. Occasionally expatriates, ethnic or religious groups might be seen as a threat to the internal security of a state, as occurred in 1991 when Kuwait expelled 300,000 Palestinians, and latterly when the political agitations of the Arab Spring were repressed. Prosperity was not the end of the story, clearly: the essential point was the use to which the oil revenues were put. We find a grotesque illustration of this theme with the so-called Islamic State (also known as Da'esh, or ISIS), which is producing oil from captured oilfields and refineries to finance its operations. The sight of an oil industry being run in this way is a reflection in a dark mirror: an oil empire that has turned to anarchy.

Oil development, however, was always an engine of social unrest. The creation of thousands of jobs in Kirkuk during the 1940s sparked changes to the social and ethnic character of the town as workers came from outside and settled there. Neighbourhoods sprang up in the old quarter, together with others housing Assyrians and Arabs near IPC's main base. The number of Kurdish employees was lower than other ethnic groups. Ethnic tensions were evident, particularly between Iraqis and Assyrians. On 4 July 1946 5,000 IPC workers went on strike. They marched through the streets and gathered at a place called Gawer Baghi, an olive grove popular with families as a picnic site, where they chanted slogans and listened to speeches. A few days later, the police charged and fired on the crowd, killing five and wounding fourteen. The strikers returned to work on 16 July.

Industrial unrest was not only confined to Iraq and Iran, and PDQ had to deal with several strikes in Qatar in the 1950s. But while such incidents might have been shrugged off as local difficulties, the problems in Iraq were not so easily dismissed. It was the heartland of IPC's oil empire, and an important supplier of oil to the West. The disturbances were generally attributed to the work of 'agitators' and political dissenters since there seemed to be no other explanation for well-paid workers going on strike. But, as the disturbances of Al Wathba in 1948 reiterated, Iraqis were sensitive to British influences.

Here was a conundrum: IPC considered that it was for the government to resolve the underlying problems, but the government was never strong enough to implement far-reaching reforms. Between censorship, outright bans and legal proceedings, the Iraqi press denounced the British. Some newspapers devised ways to get round bans, reappearing under different names: *The People* became *Voice of the People* and then *Echo of the People*, for example. IPC management remained aloof, taking the view that any form of public response would only inflame the situation. This simply allowed accusations to go unchallenged. Eventually IPC did recognize a need for a public relations department and attempted to counter its negative image in the Arab media; but by then the damage had been done.

The modern reader will have a sense of déjà vu at this point. As in Iran, there was virtually no interaction between company personnel and local inhabitants. A British diplomat visiting the oil sites in Iraq complained of the 'luxury' and 'remoteness' of the living arrangements for company staff.[3] Interaction between management and workers tended to be through limited, formal channels. Those who did mix with Iraqi politicians at company functions often found it a surreal experience, for they could be charming one day and make a virulent anti-British speech the next. On the other hand, in the field there was a degree of teamwork between the oilmen and Iraqis, drillers and workmen, in situations where everyday problems required a good working relationship between them; otherwise official structures ruled.

Everette DeGolyer had something to say about all this. He recognized the importance of maintaining cordial relations between local people and the skilled and technical employees brought in from outside. Language, political and social differences, and religion formed part of the barrier between them, but the economic disparity between them was the greatest peril. The technical men brought expertise, commanded high wages and were cosseted in their camps. They were transient, earning enough money in a difficult climate in order to return home and possibly retire on the proceeds after only a few years. They made little effort to learn the language, especially if it was Arabic, which was perceived to be difficult to learn. Local workers were unskilled and

Workers being transported to the Abadan oil refinery, 1947.

earned low wages, even by the standards of their own country. A few might qualify professionally and rise to the middle and higher-ranking jobs. All the same, a large number of local people would seek work with the oil company with the result that the company would feel no pressure to raise wages to a more acceptable level.

Mexico, where American and British oil companies pioneered oil operations in the early 1900s, provided some valuable lessons. As DeGolyer observed of the American companies:

> Men came down from the hills, brought a meagre supply of food with them, worked for a few days, slept in the brush, received their wage and went back to their homes. Skilled labour, almost altogether American drillers, their helpers, mechanics, and engineers, on the other hand, were properly housed, well fed, received medical attention, were paid a higher wage than at home, and generally received superior treatment.[4]

An oil well was expected to last only a few years; apart from a few notable exceptions, no Mexican occupied a position of substance in the companies.

The challenge was not to repeat the mistakes of Mexico. Through the camp system, oil companies became paternalistic, assuming a responsibility for their workers that went beyond the payment of wages, in some cases building townships in the process. They provided social welfare programmes, recreational facilities, medical and other services. Their most significant contribution came in the field of education, where the company would assist the government in providing classes and trade schools for workers, tradesmen and clerks and sponsoring students to study at universities abroad. In the undeveloped Saudi Arabia of the 1940s and '50s, Aramco provided many of the public services that a state would have provided. In the Eastern Province, they built schools and roads, operated a hospital and clinics, constructed workers' housing and supplied electricity.

And yet the disparity between the American employees and Saudi workers endured. There were murmurings in the u.s. diplomatic corps that all was not well with the Saudi camps. Cables were sent expressing concerns about the medical director's lack of interest in the Saudis' healthcare, and the state of the workers' accommodation.

The main cause of discontent was the difference in living conditions between American and Saudi workers.

In September 1953 leaflets criticizing the company and rumours of a strike began circulating among the Aramco workforce. When the Saudis arrested the ringleaders, more than five hundred workers attended a meeting in Dhahran. An angry mob stoned a passing USAAF bus and smashed its windows. On one day in October, 90 per cent of the Saudi workforce were absent from work. Saudi troops moved in and arrested more than a thousand workers, went into the Aramco camps and began stopping all those entering and leaving them in an attempt to identify troublemakers. The strike leaders were banished to other parts of the country and five foreign nationals deported. The action had the desired effect and the remaining Saudi employees quickly returned to work. The Saudis considered the strike a communist plot, the Americans saw it as a protest against the government, while Aramco looked again at the conditions of its workers and raised wages.

In contrast to Aramco, which had to deal with a single government and people, the IPC group was spread out across the region dealing with many different governments and populations. Its area of operations covered Iraq, Syria, Cyprus, Lebanon, Jordan, Qatar, the Trucial Coast, Oman and the Aden Protectorates. By 1958, for example, it had 15,000 employees in Iraq and 4,500 in Qatar, compared with 20,000 employed by Aramco in Saudi Arabia. Overall, there were some 100,000 oil industry employees in the six main producing countries of the Middle East, out of a population of 30 million. It was a vast kaleidoscope of people and cultures.

In spite of that, opportunities for indigenous workers to climb the ladder were limited. The number of expatriates employed by IPC rose from 140 (in 1941) to 814 (in 1949), about 4 and 6 per cent respectively of the total number of employees: they held all the senior posts in the company and there was no training programme to replace them with Iraqis. Many oil companies focused on the narrower band of workers' welfare and education, not concerning themselves overmuch with the wider implications of oil wealth; as in Iraq, oil executives would have taken the view that social issues were a matter for the government rather than themselves, as indeed they were. In the realm of workers' housing, for which the oil companies had a responsibility, there were some glaring anomalies.

Manucher Farmanfarmaian described how 'Paper City' in Abadan had grown up in the shadow of the oil refinery. In the summer the buildings were sweltering hovels, and in winter, without electricity and heating, they were a poor refuge from the bitter cold and the all-pervasive rain and mud. British managers with their 'pressed ecru shirts' had their own air-conditioned offices, and comfortable dwellings separated by well-manicured lawns and rose beds, with tennis courts, swimming pools and clubs – all far beyond the reach and imagination of the ordinary Iranian. And, as if they needed reminding, there were notices dotted about stating that particular facilities were 'Not for Iranians'.[5]

The causes of the post-war industrial unrest in the Iranian oil industry – the wildcat strikes and rioting – were surely triggered in part by these conditions and by a failure on the part of Anglo-Iranian management to address them. Trade unions remained illegal. Elsewhere, policies of integration – employing nationals as well as meshing company operations with the local economy, ordering equipment and materials through local suppliers – were introduced, but these were patchy and not always at a pace that national governments preferred.

In Saudi Arabia Tom Barger urged that American expertise should be used to assist the government in developing Saudi society. Barger was a geologist who had taken part in the early exploration of the desert and later rose to become the chief executive officer of Aramco. The company went some way towards his aspiration. It helped to create new communities outside the oil camps by granting generous loans to house buyers and by building schools; all other tasks of construction and administration remained the responsibility of the Saudi government.

There were limits to what the company could achieve. Clearly, providing these facilities in their entirety would have been a mammoth task. The wealth drawn from the oil industry provided the government with the means to address these issues, yet the result was not entirely successful and today, Saudi Aramco is only one of a few 'islands of efficiency' in a sea of state organizations.[6]

In the 1970s regulatory structures remained undeveloped and ineffectual while traditional ways of doing business evolved exponentially with the rise in oil revenues. Iran was an object lesson in how not to manage the state's oil revenues; political graft was endemic in court circles and among members of the royal family. It was rarely

Shanty-type housing in Abadan, 1951.

confronted, and then only in relation to minor officials and not the higher echelons. In Iraq the auction of oil contracts after the removal of Saddam Hussein's regime in 2003 was accompanied by a network of middlemen and corrupt officials dealing with everything from service contracts to pipelines.

A distinction is to be drawn between those companies that legitimately partner local firms in order to win contracts through their expertise and others that use middlemen to bribe corrupt officials. For example, recent news reports have suggested that hundreds of major international corporations relied on a Monaco-based company, Unaoil, to secure lucrative contracts in Asia, Africa and the Middle East. It was claimed that Unaoil had bribed local officials with money, gifts and benefits in kind. The allegations are currently being investigated by UK and U.S. law enforcement agencies.

If the image of late-night meetings to hand over bundles of 'baksheesh' seems outdated now, it is only because such transactions have morphed into a more subtle and nuanced form. This is not a simple matter of cultural differences between West and East. The demonstrators who took to the streets during the Arab Spring of 2011 did so for a variety of reasons, but including a desire to protest against corruption and waste. Anyone thinking that things have changed in today's Middle East is mistaken. At any one time, the fixers and lobby-ists, the officials and the middlemen, will be in the thick of it – and not always on the side of the angels.

But who are the angels? → Speaking from a religious POV... demons like Lucifer were once angels too. Is that what's being referenced here?

ELEVEN

SISTERS AND BROTHERS, 1945–80

AT THE END OF the Second World War a former resistance fighter by the name of Enrico Mattei was appointed as a commissioner in northern Italy. His brief was to wind up the activities of the state oil company, Azienda Generale Italiana Petroli (AGIP), which had failed to live up to the promise of the fascist years to find new sources of oil and gas, having been involved in Mosul through the fated BOD venture of the 1930s, among other things. In the absence of a strong post-war Italian government, Mattei was able to disregard his orders and, encouraged by earlier surveys, he recommended drilling and struck the rich gas deposits of the Po Valley. These became the foundation of his financial strength, but when he set about looking for oil, he was less successful. Italy lacked its own sources of crude and, when he looked to the Middle East, Mattei found the oil majors well ensconced. He called them the *Sette Sorelle*, the 'Seven Sisters'; it was a name that stuck.

Despite the degree of kinship that was implied, relations between the oil majors were not always sisterly. Many of the petroleum alliances of the early twentieth century sprang out of a mutual rivalry between the original 'big' sisters, Royal Dutch Shell and Jersey Standard (later Exxon). At that time Anglo-Persian was small by comparison, but its oil discoveries in Iran marked the rise of Middle Eastern oil, bringing the company great wealth and creating a corporate behemoth that became an imperial institution in its own right. After the start-up years, when it was financially strapped and faced the prospect of being taken over by Royal Dutch Shell (the 'Shell Menace'), Anglo-Persian shook off its difficulties and became the richest oil company in the world. It had enough oil – too much in fact – but little marketing skill, and its dependency on Iranian oil was a strength and a weakness. Only when nationalization exposed this vulnerability did executives wake up and transform the company into the global player we recognize today as British Petroleum (BP).

Evidently Mattei did not use the term 'sisters' in a literal sense, since he was scornful of the power that the seven companies wielded. Their histories were littered with trade-offs and takeovers. Royal Dutch had emerged from the Sumatran jungle to embrace Sir Marcus Samuel's Shell Transport and Trading Company in order to ship oil from the East Indies to Western Europe. Royal Dutch Shell's participation in IPC heralded the start of its involvement in Middle Eastern oil. It remained crude short, lacking access to the sources of oil, and was always buying oil from other companies. Hence, in 1948, it traded its support for the Red Line Agreement in order to buy oil at preferential prices, dropping its opposition to the American partners in IPC buying into Aramco.

True, some sisters were closer than others. Jersey Standard, strong in marketing networks but also lacking access to oil, made good its deficit by joining its compatriots in the Saudi venture. Jersey executives considered themselves as the mediators of the international oil business and had close links with Washington, which came in handy when it was necessary to fall back on diplomatic support. Often regarded as the true heir to the former Standard Oil, the company accentuated the connection in its use of the trade name 'Esso', which was a phonetic version of the 'S' and 'O' in Standard Oil.

The other American partner in IPC, Socony-Vacuum, was the third largest U.S. oil company. The latter part of its name was derived from a 1931 merger with the Vacuum Oil Company, which had invented a process for distilling kerosene from crude oil in a vacuum. The company's strength was in the Far Eastern markets, making them attractive partners in the eyes of the Aramco shareholders. Its interests often coincided with those of Jersey Standard. Indeed, after Jersey Standard became Exxon and Socony-Vacuum became Mobil, both firms merged in 1999 to become ExxonMobil.

The Texas Oil Company (later Texaco) had built up a marketing network based on distributing Texas crude. In the 1930s it was impressed by Bahrain's relative proximity to its own Far Eastern markets and so bought a 50 per cent share in Bapco and Casoc, with their oil being marketed through a new company, Caltex. Gulf Oil was a member of the IPC group, but lost their interest in Bahrain through their partners' opposition and left the consortium. They turned to Kuwait, joining Anglo-Iranian to form the Kuwait Oil Company. SoCal had already set the ball rolling in Saudi Arabia with its oil strike at Dammam in 1938.

On a Western-centric view, these were great achievements in themselves. Yet none of these companies was able to develop the oil resources of the Middle East entirely on its own. Although the end profit was great, the start-up costs were formidable.

The experience of SoCal is a case in point: in the 1920s the company, being crude short outside the United States, focused its exploration on countries in Latin America and Southeast Asia. At a cost of some $50 million and no major discoveries, less determined companies might have thrown in the towel. SoCal's 'absolute determination to find oil' drove it on, leading it to concessions in Bahrain and Saudi Arabia.[1] Then the sheer cost of developing the Hasa concession nearly bankrupted the company and forced it to seek other partners: the Texas Oil Company in 1936, and Socony-Vacuum and Jersey Standard in 1948. In short, there were sound practical reasons for bringing these companies together; unfortunately a consideration of indigenous aspirations was not one of them.

In this way companies that had once been rivals came together, bound together by circumstance and commercial opportunity. The Seven Sisters would dominate the production of Middle Eastern oil for many decades to come. Nevertheless, they were all slaves to one master: the law of supply and demand. A glut of oil brought lower prices, and oil shortages brought higher prices and – depending on margins – fluctuations in profit. The key was to command the supply of oil and hence the price. While not completely controlling global prices, the oil majors achieved a measure of success in dampening down market volatility through the mechanism of 'posted' prices.

They were able to fix their prices, and therefore the amount they paid their host governments, through this device. The posted (published) price of oil was not its price on the open market, but a notional price at which the oil majors sold their crude oil at the point of shipment. The profit was then calculated by deducting the cost of production and transport to the ports. The essential issue was that the price was fixed, and therefore profits determined, by the oil majors. They were to some extent able to absorb losses on their downstream operations (refining, distribution) through the posted prices system. Ultimately there came a point when market prices were too low to sustain the posted price, which eventually had to be cut in order to reflect the position, thus reducing the amounts paid to the producing governments. When this happened, the consequences could be severe.

Western governments attempting to take control of the process, as for example with the Anglo-American Oil Agreement of 1944, found their way blocked by the vested interests of the oil industry. The U.S. administration considered funding the Trans-Arabian pipeline project and buying into Aramco, but both initiatives failed. Washington nevertheless encouraged U.S. oil companies to participate in Middle Eastern oil, providing tax breaks and thus enabling them to increase the royalties they paid to the producing governments. Across the Atlantic, Whitehall continued to exercise a degree of influence over Anglo-Iranian through its 51 per cent shareholding, though proving to be rather less flexible than the Americans.

Middle Eastern oil was especially coveted because it was cheap, good quality and plentiful. But the high initial cost of development in the region was prohibitive for many Western oil firms, and the region's different culture and customs made it difficult for a company without the necessary contacts to operate successfully; all these factors favoured the formation of large consortia. The other side of the coin was that the exclusion of the smaller outfits created a rising sense of unfairness. In the 1950s, the U.S. Federal Trade Commission investigated what was described as the 'International Oil Cartel' of major oil companies, action was started for alleged overcharging for oil prices and the Justice Department began anti-trust proceedings against certain international oil companies. Although their outcomes were inconclusive at the time, these actions by the U.S. government against its own companies did spark considerable interest – and bewilderment – in the oil capitals of the Middle East.[2]

All the while, Enrico Mattei as chairman of the Italian state-controlled company Ente Nazionale Idrocarburi (ENI), railed against the Seven Sisters. He was referring to the largest Anglo-American oil companies: British Petroleum, Gulf Oil (merged with SoCal), SoCal (now known as Chevron), Texaco (merged with Chevron), Royal Dutch Shell, Jersey Standard (Esso/Exxon) and Socony (Mobil). It was an exclusive club that, by Mattei's definition, omitted CFP (Total)

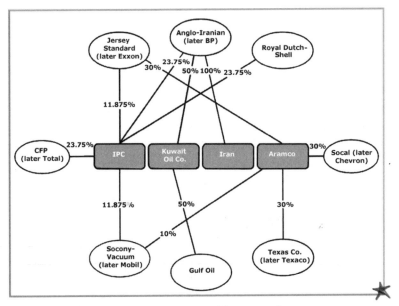

The oil majors' shares in the four main Middle Eastern oil concessions, 1948.

because that company was not part of the Anglo-Saxon elite. For the same reason, AGIP, the reborn petroleum arm of ENI, was left out in the cold – hence his annoyance. The time would come when the petroleum world would be turned upside down; but for now it needed more than mere words to change things.

SHORTLY BEFORE DAWN ON 11 December 1949 the American geologist Paul Walton was picked up from the ramshackle Kandara Hotel on the outskirts of Jeddah and driven to a nearby airstrip, close to today's downtown area of the city. In those days the desert runway was a primitive affair, illuminated with kerosene lamps and resembling a U.S. highway construction site from the 1920s. There, barely visible in the flickering light, was a parked Saudi Arabian Airlines C-47 Skytrain. TWA employees staffed the airline and the pilot was American. Among the passengers was a Russian mechanic with stainless steel false teeth, and – more to the point – a Saudi named Abdullah Tariki and his American wife. In his early twenties, Tariki was the only Saudi graduate geologist in the country at that time. This was the same man who, years later, would become Saudi Arabia's first petroleum minister.

Walton was employed by the eccentric millionaire J. Paul Getty, whose oil company, Pacific Western Oil Corporation (later Getty Oil), was not in the same league as the Seven Sisters. Even so, Getty was quite prepared to tangle with the oil majors when it suited him. 'The meek shall inherit the Earth, but not its mineral rights' was a famous saying attributed to Getty.[3] Unlike many of his contemporaries, Getty was willing to talk directly to petroleum geologists in search of new places to drill. It was this readiness to listen to the man on the ground that brought him into contact with Walton, who had been employed by Casoc in the 1930s and had considerable knowledge of the Saudi Arabian oilfields.

Having failed to obtain an oil concession from Baghdad in 1932, Getty had been casting about for a new prospect in the Middle East. The Neutral Zone, a territory shared between Saudi Arabia and Kuwait, was a British solution to the predicament of defining frontiers in areas where bedouin roamed. The bedouin had no fixed boundaries, only grazing areas that fluctuated with the seasons. Delineated at the Uqair conference in 1922, the zones (there was another one between Saudi Arabia and Iraq) sidestepped the frontier issue, and gave the British authorities the opportunity to create a buffer between the two states. Initially they were nervous about any oil development there but, having little influence in Saudi Arabia by now, were powerless to stop Getty making his approach.

And so Walton found himself on an aeroplane heading for the Kuwaiti/Saudi Neutral Zone with instructions to carry out an aerial survey of the area. The aircraft took off and headed northeast over the Mahd ad-Dhahab gold mine, then east to the town of Buraida, where the crew encountered fog and flew low in order to get their bearings. Sitting in the cockpit with the captain, Walton recognized the Anseb Oasis and navigated a course from there to the Neutral Zone. After the fog had burned off, they approached the Kuwaiti Neutral Zone, passing the derricks and gas flares of the Burgan field on the way.

Then, as only a geologist can, Walton became excited by the shape of the ground. There were small outcrops that seemed to indicate the top of an anticline. Tariki, who had been standing behind him, had also seen the outcrops, and the purpose of his presence on the flight deck was immediately clear: he was to report back to his boss, Abdullah Suleiman, the Saudi minister of Finance.

Having obtained a favourable report from Walton, Getty obtained a concession for the Neutral Zone that included a groundbreaking

55–45 profit-sharing clause in favour of Saudi Arabia. A Kuwaiti concession for the same territory was granted to the American Independent Oil Company (Aminoil), which took over as the operating company for both concessions. Once Aminoil had drilled five dry holes and were short of options, Getty persuaded them to drill on Walton's anticline. As a result, the Wafra giant oilfield was discovered in 1953. That in itself was no mean achievement but, perhaps more significantly, Getty's profit-sharing agreement eroded the 50–50 deals on which the Seven Sisters had made their stand; for the oil majors, Getty was the proverbial canary in the coal mine.

The independents were on their way. In 1953 Enrico Mattei entered the oil business in Egypt, taking the view that the quickest way to get started was to buy into a company already operating there. The event that outraged him occurred in 1955 when independent companies joined the Iranian concession, leaving ENI out in the cold. Revenge was not long in coming. Two years later Mattei brokered an oil deal with Iran, using the so-called 'Mattei Formula' of a 75–25 profit share in favour of the host country. While the boardrooms of the oil majors might have echoed with sounds of astonishment, there was also recognition that, once the deal had been done, the days of 50–50 agreements were as good as over.

In 1958 Japanese oil companies gained a foothold through the Arabian Oil company, which signed agreements to explore the offshore Neutral Zone. Saudi Arabia and Kuwait were to receive 56 per cent of the profits and Arabian Oil 44 per cent, another nail in the 50–50 concept. In Libya, new concession agreements were intentionally drafted to exclude any one company dominating its oil industry: 51 concessions were granted to seventeen companies and at least half of the oil, when it began to flow, came from independents.

But the sisters were by no means finished.

IN SEPTEMBER 1956 A curious pamphlet was circulated among U.S. oil companies in the Middle East. Dressed up as an official Egyptian document, it urged the creation of an Egyptian-controlled committee that would administer all the Arabs' oil and then allocate it to 'friends' and deny it to 'enemies'.[4] If true, the notion of Egyptians exploiting the oil resources of other Arab countries would have been highly provocative, and in direct conflict with the brotherly principles of Arab nationalism.

U.S. officials dismissed the document as a fake, however, and it was later identified as a British-inspired piece of black propaganda, a clumsy attempt to play on Arab fears of an Egyptian takeover of their oil and thus undermine the message of Colonel Nasser and the anti-Western broadcasts of Cairo Radio. There was no doubt about the potency of his message – at the time of the Suez Crisis there were disturbances across the region. Unidentified saboteurs blew up pipelines between Dukhan and Umm Said in Qatar, although Aramco's Tapline was left untouched.[5]

There was more to the situation than Egyptian megalomania. A new generation was bringing a growing self-awareness to the Middle Eastern oil states, and the customary methods of doing business, derived from the predominantly agrarian and trading economies of the region, were ill-suited to the needs of the petroleum world. The older, conservative order was being replaced with a younger breed of educated executives, men who understood the workings of the oil industry and were not afraid to confront the oil majors. The notion that crude extracted from the ground belonged to the oil company rather than the host country was passé. It was time for a different agenda: national control of oil resources was increasingly seen as a birthright, not something to be given away with a cup of coffee, haggling and a handshake.

In different circumstances, the Seven Sisters might have shrugged off the Mattei Formula and its permutations as mere blips. But when seen against a background of wider changes taking place in the Middle East, they were the warning signs of seismic shifts to come. The aftermath of the Suez Crisis had seen a left-wing government come to power in Syria, the union of Egypt and Syria in the short-lived United Arab Republic and the removal of the Hashemite regime in Iraq. Soon the British would no longer hold the Gulf rulers in their sway; the political foundations of the oil companies' presence in the region were being eroded.

And yet, believing in their own primacy, the sisters thought they could ride out the storm. When the Suez Crisis demonstrated the vulnerability of the West's oil supplies, their answer was to bypass the problem by accelerating the construction of supertankers to sail around the Cape of Good Hope. They held on to the fiction of posted prices. The problem came when the market was awash with oil, as it was when new sources came on stream and Russian oil flooded into

The oil pipeline between Dukhan and Umm Said in Qatar ablaze, December 1956.

Europe, bringing down the price of oil. The oil majors, fearful of losing their margins, decided to reduce the amount they paid to the producing countries for their oil – the posted price of oil.

They began in February 1959 by dropping the price by 10 per cent and then again in 1960 by about 7 per cent. The first move was led by BP and the next by Jersey Standard: the sisters were so interconnected that when one cut its prices, the others followed. It was not entirely without debate, and there was significant opposition to the second cut from members of the Jersey board, notably Howard Page, who warned that 'all hell would break loose'.[6] The chairman of Jersey, Jack Rathbone, had little sympathy for the nationalists, however, and was determined to press ahead. There was talk of compensating the oil-producing countries for their losses but nothing more. The cuts, when they came, were harsh.

After the first cut, the four largest oil-producing countries lost £132 million (£2.8 billion today) a year between them, and the second one had disastrous consequences, not only in financial terms but for Western influence in the Middle East. The cuts provided more ammunition for nationalists like Nasser, even if his message was not universally acclaimed across the Arab world.

THE MAHDI YACHT CLUB, a collection of buildings on the bank of the Nile with a single tree to shade visitors from the sun, was the venue for the next stage in the petroleum tug-of-war. As the Arab Petroleum Congress was taking place in Cairo in April 1959 a small group slipped away to meet under this tree. They were representatives of the Arab oil countries and Iran, together with Venezuela's Perez Alfonso and Saudi Arabia's Abdullah Tariki in attendance. After some hesitation, they drew up a gentlemen's agreement about meeting regularly in future and exchanging information about conditions in the oil industry.

Despite all the trappings of secrecy and intrigue, they produced an anodyne document, peppered with terms such as 'whereas this' and 'whereas that', and making no mention of oil prices or quotas.[7] It avoided any suggestion that they were ganging up against the oil companies. It was still an explosive document: it was the first time that representatives of the oil-producing nations had agreed to coordinate their efforts, and the meeting sowed the seed of OPEC.

What really made the agreement take firm root was the second price cut of August 1960, which came at a particularly sensitive time in Iraq where Qasim was negotiating with IPC. The Cairo conference had demanded that the sisters consult them before imposing any more price cuts, but their demand was ignored. Now there was outrage – even the pro-Western shah was appalled. In September a meeting of the five main oil producers, Iran, Iraq, Kuwait, Saudi Arabia and Venezuela, was convened in Baghdad. They might have been 'walking in a mist', but they were determined to fight back.[8] Under the guiding hands of Perez and Tariki, the newly formed OPEC passed a resolution that oil prices should be restored to the pre-August level.

On that fateful day they set in motion a process that would turn the oil landscape upside down – eventually. With its headquarters in Geneva (moving to Vienna in 1965) and Fuad Rouhani as its secretary-general, OPEC made little impact in its early years. The Seven Sisters, hoping that the organization was a flash in the pan, tried to ignore it. As Rouhani remarked, the oil companies pretended that 'OPEC did not exist'.[9]

They could afford to be stand-offish. In 1960 they controlled 85 per cent of global oil exports, using their pipelines and tankers to deliver the crude to their refineries and then marketing the oil through their outlets. Their position was not unassailable, since new sources of oil were undermining their monopoly and new independent companies

Sheikh Ahmad Yamani (third from left) at an OPEC press conference in 1973.

were appearing all the time, but they were not seriously threatened by OPEC at this time. They played one government against the other as they continued to control the global oil market. Secret agreements with Saudi Arabia and Iran enabled them to pay lower prices for their oil than other companies.

OPEC pressed on: over the coming meetings, members demanded a renegotiation of all concession agreements and required oil companies to negotiate through OPEC and not with individual states. Meanwhile, the oil-producing countries were sending increasing numbers of students abroad for technical training, thus building up their own talent pools. There were no further reductions in the posted price of oil and member states did gain an increase in royalties (around four cents a barrel). But an underlying disunity – the conservatives versus the progressives – endured; there was too much posturing and too little action. An OPEC document, 'Declaratory Statement of Petroleum Policy in Member Countries', set out the right of all countries to sovereignty over their natural resources, but despite this it was only a statement of intent, after all. There was no consensus about regulating production or fixing prices.

By now, the old faces were fading from the scene. Sheikh Tariki fell out of favour and was replaced by a young lawyer named Ahmad Zaki Yamani. By 1969, five extra members and many discussion papers later, OPEC states had achieved little towards gaining control of their oil resources. Momentous change was on the way, that much was certain, though not even the most prescient members could have predicted exactly how it would take place.

IN 1962 A GAS well fire in Algeria called 'The Devil's Cigarette Lighter' burned for six months before Red Adair put it out. Certainly it was a long-burning fire, if not as long as the figurative one that had been burning in the Middle East since the rise of nationalism. All that was required was something to flare the region into a greater flame, and this came in June 1967 upon the outbreak of the Six-Day War.

Saudi Arabia, Iraq and the Gulf producers banned oil exports to the UK and USA because of their perceived complicity in the war. It was an impulsive decision, a bitter reaction among leaders to their fellow Arabs' defeat at the hands of the Israelis. It was also a strange decision in that it overlooked other more effective measures such as full oil nationalization. But the leaders were angry and were in no mood for well-made plans. They wanted revenge, even if it meant heavy financial losses for their own states. And those losses were high: by the end of June, Saudi Arabia had lost £11 million (£183 million today) and Kuwait's national income had fallen by 40 per cent. Other producers moved in to fill the void: Venezuela and Iran (who did not join the embargo) increased their production to meet the shortfall, as did Texas. By July the embargo was in ruins and the Arabs in disarray.

Here was an important lesson for Arab leaders such as King Faisal of Saudi Arabia: oil and politics did not mix well when oil was cheap and plentiful. In January 1968 in an attempt to distance themselves from the more extreme members of OPEC, Saudi Arabia, Libya and Kuwait formed a breakaway group, the Organization of Arab Petroleum Exporting Companies (OAPEC). Its articles required that oil should be a member's main source of income – thus excluding the more radical regimes – which was later amended to an 'important' source of income.

In the sisters' minds, all this confirmed that OPEC members were incapable of acting together. Yet there were other threats to the sisters' dominance, the spread of independent oil companies among them. The problem surfaced in Libya, where independents proliferated. In September 1969 Colonel Muammar Gaddafi overthrew the corrupt King Idris in a bloodless coup. Allied with Algeria, Gaddafi embarked on a radical campaign against the West.

Of the independents, Armand Hammer's Occidental Petroleum was the most exposed. A loner in the petroleum world, Hammer had links with Russia, but none with the oil majors. Occidental had achieved spectacular success in Libya, becoming the country's largest producer. But, when Occidental came under pressure from Gaddafi in 1970, Hammer found himself alone, dependent on Libyan oil and with no alternative supply to fall back on – Jersey Standard could only supply oil at third-party prices, which was unacceptable.

Hammer had no choice; he caved in to Gaddafi's demands. He agreed to an increase in the price of oil by 30 cents per barrel and in tax from 50 to 58 per cent. A month later, after more pressure from the Libyans, the oil majors operating in the country agreed to an increase in the posted prices of oil. For the sisters, it was a dangerous turn of events. It set a precedent for other countries to follow and, sure enough, new demands came rolling in.

Now it was the oil companies' turn to find unity, or at least attempt to do so: 24 of them agreed to negotiate price rises with OPEC as a whole rather than with individual countries. The shah of Iran strongly criticized the move, stressing that the influence of moderates would be lost among the more strident voices in OPEC and urging the oil companies to make agreements with the Gulf countries as a separate bloc. The British and American governments, which had initially supported the oil companies, saw merit in the shah's suggestion with the result that the united approach against OPEC began to unravel.

Accordingly, the companies settled with the Gulf members of OPEC. The Tehran Agreement, as it was known, was signed on 14 February 1971, giving those states an increase in the posted price of oil of 35 cents per barrel, with annual increases of 5 per cent and 2.5 per cent for inflation. The net result was that the price of Gulf light crude rose to about 50 cents per barrel. Whereas the agreement was dressed up as a reasonable compromise, in fact it represented a major power shift towards the oil-exporting countries of the Gulf. An embargo was issued against any oil company not paying a minimum 55 per cent tax rate. The fact that the new posted prices of oil were fixed for a period of five years was some consolation for the oil majors, but their control over the supply (and therefore the price) of oil was effectively over.

That was not the end it. On 24 February 1971 President Houari Boumedienne of Algeria announced the nationalization of 51 per cent of French oil assets in his country. In April the Libyans came to an agreement with the oil companies known as the Tripoli Agreement. The posted price of oil was increased by 90 cents, and Libya's oil revenues raised by 50 per cent, effectively leapfrogging the Tehran Agreement of six weeks before.

In July, a new front opened up. OPEC renewed its demand for greater participation in the oil companies – in other words, partial nationalization. In December, in response to the Iranian invasion of Abu Musa and the Tunbs, Colonel Gaddafi nationalized BP's interests in Libyan oil operations. The nationalization bandwagon was gathering pace again.

Relations between IPC and the Iraqi government were increasingly strained. Freight prices began to fall, the result of the new supertankers that were carrying oil to the West, and Persian Gulf crude was an attractive prospect, certainly when compared with Iraqi crude. A mild winter in 1971/2 brought a surplus of crude to the global market, again lowering prices. There was more trouble to follow: in order to compensate for declining margins and to stabilize prices, the IPC group reduced its production from Iraq. In Iraqi eyes, their actions seemed like a cynical ploy to settle old scores.

At this point, the Russians entered the scene, providing a much needed outlet for the oil that INOC was producing from the North Rumaila field. The new strongman of Iraq, Saddam Hussein, travelled to the Kremlin and signed an agreement to that effect. The Iraqi government then demanded that IPC restore the Kirkuk field to full production or face immediate nationalization. Just as talks were due to reconvene, Saddam's words took on a menacing tone as he promised to bring the oil companies 'to their knees'.[10]

He followed it through. On 1 June 1972 Baghdad nationalized all IPC operations in Iraq. In order to maintain oil production while the handover was made, the Mosul and Basra Petroleum Companies were given a temporary reprieve while the handover of IPC's assets took place. The Syrian government nationalized the oil pipelines on their own territory, thus pre-empting any Iraqi claim over them.

Iraqis on a cart pass by a poster of Saddam Hussein in Baghdad, 1980.

The oil majors were shocked and bemused: how on earth could the Iraqis market their oil? Once fortified, the IPC group tried to make a stand. It announced that it would 'chase the oil', suing any company that might purchase oil from its confiscated concession.[11] But if IPC executives really thought this would do the business, they were mistaken. OPEC members resisted their threat, supporting Iraq with offers of financial help and capping their own oil exports. The French broke ranks and secured an agreement with Saddam that CPF could keep its 23.5 per cent share of Iraqi oil. It was the start of a long relationship between Baghdad and Paris revolving around arms, technology and nuclear development.

As lawyers delivered unwelcome news to the IPC board – they doubted the strength of IPC's case – the shareholders found themselves increasingly isolated. Whitehall had no designs on the Iraqi oilfields. There was plenty of oil in the world, Arabian oil could fill the gap left by the loss of Iraqi oil – about 3 per cent of imports to the UK at the time – and there was the promise of significant oilfields in the North Sea to come in a few years' time.

Washington agreed. The Nixon Doctrine was in full swing: since this aimed at improving relations with Iran, Saudi Arabia and Israel, the Americans were hardly likely to support a return to colonial times. With their options dwindling, the IPC group decided to capitulate. In

February 1973 they gave the Mosul Petroleum Company to the Iraqis for no cost, agreed to expand Basra operations and to settle their claims for the loss of the Iraqi concession.

As it was, it would take another six years to conclude the IPC saga. Upon the outbreak of the Yom Kippur (Ramadan) War in October 1973, the Iraqi government nationalized the shares of Shell, the American companies and Partex in the last remaining IPC associate company, Basra Petroleum (BPC). This was done in retaliation for their respective home governments' support for Israel. Even those on the periphery were punished: Portugal was targeted because it had allowed U.S. aircraft supplying Israel to refuel in the Azores. The Iraqis nationalized the remaining British and French interests in BPC two years later.

That left the question of compensation, but talks came grinding to a halt, and were only revived after another convulsion in Iran. Disruptions in the Iranian oil industry brought their exports to a halt, and only began to pick up after the shah had left the county for exile. The IPC group, worried that the Iraqis might take copycat measures, decided to end the dispute once and for all.

Presently, the parties met in Baghdad and the group agreed to pay the Iraqi government £55 million (£255 million today) in outstanding revenues. The old customs house where they gathered, a relic of Ottoman times, was an appropriate setting for the final demise of IPC, at least as far as Iraq was concerned. One of the great beasts of the Middle Eastern oil industry, it had risen from whispered transactions in the corridors of Constantinople to a commanding position in the world of oil. And now, like those early deals, its fate was sealed in traditional style, with a handshake and a weary smile.

OPEC MINISTERS WERE IN Vienna when they first heard the news of the Yom Kippur War. They were about to meet the oil companies in order to renegotiate the Tehran Agreement, but instead chose to stay in their hotel rooms and await the outcome of the conflict. When they emerged from their rooms, it was to a new petroleum scenario. Arab OPEC members proceeded to impose a 5 per cent cut for every month that Israel remained in Arab-occupied territories, and until Palestinian rights were restored.

In December Libya imposed the highest oil price ever known – $18.76. Overall, the price of crude rose fourfold from $3 per barrel to $12 by 1974. As the Americans resupplied Israel after the war, Arab

OPEC countries banned petroleum exports to the United States, an embargo that was extended to other countries that supported Israel including the Netherlands, Portugal and South Africa. The Americans, more dependent on imported oil than before, were in a vulnerable position. It led some to suspect Secretary of State Henry Kissinger of contemplating military action in the Middle East in order to prevent the 'strangulation' of the industrialized world.[12]

OPEC's was a three-pronged attack – price rises, production cuts and an embargo – on the established order, and brought a variety of responses. In Great Britain Prime Minister Edward Heath, through the government's 51 per cent stake, secretly applied pressure on BP to meet the UK's oil supply from its Iranian sources, to the detriment of its other customers. Other industrialized nations had stockpiles of oil that saved them from the early shocks. Nevertheless, they needed U.S. assistance to secure alternative supplies of crude; there was simply not enough oil to go round. To add to these troubles, OPEC members made the lifting of the embargo dependent on the United States effecting a peace settlement between Egypt and Israel. In the event, the withdrawal of Israeli troops from the west bank of the Suez Canal was enough for the embargo to be lifted in March 1974.

These events had another significance. The embargo brought a new direction to energy policy in the United States. President Nixon announced Project Independence, the start of a drive towards reducing the country's reliance on oil imports from the Middle East. That in itself was not a great success, but it did bring a shift in the energy market, marking the start of oil's decline as an economic weapon. Today, although the consumption of oil is now higher than ever, its share of the overall energy market has fallen from about 50 to 30 per cent. Consumers have turned to cheaper, alternative forms of fuel, and the ability of OPEC to cause severe economic shocks in the world has never quite equalled the heights of 1973: oil is still a powerful sword, but its edge has been dulled.

Over the coming years OPEC was further weakened by other issues: individual states cheating on the oil quotas set by their fellow members and oil companies trading on the spot market where oil could be bought and sold at extortionate prices, for example. In 1979, when the group met in Abu Dhabi, the then president Sheikh Otaiba suggested blacklisting offending companies and refusing to sell oil to them.

Behind the posturing and politics, however, an important structural change was taking place. After a gradual start, Qatar and Kuwait had achieved full nationalization, and Saudi Arabia was on the verge of completing its full purchase of Aramco, eventually changing its name to Saudi Aramco. The Abu Dhabi government's stake remained at 60 per cent on the basis that its nascent oil industry would benefit from the shared experience and skills of the Western oil companies; memories of Iraq and Iran were still fresh in the mind.

In this way the future shape of the oil industry was made. Unfair concession agreements lasting 65 or 75 years were consigned to the past; production-sharing agreements and service contracts were the thing of the future. All in all, the Arabs had seen astonishing success. Barely half a century had passed since their leaders received the oilmen into their tents and haggled over terms, and now they were masters of all they surveyed. As the 1970s drew to a close, and the season turned to autumn, the star Canopus was rising over the desert, traditionally marking the moment when the bedouin began their annual trek to fresh pastures. It was time for renewal and change.

TWELVE
KINGS AND CARTELS,
1968–86

IN THE 1970S TEHRAN was humming. Iran was one of the world's top export markets and a favourite destination for the arms salesmen of the West: the commercial boom was in full swing. Such was the pressure from visiting businessmen on accommodation that the Hilton ballroom was turned into an enormous space with five hundred beds. In the mass-production car factories, as the government liked to point out, workers earned more than their British counterparts.

The shah's vision of a modern progressive country was expressed in the 'White Revolution' of the 1960s and, later, in the drive for the 'great civilization'. Then the problems started to appear: as villagers streamed into the cities, shanty towns sprang up all around. The ports were blocked with ships waiting for up to five months to unload, and the transport system was broken. The affluent class in the towns and cities of Iran, with their newly acquired refrigerators and washing machines, had to endure electricity cuts for eight hours a day. They could afford to buy cars, but now the production lines were clogged up, and the streets were jammed with traffic anyway.

It was all down to oil and the wealth it had generated. The hike in oil prices that followed the Tehran Agreement of February 1971 paled in comparison with the oil price shock that followed the Yom Kippur War less than three years later. As more than five million barrels of oil a day disappeared from the global market, Iran pumped more crude to meet the shortfall.

The shah frequently iterated that he would not use oil as a political weapon, refusing to join the Arab oil boycott of 1973 and speaking out against it. All the same, he took a firm line on the matter of oil prices, supporting the Arab OPEC countries in their demands. He pressed on

ar reaching
ries of
orms in
n; launched
Shah in
63, and
ted until
79,

with his requests for arms, offering the United States discounted oil in return for American military hardware. His government had lengthy talks with the consortium operating the Iranian oilfields for an increase in the price of oil, which culminated in an extra 5 per cent share of the profits from its operations.

In disorderly haste or Confusion.

Amid the helter skelter of Middle Eastern politics, the shah was emerging as a statesman, though not always for the right reasons – his action in seizing the Gulf islands brought condemnation across the Arab world, for example. Even the Americans' appreciation of the shah was qualified: rising oil prices were good for Iran, but disastrous for the United States. Higher prices damaged its economy and forced the Americans to look for ways to break the OPEC stranglehold. 'I think you must develop alternative sources,' the shah helpfully advised President Gerald Ford, 'because in 25 years this will be out.' At the time they were discussing the possibility of the United States receiving Iranian oil in return for military arms and equipment.[1]

It was the old dilemma. Surely there was some way of granting the shah's wish list in return for oil? Hand-wringing Pentagon officials worried about Iran's technical abilities and the threat to stability if Iran built up its arsenal to such an extent that it rivalled or even outstripped Western influence in the region. Others fretted that this would make the U.S. overly dependent on Iranian oil. And the more astute advisers pointed out the scope for political scandal if news of any secret deals with Iran ever leaked out.

It was only when Washington woke up to the fact that the shah was not really on their side that attitudes changed. For the CIA, which had a long memory, it was mortifying to see their protégé develop his own voice. As one official remarked: 'He was our baby and now he has grown up.'[2] For the shah, there was no going back. In 1974 he had made it clear that he would not countenance a fall in oil prices; in fact he was talking about a 10 to 15 per cent oil price hike. Since Iran's five-year plan relied on rapidly rising oil revenues this was no great surprise, even if difficult for the Americans to swallow. In President Richard Nixon and Secretary of State Kissinger, the shah had strong allies, but then the Watergate scandal reached its climax and Nixon was gone.

On 15 May 1975, amid a fanfare of silver trumpets, a red carpet and the boom of a 21-gun salute, which left its smoke drifting across the White House lawn, the shah and his entourage arrived. As President Ford greeted his guests several hundred Iranian students

The Shah with President Gerald Ford in the White House, May 1975.

shouted 'Down with the Shah!' and brandished posters outside the gate. In the meetings that followed, at Kissinger's insistence, Ford avoided raising the touchy issue of oil price – apart from one occasion when Kissinger was briefly out of the room – but the shah sidestepped the issue.

Having successfully navigated his way through the talks without mentioning the taboo subject, the shah had a surprise in store. On 17 May he gave a press conference at which he announced an oil price rise; some Iranian officials mentioned a figure of 35 per cent. It was an astonishing move, and one that presented opponents of the shah, such as Treasury Secretary Bill Simon, with the opportunity to cultivate the Saudis as a viable alternative to the Shah. The focus now shifted to Riyadh and the next moves of the Saudi regime.

The death of King Faisal in March had already ushered in a new set of politicians under a new king, men who were willing to use oil as a political weapon. Alarmed by Iran's military build-up in the Gulf region, they saw oil prices as a means of restraining the shah's ambitions. And so, while the Saudis quietly cultivated the American administration, relations with Iran began to decline. Henry Kissinger remained a staunch supporter of the shah and agreed an increase in military supplies, but even he recognized that the shah's development programme needed to slow down. The last thing the Western economies needed was a rise in the price of oil, and Iran's Achilles heel – its inability to lead on the issue – would soon be exposed.

IN DECEMBER 1976 AN OPEC meeting was held in Doha, Qatar, in the Gulf Hotel overlooking West Bay. A year had passed since a terrorist group led by the infamous Carlos the Jackal had held twelve OPEC ministers hostage in Vienna, and security was tight. An American said to resemble Carlos was detained and threatened with deportation. Outside the hotel, Qatari troops were camped alongside their Land Rovers with cannons mounted on the rear, helicopters flew overhead and a fast patrol boat was anchored in the bay. The deputy commander of the country's armed forces stalked the hotel lobby, walkie-talkie in hand as OPEC delegates came and went in motorcades, guarded by steel-helmeted policemen and heavy machine guns.

The oil minister for Saudi Arabia, 46-year-old Sheikh Zaki Yamani, who had been one of the Vienna hostages, always travelled with a bodyguard now. He was one of the last to arrive at the meeting and the first to leave, though not because he was unhappy with the security arrangements. When members voted for a 10 per cent increase in the price of oil, Yamani led a walk-out of the Saudi delegation. Upon his return the following day, he announced that the Saudis would raise their prices by 5 per cent and no more.

It was a bold move. In effect, Saudi Arabia had decided to undercut the price of Iranian crude and boost production. Prices would fall, and then be followed by a freeze; the Saudis would take over the leadership of OPEC and condemn Iran to financial disaster. The outcome was a mixed bag for Washington: their alliance with Riyadh was sealed and a series of lucrative arms deals assured, the OPEC cartel was weakened, but the shah was doomed. And yet, despite his foibles, the Americans still saw the shah as a force for stability in the region. U.S. defence analysts predicted that, since Iran had bounced back from a price fall in 1975, it would do the same in 1977.

They were wrong. Without massive oil revenues, the shah's regime could not hope to survive. The Tehran government had committed itself to ambitious development plans based on ever-increasing oil revenues. Now it urgently sought a $500 million dollar loan from a Western banking consortium, but it was too late; Iran had over-reached itself. 'We're broke,' the shah despaired. 'Everything seems doomed to grind to a standstill, and meanwhile many of the programmes we had planned must be postponed. It's going to be very tough.'[3]

The disruption that followed – the shortages, the blockades, the strikes – was bound to reflect personally on the shah. Even before the excesses of Persepolis, he had clearly identified himself as the head of a modern, progressive nation modelled along Western lines – one that was now coming apart at the seams. There was a grim irony in the fact that the economic downturn should coincide with a reform programme towards greater press freedom and the better treatment of political prisoners. But it was the economy that dictated the course of events, and by 1978 the great economic push was as good as over. Inflation was high and prestige projects dependent on oil money were left trailing in the wind.

Western influences unsettled the country and the spread of urbanization eroded the traditional ways. Iran's friendly relations with Israel jarred at a time when support for Palestine was growing among a disaffected youth. Israel, without its own oil, had originally been supplied by the British, but high prices in the mid-1950s persuaded it to buy about half of its oil from the Soviet Union. After the 1956 Suez Crisis, Arab pressure forced the Israelis to turn to Iran for its oil supplies. Today, a curious legacy of the shah's policy remains in the Israeli desert: a mysterious pipeline running from Eilat on the Red Sea to Ashkelon on the Mediterranean. In fact, this was conceived at the time of the Arab–Israeli War in 1967 as a means of allowing Iranian oil exports to bypass the Suez Canal.[4]

The real turning point came when religious leaders such as Ayatollah Khomeini, who was living in exile in Paris, became the focus of anti-shah dissent. A mixture of religious and anti-Western feelings provided a powerful recipe for dissent. The placard waving that dogged the shah as he travelled abroad was more than the passing antics of a few disgruntled Iranian students, since the grievances were now rooted in the history and character of his people – the shah had lost the trust of the nation. And when the protests became widespread, they brought the shah's whole gleaming structure crashing down.

The disturbances began in January 1978, leading to riots and destruction that were eclipsed seven months later by the death of some 400 people in the Cinema Rex fire in Abadan. In September protests spread to the oil industry and continued on and off for the next five months. At first, workers at the Abadan refinery demanded higher housing allowances, which the government ignored.

On 8 September a crowd erected tents in front of the refinery. The following day, which came to be known as Black Friday, government troops advanced and shot dozens of protestors. Seven hundred workers at the refinery went on strike for higher wages and called for an end to martial law. By the end of the month the strike had spread to other oil centres and the oilfields. A cycle of unrest and repression then followed in which Iranian workers, by their actions, managed to reduce exports of Iranian oil to less than one-tenth of their normal volume.

At another time the loss of Iranian oil might not have had a dramatic effect on global oil prices, since they amounted to only about 4 per cent of consumption. Panic hit the foreign markets, however, as buyers hoarded oil supplies. This in turn triggered fuel shortages at the pumps. In the United States queues at petrol stations were reported as being longer than during the 1974 crisis. Whereas some drivers suspected the oil majors of a trick to exploit the situation, it was really OPEC's tight grip on production that caused prices to rise. Only when the output of industrialized countries began to slow down, and the use of oil was reduced, did prices begin an overall decline that would last for the next twenty years.

The shah's position was becoming impossible, despite concessions to the opposition and measures to moderate his regime. On 17 January 1979, facing widespread protests, he left Iran with his family. Two weeks later Ayatollah Khomeini returned to Tehran and began to consolidate his power, eventually being proclaimed Supreme Leader of the Islamic Republic of Iran.

The country's oil industry made a show of getting back on its feet. In March, after the striking oil workers had returned to work, a crowd of government officials and employees gathered to witness the rebirth of the industry. Hassan Nazih, the new director of NIOC, pressed a button that was meant to start the flow of crude oil into a waiting supertanker – and nothing happened. There was a five-minute delay as technicians scurried about and repaired an electrical malfunction in the pumping equipment. It was a minor delay and an embarrassment for the authorities, but it also seemed to epitomize all the troubles arising from the ageing structure of the oil industry at that time.

Relations between Tehran and the West deteriorated. In November 52 diplomats and citizens were taken hostage in the U.S. embassy in Tehran. Despite their release two years later bringing a brief respite, Washington steadily ratcheted up sanctions from 1984 over issues such as terrorism, human rights and nuclear weapons. These measures culminated in 2012 when the United States and the European Union (EU) imposed a new set of oil sanctions.

Although none of them was fatal to Iran's oil industry, the sanctions added to its overall decline in the global petroleum rankings and confirmed the ascendancy of its great rival on the other side of the Gulf, Saudi Arabia, as the leading power in OPEC. More than twenty years had passed since the shah had died in exile, but now the proclamation of his passing seemed more apt than ever: the king of Iran is dead, long live the king of Saudi Arabia.

THE CLANK AND RUMBLE of construction reverberated around the cities of Saudi Arabia as hard hats mixed with *ghutras* on the dusty streets. In Jeddah, old, sun-soaked houses of the Ottoman period were reduced to rubble. Riyadh, once a huddle of mud-brick dwellings, was now giving way to highways and skyscrapers, shopping malls and office blocks. Where camels once roamed, cars swept along desert highways and jet airliners roared above. The time when electricity, paved streets and Western-style consumer goods were scarce luxuries was past.

[*ghutras* = traditional Arabian headdress]

There was still much to be done: the need for more running water, more telephones, more landscaping and more education for drivers was obvious. Derelict cars and unfixed water pipes were a problem though, as the U.S. ambassador put it, 'Riyadh no more than Rome was built in a day.'[5] It was a story being repeated around the oil-rich Middle East: the 'arish and mud-brick dwellings of the old Gulf towns were being uprooted in an eruption of concrete, glass and chrome.

The kingdom had emerged from the stresses of the King Saud years on a more balanced footing under Faisal. Whereas corruption and confusion had once reigned, the new order was marked by financial stringency and family reconciliation. The House of Saud, having disposed of one ruler, closed ranks around the new one. The deposed leader might try his utmost to regain power, at one point chartering a plane full of troops and equipment to retake the throne, but the CIA was already on the case and the flight never got off the ground.

In Iran the Americans had secured a Faustian pact with the shah in an oil-for-arms deal, and now they sought a similar arrangement with the Saudis. Since the decline of British influence after the Second World War, the United States was now the predominant foreign power in the land with the Dhahran airbase and control of the country's

Secretary of State Henry Kissinger meets King Faisal of Saudi Arabia, 1975.

oil infrastructure through Aramco; even after nationalization, Saudi Arabia would remain dependent on American know-how to operate its complex oil industry.

At the heart of the kingdom's oil strategy was the soft-spoken and flamboyant Sheikh Yamani. To most Westerners in the 1970s, Yamani was the embodiment of the modern, oil-rich Saudi Arab. He was equally at home in a *majlis* of his native land as in a conference room in New York, as much at ease in a traditional *thobe* as in a business suit. Born in Mecca and a lawyer by profession, he had degrees from Cairo University and Harvard Law School. The royal family had appointed him legal adviser to the Council of Ministers and then oil minister, and he developed a close working relationship with King Faisal.

Saudi Arabia was incredibly rich, so rich that it earned more money than it could possibly spend. Money went into the royal coffers or was invested in foreign banks, which created a massive international market in Arab petrodollars. And yet, heedless of the eye-watering revenues, some things did not change. There was a fundamental contradiction between this new-found wealth and the moral and religious stringency of the Wahhabi faith. The old conflicts in society endured: the tensions between the strict radicals who were implacably opposed to change and the modernists and reformers who wanted to progress in economic and social matters within the framework of an Islamic state. The *ulema*, the religious body designed to advise successive monarchs on religion and policy, remained a potent force in the political structure of the kingdom and advised the king on a range of issues.

In photographs of the time, Faisal appears lean and worn, and always with a serious expression on his face. He took firm control of government affairs, bringing in a strict austerity programme. He did something unheard of in King Saud's day: he balanced the books, reduced the national debt and increased oil production. He introduced free education and medical services, and a new landscape of hospitals, schools, housing projects and factories was soon springing up. A water well-drilling programme brought the bedouin in from the desert to settle for the sedentary life, preferring Toyotas to camels. In the meantime, Saud's old residence – Nasiriyah Palace in Riyadh – stood deserted, a symbol of past extravagance now gathering dust.

In foreign affairs Faisal stood out as a natural leader of the Arab world, taking the lead on the 1973 crisis and the call for an oil boycott against the United States. He was a devout man, and his rule saw the use of oil money to disseminate Islam across the globe. Saudi Arabia's credentials as the centre of the Muslim world were compelling: as the birthplace of the Prophet Muhammad, the keeper of the holy places of Medina and Mecca, and the destination of millions of Islamic pilgrims performing the Hajj every year.

The oil boom presented an opportunity to expand that role. In an age of Arab nationalism, Faisal travelled abroad to preach a message of pan-Islamic brotherhood. He initiated the building of mosques and religious schools in Asia and Africa, diverted funds into organizations such as the Islamic Solidarity Fund and founded the Islamic Development Bank. And the concept of Muslim brotherhood was boosted in the 1980s when the Saudi government provided funding to the Mujahidin in their struggle against the Soviets in Afghanistan. But after the 9/11 attacks, the spread of Wahhabism was seen in a different light. Saudi Arabia came under a cloud of Western suspicion because of its global Islamic connections.

Back in the 1970s, relations between Saudi Arabia and the United States were based on two underlying presumptions: that the Americans needed Saudi oil and that both shared an antipathy towards communism. Within these parameters, the 'special' relationship between Riyadh and Washington could – and did – withstand a certain degree of stress. America's friendly relations with Israel were a constant irritant and yet the relationship survived, albeit with considerable difficulty at times.

Diplomats like Henry Kissinger took Faisal's actions during the 1973 crisis badly, considering the oil blockade to be little short of blackmail. During his shuttle diplomacy to resolve the crisis, Kissinger himself probably harboured dark thoughts about Saudi Arabia's role in the affair, but would never have seriously considered breaking off relations: the kingdom was too important in terms of combating communism in the Middle East. That Faisal himself should agree to supply u.s. forces in Vietnam with oil despite the embargo, and was a prime mover in getting the embargo lifted in March 1974, was a clear indication that this was a disagreement between friends. The real problem would come later when the threat of communism declined and reliance on Saudi oil appeared to be dwindling; then the common ground was not so easily found.

FAISAL MET HIS END in March 1975 when his young nephew pulled out a gun and shot him twice; he died in hospital a few hours later. It fell to his successor, King Khalid (1975–82), to deal with the ongoing issue of oil prices. By 1979, with estimated reserves of roughly 150 billion barrels, Saudi Arabia held one-quarter of the planet's oil.[6]

The key to the country's success in controlling oil prices lay in its ability to vary output, reacting quickly to demand. It was not an exact science, fixing prices: on occasion the Saudis could get it wrong by pumping too much or too little oil out of the ground. In the early days of their primacy, they occasionally got it wrong, operating on a trial-and-error basis and misreading the market. In two instances, their decision to reduce oil prices coincided with the arrival of new administrations in Washington that were considering the kingdom's requests for more arms. The Saudis consistently produced more oil than necessary and yet, unlike Iran, restricted their spending. If production dropped to as low as five million barrels, they still could cover their domestic economic needs. This in turn brought the flexibility required to become a swing producer.

There was more to it than simply extracting more money or political pay-offs from the West, however. Oil could not be used in complete isolation since excessive price rises brought a basket of economic woes elsewhere: inflation, recession and political instability. It was apparent to the Saudis that what they did in the realm of oil pricing could seriously affect the world around them and might destabilize the kingdom itself. Their ability to lead on price was constantly being eroded, too.

Oil tankers under U.S. Navy escort in the Gulf, 1987.

In 1979 they restricted production to 8.5 million barrels to mark their disapproval of the peace treaty between Israel and Egypt, but the next four years brought an overall drop in the oil price of almost 40 per cent. New discoveries, new producers and improved fuel efficiency all contributed to a falling demand for Saudi oil.

In late 1985 the country abandoned its swing-producer role, increased production and aggressively moved to increase market share. Other OPEC members also increased production in order to maintain their own share of the market. At the forefront of this strategy was Sheikh Yamani but, behind the scenes, the king was the final arbiter of such matters. In 1986 Sheikh Yamani was officially rebuked for predicting that oil would fall to $8 a barrel. Actually, the writing was on the wall as far as his tenure as petroleum minister was concerned. In October, after King Fahd (1982–2005) had indicated that the price of oil should be set at $18 barrel, Yamani attended an OPEC meeting without making any mention of that figure. His dismissal followed ten days later, leaving him to hear the news on the radio.

It was clear that the royal family made the decisions and left the government to carry them out. A number of prominent posts – first and second deputy prime minister, defence, interior and foreign affairs – were held by members of the royal family. A consultative body, the Supreme Petroleum Council, advised the king. It ensured that a wide range of views from the political to the financial were heard before decisions were made, acting on the traditional practices of consultation (*sura*) and consensus (*ijma*).[7] This is a common feature of the modern Arabian monarchies.

Be that as it may, whatever the political structure of the kingdom, the sheikhdom or republic, it would take only one leader to threaten the stability of them all. And so the time has come to consider the great tragedy of Middle Eastern oil: Saddam Hussein and the descent into war.

THIRTEEN
A CAMEL RIDE TO ARMAGEDDON, 1980–2003

O N 22 SEPTEMBER 1980, after weeks of border skirmishes, Iraqi troops invaded Iran. In the first stages of the conflict, the Iraqi advance was swift, and Saddam Hussein's troops occupied the city of Khoramshah with relative ease. The Iranian military, which was still reeling from the convulsions of the Iranian Revolution a year before, was disorganized and offered little resistance. Fortunes changed when the Iranians regrouped and, unified under the religious leadership of Ayatollah Khomeini, fought back in numbers. Iraq had overstretched itself and retreated to its original borders. The war might have ended there except that Khomeini wanted it to continue. Iraq could not lose face; Khomeini could not lose the war. The result was a stalemate.

Meanwhile, despite their differences, OPEC members tried to conduct their business as usual. In December 1980 they met among the palm trees of Bali and agreed to raise the ceiling price of oil to $41 a barrel. There were some tense moments. The Iranian delegation protested against Iraq's detention of their oil minister and even displayed a poster of the minister in a chair reserved for their chief delegate. The Iraqi delegation for their part arrived fully armed for the conference, carrying seventeen guns between them and even wearing their weapons inside the conference room. With Saudi Arabia and Libya already at each other's throats over alleged U.S. surveillance flights over Mecca, it was a remarkable achievement that the fractious meeting should have reached any decision at all, let alone one as contentious as raising the price of oil.

The United States was not indifferent to the conflict. The Carter Doctrine, which had been announced earlier in the year, recognized the strategic importance of the Arabian oilfields and the need to protect their oil flows as a vital interest, indicating America's determination to protect the Gulf from invasion. The Rapid Deployment Force was established in 1981 as a contingency for u.s. intervention. Two years and a name change later, the Central Command (Centcom) was in place and able to requisition up to 300,000 troops from existing military units. The Gulf states remained wary of inviting u.s. troops onto their soil, therefore Centcom's headquarters were thousands of miles away in Florida with a small command aboard the uss *La Salle*, the flagship of the Middle East force in the area.

On 10 June 1982 Saddam Hussein tried to extricate himself by proclaiming a unilateral ceasefire, but this was rejected. Iran demanded the removal of Saddam and compensation for war damage. When Iraq refused this demand, Iran launched Operation Ramadan, in which Iranian forces attempted to capture the city of Basra, the first of many such attempts. With indiscriminate ballistic-missile attacks on cities and the use of chemical weapons initiated by Iraq, this war was particularly shocking. Iraq attacked oil tankers loading oil at Iranian ports and Iran did likewise to ships loading at Iraqi ports. With various provocations, the war seemed to invite Western intervention; the United States protected oil tankers and skirmished with the Iranians, but otherwise held back.

A lack of maintenance, spare parts and skilled workers had cut Iranian oil production to one-and-a-half million barrels per day. Iraq had suffered too, and the loss of its oil supplies was potentially more damaging to the West – their exports averaged about 11 per cent of OPEC's total. After eight years in which more than half a million lives were lost and some $230 billion dollars were expended, the conflict ended in deadlock. In August 1988 Ayatollah Khomeini agreed to a ceasefire, declaring: 'Taking this decision was more deadly than taking poison. I submitted myself to God's will and drank this drink for his satisfaction.'[1] Peace followed and it appeared that u.s. policy objectives had been achieved: the Gulf and Arabian oilfields were secure and Iranian influence in the region had weakened.

The danger to Middle Eastern oil had not passed, however. The deployment of u.s. forces marked an escalation of American military involvement in the region, and the end of the war left a combustible mixture in the air: radical Islam, an alliance between Iran and Syria and a bankrupt Iraq seeking to maximize its revenues in order to avoid financial collapse. The American preference for Iraq would be short-lived; the fuse for the next war was set and burning.

BELIEVING THAT HE HAD saved the Arab world from the threat of Iran, Saddam Hussein found his fellow rulers remarkably ungrateful. Iraq emerged from the war owing large debts, which he expected his creditors to write off. He demanded that the emirate of Kuwait forgo some $20 billion in loans, for example. Barely two years after the end of the Iran–Iraq War, Saddam was making threatening noises towards both Kuwait and the United Arab Emirates. He accused those countries of 'stabbing Iraq in the back with a poisoned dagger'.[2]

In Saddam's eyes, their crime was to produce too much oil, thereby adding to a glut in the global market and keeping prices low, defying his drive for higher prices. He also accused Kuwait of 'stealing' Iraq's resources by taking oil from the Rumaila oilfield, which straddles the frontier between the two countries. At the centre of the dispute was an old territorial claim, the same one that General Qasim had pursued in 1961, that Kuwait had once been part of the province of Basra under the Ottoman Empire. In 1990, however, Saddam's words were seen as hectoring and few took his threat of an invasion of Kuwait seriously.

This was most vividly illustrated by a meeting between the u.s. Ambassador to Iraq, April Glaspie, and Saddam Hussein on 25 July, at a time when Iraqi troops were massed on the Kuwaiti border. There are differing accounts of this meeting, but the fact that Glaspie failed to warn Saddam strongly against the use of force was surely a reflection of the Bush administration's policy at that time, to deepen and improve relations with Iraq. An Arab solution to the problem was preferred; u.s. policy makers simply did not believe that Saddam was foolish enough to invade Kuwait.

Except that he was. Iraqi troops occupied Kuwait City, meeting only a few pockets of resistance from local troops. The emir, Sheikh Jaber al-Ahmad Al Sabah, had already fled with his family to Saudi Arabia by helicopter. Purporting to legitimize the old claim, Saddam annexed the emirate and renamed it the nineteenth province of Iraq. By now Saddam controlled 20 per cent of global oil reserves, with another 25 per cent beckoning across the border in Saudi Arabia. And there a new danger lay, for King Fahd's army of 65,000 men was no match for Saddam's million-man army no matter how ramshackle it might appear to be.

Away from the battlefield, the loss of oil was not immediately apparent. Supertankers waited off the u.s. shore to discharge their cargoes; Saudi Arabia and Venezuela could easily make up any shortfall.

USAF fighters fly over burning Kuwaiti oil wells during Operation Desert Storm, 1991.

Undeniably, the industrialized nations had learnt a valuable lesson from the fuel scares of the 1970s. The U.S. now had 590 million barrels of crude oil stored away in caverns carved out of salt domes in Texas and Louisiana, enough to meet demand for about 34 days, while Japan had enough reserves for 142 days. For all that, there was still potential for Saddam to cause long-term damage to the West if he invaded Saudi Arabia.

The UN Security Council demanded that Iraqi troops withdrew, and the United States and Russia united to condemn the invasion. The critical question of whether foreign troops would be allowed on Saudi soil was answered when King Fahd agreed to a large U.S. deployment. In October the military operation to expel Iraqi forces from Kuwait – Operation Desert Shield – began. Over the following weeks a U.S.-led coalition of two dozen nations brought more than 900,000 troops into the area and stationed most of them along the Saudi–Iraq border.

On 15 January 1991 the UN deadline for withdrawal passed without response. Operation Desert Storm began with a five-week bombardment of Iraqi command and control targets from air and sea. A ground invasion followed in February with coalition forces rapidly driving into Iraq from Kuwait and calling a ceasefire within 100 hours. In a last-ditch move to frustrate the Allies, Saddam ordered the Kuwaiti oilfields to be set alight, and the oil taps to be opened into the Gulf.

Images of black smoke and oil-smothered seabirds, burnt-out cars and lines of weary Iraqi troops surrendering against a backdrop of burning oil wells became imprinted on the collective memory.

While protecting oil supplies from Arabia and the Gulf was central to Allied war aims in the first war, the issues were not so well defined in the approach to the second. The decision made in 1991 to leave Saddam Hussein in place left a slow fuse burning, and Saddam went on defying the West whenever he could. The Iraqi oil industry managed as best it could; since nationalization, Russian commercial interests had been heavily involved in Iraq, and Russia was the main customer of Iraqi oil. The United Nations attempted to punish Saddam for his humanitarian breaches by imposing oil sanctions, but then alleviated them with an oil-for-food programme that allowed Iraq to export a certain quota of oil in exchange for food. Saddam's regime still sidestepped the worst effect of sanctions: oil smuggling in small dhows was rife in the Gulf, and the oil-for-food programme was widely abused.

In the latter years of Saddam's rule, the focus came to rest on his supposed stock of biological and chemical weapons of mass destruction (WMDs). In September 2002, Whitehall's infamous 'dodgy' dossier asserted that Saddam's military planning allowed for some of his WMDs to be ready within 45 minutes of an order to use them, a claim endorsed by the British prime minister, Tony Blair.[3] Even though weapons inspector Hans Blix found no WMDs in Iraq, and the United States failed to convince the UN Security Council to intervene, President George W. Bush approved U.S. military action. On 17 March 2003, with his forces already in place, Bush gave Saddam an ultimatum to leave Iraq within 48 hours; Saddam refused. Three days later, Operation Iraqi Freedom began with an aerial campaign of bombing key targets followed by an invasion of Iraq. On 9 April U.S. forces occupied Baghdad and on 13 December Saddam Hussein was found hiding on the outskirts of Tikrit. He was subsequently put on trial and executed.

The connection between oil and war was often made in the approach to the war, with anti-war protestors claiming that the West wanted to invade Iraq in order to take control of its oilfields. 'No Blood for Oil!' was a popular slogan against both Gulf wars. There were other explanations for the war, certainly: the potential threat from Iraq's WMD programme, and a desire to promote a Western-style democracy in Iraq. The 9/11 attacks raised the possibility of a visceral

U.S. response against the Arab world in some form or another, and the irritant Saddam certainly presented a target.

When no WMDs were found, and other motives seemed to fall away, the one great question remained: if the war was not about biological and chemical weapons, or democracy, then what was it about – oil?

THE SIGNS WERE THERE. As early as the winter of 1973, at the height of the Arab oil embargo, suspicions arose that the United States was planning to invade the Middle East and seize the Arabian oilfields. One day in November, Lord Cromer, then the British ambassador in Washington, had a fraught conversation with U.S. Defense Secretary James Schlesinger, in which the latter said he could not rule out using force in the region. Alarm bells were ringing in Whitehall when, six days later, U.S. Secretary of State Henry Kissinger warned that if the embargo continued, America would have to decide what countermeasures to take. On 28 December the Joint Intelligence Committee in London prepared a paper for the British cabinet entitled 'The Middle East: Potential Use of Force by the United States'.[4] But then the moment passed and the paper disappeared into the archives 'to be kept under lock and key'. That did not prevent it being the source of considerable excitement in the British press when it was released into the public domain thirty years later.

In truth, thoughts of invasion at that time were probably those of Schlesinger and others in the Defense Department, whom Kissinger dismissed as 'crazy'.[5] However, the notion of an American invasion livied on, if only in the imaginations of a few. In January 1974 *The Economist* observed: 'Some Arab commentators are already painting a lurid picture of American marines swarming ashore at any moment to seize the oilfields. Saudi Arabia and Kuwait have placed explosive charges around their principal fields.' If such contingency plans existed, the article continued, it was likely that the Arabs could destroy the oilfields before U.S. troops ever reached them. Otherwise, some U.S. officials were thinking that the CIA might help install more amenable rulers in the Gulf as a last-ditch measure to control oil prices. 'Memories of Dr. Mossadegh,' the writer concluded, 'are very much alive in Washington these days,' suggesting that the idea of a CIA-backed coup was being considered in the highest circles.[6] The story was speculative but convincing enough to cause the American ambassador to

Iran to urge against American 'muscle flexing', which simply fanned 'emotionalism and inflexibility in the Middle East'.[7]

In 1975 an article in *Harper's* magazine supposed that America's economic and political problems could be solved if the larger Arabian fields were taken over and run by oil workers from Texas and Oklahoma. At the same time, a spate of similar stories appeared in other magazines and newspapers. James Atkins, who was then u.s. ambassador to Saudi Arabia, surmised that the original story came from a background briefing, probably from a high official source. One writer has suggested that the idea of military intervention sprang from a group of hard-line thinkers, eventually known as 'neoconservatives', many of whom were in positions of influence when the Second Gulf War erupted almost thirty years later.[8]

Western officials freely admitted the part played by oil in bringing about the First Gulf War, though they stayed remarkably tight-lipped about oil as a motivation for the second. Tony Blair, in a statement shortly before the invasion of Iraq in March 2003, said:

> The oil conspiracy theory is honestly one of the most absurd when you analyse it. The fact is that, if the oil that Iraq has were our concern, I mean we could probably cut a deal with Saddam tomorrow in relation to the oil. It's not the oil that is the issue, it is the weapons.[9]

But the real issue was about oil as a weapon not a fuel, about the control of oil as a means of exercising power, about whoever had their 'hand on the spigot'.[10] Washington certainly saw oil as central to the problem of Saddam. It was inextricably linked to his ability to project his image and influence the Arab world.

In 2001 Vice President Dick Cheney commissioned a report on energy security that noted Saddam's potential to destabilize the flow of oil to the markets, his willingness to threaten to use the oil as a weapon and use oil exports to manipulate the markets. The report recommended:

> The United States should conduct an immediate policy review toward Iraq including military, energy, economic and political/diplomatic assessments. The United States should then develop an integrated strategy with key allies in Europe and Asia, and

with key countries in the Middle East, to restate goals with respect to Iraqi policy and to restore a cohesive coalition of key allies.[11]

Some commentators have asserted that this proves the United States went to war in order to stabilize world energy supplies.[12] Then again, the authors of the report made no recommendation for military action; indeed calls for military assessments rather than action were only part of an overall strategy for dealing with the oil problem.

On 11 September 2001 television images of the Twin Towers in New York collapsing as a result of terrorist attacks were beamed across the globe. In Washington and Whitehall there was an urgency that something had to be done: within hours of the attacks Blair was telling Bush that 'we are better to act now and explain and justify our actions than let the day be put off until some further, perhaps even worse catastrophe occurs.'[13] At that stage Blair was suggesting that sanctions be imposed and pressure put on regimes to end the worldwide trade in biological, chemical and other WMDs.

As a result of the attacks, however, hawkish neoconservative figures in the White House, such as Dick Cheney and Donald Rumsfeld, gained the upper hand in U.S. foreign affairs. Within twelve months plans were being prepared for a pre-emptive attack on Iraq, and Blair had pledged his support to Bush in that endeavour. As Carne Ross of the UK mission to the UN observed: 'As 2002 drew on, it became clear that the U.S. had a different agenda and had [a] waning interest in negotiating a diplomatic way forward at the UN.'[14]

The fact that Iraq was a major oil producer was always in the mind of the war planners, since the country's ability to recover after the war depended on its oil revenues. The Bush administration discussed the possibility of French and Russian oil companies becoming engaged in Iraq, and BP and Shell were worried about being left out. In meetings with the Foreign Office it was agreed that oil was a strategic concern and that both companies should take part in the bidding for oil concessions at the end of the war.

It has since emerged that the Americans were determined to shape the reconstruction of the Iraqi oil industry. Washington insisted that the Coalition Provisional Authority (CPA), a new body that was to govern Iraq post-invasion, should control the post-war oil industry. This was against British advice that the UN, the World Bank or an Iraqi body should be involved. To make matters worse, the head of the CPA reported directly to the U.S. Secretary of State without any reporting line to Whitehall. Not that the British were doing too badly in other sectors, however. Up to August 2003 an analysis of Bechtel subcontracting by nations placed Iraqi construction firms first with 36 per cent, American second with 28 per cent and British third with 16 per cent; UK firms dominated the private security business.

As it turned out, Washington insisted on having an oil law as part of Iraq's reconstruction, permitting long-term contracts with international oil companies and allowing foreign companies to control and manage Iraq's oil resources for 25 years, a reversal of everything that had gone before. The Iraq National Oil Company would retain only 17 of Iraq's 80 known oilfields. The question is why Washington thought it necessary to almost privatize the Iraqi oil industry rather than rebuild its nationalized structure – and that, surely, was about the control of oil.

It is clear that the United States wanted to blunt Saddam's use of oil as a weapon, but plans to act on this were rudimentary and, in any case, the point was overstated. Saddam might have found ways to bypass sanctions, but Iraq's ability to act as a swing producer was severely limited. The West could meet any Iraqi shortfall in other ways: the global market could pump more oil from Saudi Arabia and other

Protestors on a 'Stop the War' march in London, September 2002.

places. Certainly Bush intended to gain control of oil *after* the 9/11 attacks for practical reasons, and removing Saddam was discussed in British circles as a 'prize' worth gaining because of the security it would bring to global oil supplies, but this was one of several unformed reasons for moving against Saddam.[15]

In these circumstances it is difficult not to conclude that the events of 9/11 provided the principal motivation for the invasion of Iraq in 2003 and played into the hands of the neoconservative group advising the White House, despite there being no conclusive evidence linking Iraq with the attacks. Emboldened by a relatively trouble-free campaign in Afghanistan the year before, Washington saw Iraq as the next in line. Exaggerated intelligence about WMDs and a tenuous link to terrorism were the pretexts for war, and the freeing of Iraqi oil from Saddam's control was a consequential, if valuable, strategic prize – but oil was not the driver for war.

FOURTEEN
THE NEW ROME

'*WAHID MARTIN! WAHID BEEWEE!*' announced the old man excitedly as he stood in the doorway of the shop, banging his camel stick on the floor. An Omani, he was trying to explain to the English visitors that he remembered two geologists – Mike Morton and 'Peewee' Melville – for whom he had worked as a rod man some fifty years before. He wielded his stick to indicate the rod he had once held up for the surveyors to take their measurements. Even in that small village shop in Awaifi, Wadi Umayri, Oman, he remembered the arrival of the oilmen whose work had started a chain of events that stretches into the modern day.[1]

This was a simple cameo from a modern oil country in the Middle East, in contrast to the images of death and destruction that appear in the Western media on a daily basis. Although there had been rebellions and upheaval in Oman, its people emerged largely unscathed with their traditions intact. The local oil industry has not fared so well, and has not escaped the blight of recent times as tumbling oil prices and lower oil revenues threatened the country's economy. Its oil reservoirs are challenging, too: in 2001 oil production peaked and then dipped until enhanced recovery programmes began. Oman has more than 150 oilfields, many of them smaller, more complex and not as productive as others in the Middle East, with the result that production costs are proportionately higher.

Now that the oilfields are maturing, the 'easy' oil having been extracted, the challenge facing PDO and the other oil companies in Oman is how to improve the amount of oil recovered. The enhanced recovery projects in progress rely on steam, polymer or gas injection to coax more oil out of the ground. Overall, these methods appear to

A liquid formed by condensati in CHEM, it's a compound produce by a condensation reaction

have had some success: oil production, including condensate is now at its highest level of around one million barrels per day. Oman is twenty-fourth in the global oil production table, with oil reserves of about five billion barrels. An awareness of the modest resources that remain in the ground has led the government to introduce programmes to diversify the economy.

Progress in Yemen was slow. In the late 1970s Shell carried out a drilling programme along the Red Sea shore. Algerian and Russian groups also showed an interest, with the latter making some promising findings in the Shabwa area. In 1982 the Italian firm AGIP made a marginal offshore discovery some 169 kilometres (105 miles) east of Mukalla. None of these efforts uncovered oil on a commercial scale. The breakthrough came in the early 1980s after Hunt Oil had instituted a seismic programme. In 1984 hydrocarbons were found in the Ma'rib-Al Jawf Basin. The Alif No. 1 well was the first discovery of commercial oil in the country. In 1991 the existence of a second petroleum basin, the Masila–Jeza basin, was confirmed when CanadianOxy struck oil at Sunah. This was soon followed by more discoveries at Heijah, Camaal and Hemiar.

Yemen had proven oil reserves of around three billion barrels as of 1 January 2014. But the country's infrastructure, particularly its pipelines, has suffered from sabotage, leading to serious interruptions to the flow of oil. Piracy has curtailed offshore activity. The U.S. Energy Information Administration estimates that Yemen's crude oil production declined from 127,000 barrels per day in 2014 to 44,000 in July 2015. Yemen is also the arena for a wider geopolitical struggle going on in the Middle East between Iran and Saudi Arabia, who are supporting opposing sides in the conflict. With a difficult political situation and little prospect of stability in the near term, the immediate future of oil exploration and production is uncertain.

Historically, the country is important for another reason. In the days of the Seven Sisters, the international oil companies (IOCs) controlled 85 per cent of the world's oil, while today the National Oil Companies (NOCs) control 90 per cent. The Seven Sisters have been replaced by an entirely different cast: Saudi Aramco, Gazprom of Russia, the China National Petroleum Company, NIOC of Iran, Petróleos of Venezuela, Petrobras of Brazil and Petronas of Malaysia. These new sisters are mostly state controlled, but the Yemeni experience shows that the smaller independent oil companies still have a part to play.

The Ghaba well site in central Oman. In the 1950s the derrick was used for the Fahud
No. 1 well before being transported to Ghaba and then abandoned after drilling had
ceased. In 2006 it stood alone in the desert, a monument to an earlier
time of oil exploration.

Ever since Getty's Pacific Western Oil Corporation gained a share
of the Saudi–Kuwaiti Neutral Zone concession, these firms have developed
areas that the larger companies avoided, whether for technical
reasons or simply because they already had too much oil. In an industry
where independents abound, those such as Continental in Dubai,
Maersk in Qatar, CCED in Oman, Crescent Petroleum in Sharjah, Hunt
Oil in Yemen – to name but a few – have achieved considerable success.
In Yemen it was the independents that made the discoveries. And
DNO, a Norwegian company also involved in Yemen, was the first oil
company to venture into Kurdistan after the fall of Saddam Hussein.

ABADAN IS THE BEATING heart of Iran's oil industry. The lights of the
refinery still illuminate the night, although the infrastructure is old
and creaking. The city has seen all the fluctuating fortunes of the oil
business: in 1980 the area was a battlefront as the Iraqis attempted to
invade Khuzestan Province. The Iranian army was unable to mobilize
quickly, with the result that the citizens took up arms to defend the city

themselves; despite repeated attacks, it was never taken. During that war the refinery was badly bombed and most of the civilian population left the city to seek refuge elsewhere. After the conflict was over, the work of reconstruction began. By 1997 the refinery had returned to pre-war production levels. Today it is run by a state company that is part of the Petroleum Ministry.

This relic of the past reminds us of the contradiction of Iranian oil. It was in Iran that the first oil discoveries in the Middle East were made; about half of the country's oil production now comes from fields that are more than seventy years old. Iran has an abundance of oil, and now gas as a result of the giant South Pars field in the Gulf. Today the country has the fourth-largest proved crude oil reserves and the second-largest natural gas reserves in the world. And yet it has never achieved the same heights as Saudi Arabia and, for certain periods, has almost disappeared from the global rankings as it struggled to overcome domestic problems, invasion and international sanctions. In short, Iran has consistently underachieved its petroleum potential.

Nowadays the future of its oil industry looks brighter with the signing of the Iran Deal in 2015 to curtail the country's nuclear activities. This in turn has opened the way for sanctions to be lifted and for Iran to return to the stage as a major oil exporter. There is much optimism that the country's oil industry will rebound from the lean years. But even if the oil wealth starts to flow again, it is highly unlikely that there will be any going back to the days of the shah.

The current leadership of Ali Khamenei remains highly suspicious of Western influence – and the constitution prohibits foreign ownership of Iran's natural resources. Foreign investors have been discouraged by a system of buy-back contracts, whereby they develop oilfields before handing them back to the Iranian government. Nevertheless, it now appears that this model has been abandoned in favour of contracts that will allow investors to retain a share of the developed fields. In the meantime, the country is gearing up to boost oil production: deals have been signed with Russian companies to build new rigs for the Gulf and plans drawn up to develop its oilfields.

There are other challenges. Since the revolution Iran has seen its population double from 37.5 million to 80 million, and the country is now the region's second-largest consumer of oil. Energy subsidies have kept the cost of petrol low and there has been a boom in the demand for motor cars. Iran's refineries, which produced just enough oil to meet domestic demand, could not keep pace. Since part of their output goes into other products, Iran actually has had to import oil in order to meet the demand. Despite protests about large gas-guzzling cars, domestic fuel consumption will continue to reduce the amount of oil available for export and therefore the amount of foreign revenues coming in.

The perception remains in the West that Iran is a difficult place to do business. As late as mid-2016 the oil majors such as ExxonMobil and Chevron were still holding back; only Total and Shell had started buying Iranian crude. Foreign investment and participation will surely be needed to improve the current infrastructure and develop Iran's oil production. Uncertainty about the political climate remains as hardliners and moderates jostle for influence, and the election of President Trump in the United States brings a host of new concerns.

In contrast with regimes of old, the government of President Rouhani appears to be pursuing a moderate agenda. The prize is both economic and political: it is estimated that the lifting of sanctions will bring one million new barrels of oil per day to the global oil market, increasing Iran's market share and altering the Middle East's balance of power in the process. In this regard, supporting Iran's resurgence suits both hardliners and moderates alike.

The motivation to bring their country out of the petroleum shadows is strong. Oil as a means of accessing wealth, power and influence is a weapon that, in this case, can be used against their great rival in the region, Saudi Arabia. With the predominantly Shia–Sunni divide between the two nations, it is clear that there is a fault line far deeper than a simple competition over oil.

In January 2016 the execution of Iranian cleric Sheikh Nimr al-Nimr among 46 other men in Saudi Arabia on terrorism-related charges triggered strong protests from Iran and its allies. Sheikh Nimr was a Shia critic of Saudi Arabia's monarchy and was seen as a figurehead by many Shi'ite protesters during the Arab Spring uprisings in the Gulf region. Since Saudi Arabia, a predominantly Sunni country, has an estimated 10 per cent Shia population concentrated in the oil-rich Hasa province, the threat of disruption to its oil production is a serious one. And since most of the country's oil comes from the province, and accounts for one-fifth of global supplies, reports of disturbances in the province are guaranteed to light up the news desks of the industrialized world.

A land of long memories: anti-American images, such as this one of demonstrators in Tehran in May 1951, still resonate in Iran today.

THE OIL CAMP LOOKED much the same as he remembered. The IPC social club, where oilmen once sipped cocktails as evening cooled, seemed to be caught in a time warp: the same dance floor, bar and table layout, the veranda and pool were still intact. The cottages and gardens, next to a schoolhouse with a small bell tower, were all there. The utilitarian offices remained, the buildings laid out in the Indian army cantonment style that had been the template for many oil camps across the Middle East. The hospital, the workshops and small refinery all lived on.

This was Kirkuk as seen in 2003 by Dr Terry Adams, a British oil adviser to the CPA, which had just taken over the government of Iraq in the wake of Saddam Hussein's defeat. Adams, who recalled how the Iraqi oil industry had been in the 1960s, found things little changed in the camp.[2]

Since the IPC days, however, the fortunes of Iraq's oil industry had been varied. By 2003 the nationalized companies were producing a creditable two million barrels of oil per day, but more than twenty years of isolation, three wars, UN sanctions and the politicization of the oil industry under Saddam Hussein had taken a heavy toll. By placing complete control of the country's oil resources in the hands of the state, nationalization handed great power to a few individuals, and decisions were made for political as opposed to economic or business reasons.

The industry that Adams saw in 2003 reminded him of the decrepit infrastructure of the former Soviet Union. Under Saddam, senior management positions had been filled with political appointees rather than qualified technocrats. Profits were diverted to elite groups, such as the military, instead of being invested in maintenance and new equipment. The drive to maximize output at all costs meant that sound reservoir management had been abandoned, causing irretrievable damage to the oilfields. A dwindling number of well-trained oilmen remained from the IPC days, but the standard of training had declined. The end of hostilities brought large-scale looting: thieves stole anything that was portable and vital operational equipment was lost.

The removal of Saddam Hussein's regime brought new problems. To progress under Saddam, senior managers had been obliged to join the Ba'ath Party. The CPA decided to purge party members from all sectors, thus causing a huge loss of expertise in the oil industry and removing a large number of technical specialists from their posts. This had a negative impact upon operations and created a group of seriously disaffected ex-employees who had lost their jobs, their position in society and their self-respect. Who better to provide saboteurs with the technical advice they needed? The ensuing campaign against oil facilities showed a high degree of knowledge that only those who had worked in the oil industry could have provided.

Predictably, the American-backed Oil Law proved to be highly controversial and the Iraqi parliament has not to date approved the draft legislation. In its absence, the bidding process was put out to auction. In December 2009 executives from the international oil companies flew into Baghdad to hear Oil Minister Hussein al-Shahrastani announce how much oil each successful company would be expected to produce, and how much Iraq's government would pay them.

What followed was, according to *Time* magazine, 'one of the biggest auctions held anywhere in the 150-year history of the oil industry'.[3] Like actors in a long-running play, the ex-IPC partners returned to the stage: Anglo-Iranian (now known as BP), CFP (known as Total), Jersey Standard and Socony (ExxonMobil) – and Shell was there too. The oil remained the property of the Iraqi state, and the successful companies were awarded service contracts under which they would be paid a fee for their services. Like Iran, there was a determination never again to be in the thrall of foreign-owned oil companies.

Oil has not brought contentment. Decades of war, instability and sanctions have destroyed the fabric of the state and impoverished the country. In the south the militias rule Basra, where the small elite that has access to the oil wealth lives in gated houses and frequents glossy malls away from the general population and raw sewage that flows through the old canals. The militias do their own construction deals with the international oil companies, but the fall in the price of oil has meant that debts have gone unpaid and many public projects have been abandoned.

In the north, the Kurdish Regional Government has made its own oil deals, signing six exploration contracts with ExxonMobil and openly defying Baghdad at the same time. It was a calculated gamble: in the face of losing other contracts in Iraq, the company nonetheless considered Kurdistan a risk worth taking. With the Baghdad government still weak and unable to reassert its authority over a virtually autonomous Kurdistan, this is the situation that pertains today.

The main bone of contention is Kurdish oil exports. The regional government has completed a pipeline that links to the existing line running to the port of Ceyhan on the Turkish coast. When jihadis attacked Baghdad's pipeline, the central government was forced to rely on the Kurdish pipeline. An agreement allowed the Kurds to receive a 17 per cent share of the national budget and to export their own oil, though its terms have never been met: the Kurds are not receiving their share of the budget while exporting more than their quota of oil. When Baghdad threatened legal action against the shippers and buyers of Kurdish oil, many of them fell away. Nevertheless, oil was still being shipped to Ashkelon in Israel for storage until European buyers could be found. There were stories of ship-to-ship transfers of oil taking place at sea off Malta. By 2016 Kurdistan was exporting 500,000 barrels of oil per day, one seventh of Iraq's total.

It was the weakness of Baghdad that brought the West an alternative source of Iraqi oil from Kurdistan, an outcome that was welcomed in the boardroom of ExxonMobil. It was a different story when, in the disruption that swept the region in the wake of the Arab Spring, an unexpected producer appeared on the scene.

AT THE END OF a twisting, dusty road in Syria lies the Turkish border town of Besalan, where grimy smugglers come to haggle over the cost of a barrel of oil. The town is littered with rubbish, being so well guarded that even the refuse collectors are not allowed in. The assortment of oil traders who meet here, many of them once fighters in the civil war, deal in crude oil that jihadis and smugglers have sold them.

The oil is pumped across the border through buried pipes to men waiting on the other side to fill their barrels. Vans and buses then lumber into town packed with the barrels for auction. Spies on street corners keep watch for the police. Although the full scale of the smuggling is unknown, some reports suggest that it is more brazen at certain points along the border where groups of men carry barrelfuls of oil on their backs into Turkey and return with the empty barrels to pick up another load. Once they have purchased the oil, Turkish traders secretly supply petrol stations, or independent operators who then set up their own makeshift filling points at the roadside.

After IPC withdrew from Syria in 1950, other companies made oil and gas discoveries there. In 2014 the jihadist group known as Islamic State (IS) emerged to control oilfields in Syria's eastern Deir Ezzor province and Iraq. By October 2015 oil production was said to be between 34,000 and 40,000 barrels a day, though this has fallen since Russian and coalition airstrikes. IS also controlled the Qaiyara field near Mosul in northern Iraq with a production of about 8,000 barrels a day of heavy oil used to make asphalt. The Bayji oil refinery, a monument to the Hashemite years, was occupied by jihadis and was the scene of fierce fighting between Iraqi government forces and militia. Eventually the government recaptured the refinery, but not before it was torched by retreating jihadi forces.

The jihadis had access to a few refineries or simply relied on makeshift apparatus set up by locals – a bizarre throwback to the days when oil was a cottage industry in Iraq – to refine the crude into petrol or *mazout* (a heavy diesel used in generators). As they controlled some oil production on an irregular basis, they were able to conduct a certain amount of business with the independent oil traders who visited the oilfields in order to buy crude. Ironically, where vehicles once appeared willy-nilly and caused lengthy traffic jams to collect the oil, airstrikes brought a more orderly system where the traders were told when and where to collect their oil. The traders then sold the oil locally or took it to a jihadi refinery, making in the region of $10 per barrel. The refined

The desert transformed: the modern city of Riyadh stretching into the distance.

product was then transported to the border where it was smuggled to towns such as Besalan.

The aerial bombing campaigns and advances by government forces aim to put an end to this trade for good, cutting off an important source of revenue to the Islamic State 'caliphate' by targeting the means of extracting the oil as well as the refineries. At the time of writing the success of these tactics, and the future of Islamic State, are yet to be told.

IN OCTOBER 2014, IN the dark and cold of a Moscow night, a Falcon 50 private jet collided with a snowplough on the runway of the city's Vnukovo International airport, killing the single passenger and three crew members on board. Russian investigators concluded that it was a tragic accident, and the incident might have passed quickly into history were it not for the fact that the passenger was Christophe de Margerie, the CEO and chairman of Total.

His loss was widely mourned. It was a mark of how far the French oil industry had come since the 1930s when Total's predecessor CFP was a small company by global standards and its executives had a reputation of being stonewalling spoilers. According to *Forbes* magazine, Total is today in the top ten of the world's biggest oil and gas producers. It is heavily involved in the Middle East, being part of several oil and gas projects in the UAE and taking a major stake in the Al Shaheen offshore field in Qatar.

De Margerie was among those convinced that there would soon be a major shortage of oil. He once said, 'Where is electricity coming from? Flowers? Maybe someday. But what's available now is from oil and gas.'[4] His remarks might sound less urgent in a period of oil glut. Yet for years industry experts had been predicting that world oil supplies would soon peak (a phenomenon known as 'peak oil') before beginning their descent into scarcity. Demand was outstripping supply, they argued, and existing oilfields were running out of oil.

They pointed to the elephant-sized Ghawar oilfield, which at one stage accounted for half of Saudi Aramco's production. Here the oil company appeared to be pumping increasing amounts of water into the reservoir.[5] Was this to maintain pressure in a dwindling oilfield? If Ghawar was in trouble, then so too was Saudi Arabia and everyone else. As Matthew Simmons observed in more vivid terms in his 2005 book *Twilight in the Desert*:

> Then, Saudi Arabian oil output will clearly have peaked. The death of this great king [Ghawar] leaves no field of vaguely comparable stature in the line of succession. Twilight at Ghawar is fast approaching.[6]

If the more imaginative sections of the Western press were to be believed, the Middle East seemed to be sliding into economic obscurity.

The doomsayers were wrong, the *Schadenfreude* misplaced. Peak oil did not materialize – not for the moment, at least – and Saudi Arabia was pumping oil as if there were no tomorrow. The global oil industry had come a long way since the days when geologists sniffed rocks for traces of hydrocarbons. Since the 1920s an array of techniques has revolutionized the way that oil companies find and extract oil. The advent of seismic equipment enabled geophysicists to examine and analyse underground rock structures, spelling the virtual demise of the petroleum geologist in the field. Seismic data and three-dimensional imaging are now used to plan the extraction of oil from subterranean reservoirs. Gravimeters and magnetometers, too, helped oilmen 'look' into the earth in order to detect anomalies in its gravitational and magnetic fields, for instance, gathering evidence that might reveal salt domes, a possible sign of hydrocarbons.

There were innovations in marine exploration and development, such as jack-up rigs, drill ships and artificial islands. Directional and horizontal drilling allowed drillers to access lateral areas far from the point where the drill bit entered the ground. The United States saw a remarkable turnaround in its oil and gas production through advances in hydraulic fracturing ('fracking') techniques. Such was Washington's confidence in its own energy resources that a ban on exporting oil from the United States, designed to protect the domestic market, was lifted.

It will be recalled that enhanced oil recovery schemes breathed new life into the older oilfields and again increased the amount of oil being extracted from the ground. Certain oil producers saw their energy portfolios enhanced by gas reservoirs: Egypt is a modest oil producer by Middle Eastern standards, but it was set to be transformed by the discovery of a supergiant gas field in the Mediterranean. As new oil discoveries added to the world's store of unrecovered resources, the advent of peak oil was pushed back still further. Reports of oil's death had been somewhat exaggerated.

Perhaps there was method in Riyadh's madness, then. Pumping oil protected Saudi Arabia's market share and recognized that OPEC is no longer an effective mechanism for controlling prices. Other motives have been ascribed to the Saudis' actions: that they wished to destroy the U.S. fracking industry, whose high costs made it vulnerable to sustained price falls; that they were trying to use oil as a weapon in order to put pressure on Russia over Syria; or that they were aiming to spoil the return of the prodigal Iranians by squeezing them out of the global oil market.

Announced in 2014 by the petroleum minister at the time, Ali al-Naimi, the effect of this 'market-share strategy' was far-reaching. It brought a global surplus of oil, but the resulting price crash slashed the revenues of petroleum states, including those of Saudi Arabia. Its government raised domestic fuel prices and lowered spending in order to narrow its deficit, possibly the largest since 1991. Economic growth might have been relatively sluggish, but it was thought that the king-dom's vast foreign exchange reserves of $582 billion meant that it could sustain low oil prices for a few more years to come.

It was predicted that, if the low oil price was maintained, then the political ramifications in the Middle East would be severe. The International Monetary Fund (IMF) predicted that many oil-exporting countries would struggle if low oil prices continued. Undoubtedly the smaller producers like Bahrain, Yemen and Oman would find it increasingly difficult to compete and their revenues would dwindle, while the larger producers would have to cut back on expensive projects. There was also a question mark about the viability of smaller states in the long term. Even in those larger states, uncertainty about the future of oil threw a shadow over the sustainability of current political structures: in Saudi Arabia difficult questions arose over the growing size of the royal family and the future allocation of a diminishing oil wealth.

On the other hand, low oil prices invigorated interest in economic reform and Deputy Crown Prince Mohammed bin Salman had a plan for the day that the oil ran out. Called 'Vision 2030', it aimed to diversify the Saudi economy and break the kingdom's reliance on petroleum, including the privatization of a part of Saudi Aramco; interestingly, this would require the hitherto secretive company to make public details of its financial arrangements for the first time. Given that a senior member of the royal family was leading the initiative, there was hope that it would not founder in the face of opposition from vested interests: previous economic reforms had been led by senior technocrats who lacked Crown Prince Mohammed's clout. The Gulf states had developed similar plans, as well as building up their sovereign wealth funds and investing abroad across a wide portfolio. The oil will continue to flow for many years, but at least these states have recognized that now is the time to make plans for a future with less reliance on oil.

At first there was no sign of any let-up in the market-share strategy with the departure of Ali al-Naimi as petroleum minister in March 2016: both the increasingly influential Mohammed bin Salman and the new minister, Khalid al-Falih, appeared to be proponents of the market-share strategy. This was demonstrated at an OPEC meeting at Doha in April when the prince insisted that any agreement to freeze oil production should include Iran, which seemed an impossible demand. Iran did not attend the meeting, OPEC was split, and the Saudis soldiered on.

There were many who doubted that the strategy could succeed. Contrary to expectations, the U.S. shale oil producers proved to be remarkably resilient in the face of lower oil prices, having cut their costs in order to remain competitive. Moreover, Saudi Arabia's ability to command the market had been undermined by two major OPEC producers, Iran and Iraq, who were determined to increase their output in any event, the former seeking to expand in the Asian markets and the latter needing oil revenues to pay for its fight against Islamic State. Outside OPEC, Russia was producing oil at its highest level for years.

It was time to change tack. Saudi Arabia's foreign exchange reserves were falling at an alarming rate – 20 per cent over two years. Riyadh announced cuts in ministers' salaries and a reduction in benefits for public sector employees, who comprised two-thirds of the workforce. In December 2016, after Russia and several other non-OPEC countries promised to curb oil production, Saudi Arabia announced that it would cut its oil production, together with other OPEC members. The immediate effect was a 15 per cent rise in oil prices; but whether the six-month agreement will hold and be extended remains to be seen.[7]

All this is being played out against a global background. Oil is no longer 'sexy', and a growing awareness of climate change and the harmful effects of fossil fuels was recognized by the Kyoto Protocol of 1997. Now, with the Paris Agreement of 2015, there is a 195-nation climate pledge to reduce emissions and restrict global warming to an increase of 1.5 per cent. The trend towards renewable sources of energy goes on. In 2015, while oil among fossil fuels accounted for 32.9 per cent of energy consumption, the use of renewable energy in power generation grew by 15.2 per cent. Worldwide, renewables accounted for 6.7 per cent of power generation. Oil is still number one, but renewables are picking up fast.[8]

Fears of peak oil, the greater use of gas and a motor industry looking towards a new era of electrically powered vehicles all militate towards a future without oil. Added to the mix are doubts about the true extent of Saudi Arabia's oil reserves, and about whether Vision 2030 is a genuine attempt to deal with the future or simply a public relations stunt. Meanwhile, the United States continues to supply Riyadh with military equipment: the underlying relationship between the two nations based on oil and weapons still endures.

One thing is certain: there are turbulent times ahead. When Ali al-Naimi left office he remarked: 'During my seven decades in the industry, I've seen oil at under $2 a barrel and $147, and much volatility in between. I've witnessed gluts and scarcity. I've seen multiple booms and busts.'[9] As a bedouin shepherd who had had risen through the ranks to hold the post of Saudi oil minister for twenty years, he had experienced both ends of the petroleum spectrum. During that time many cities of the Middle East were transformed by oil. Today,

Secretary of State John Kerry (third left) at a meeting with Deputy Crown Prince
Mohammed bin Salman (second right) in Riyadh on 23 January 2016.

conurbations such as Riyadh, Kuwait and Abu Dhabi owe their rapid
growth to the wealth and activity generated by oil. In contrast, parts of
Iraq and Syria are still in conflict, while Iran is emerging from decades
of economic sanctions. There are those that have largely missed out on
the oil boom: Amman in Jordan, for example, lives on, facing different challenges than the shimmering oil-rich capitals, and feeling the
economic aftershocks of events more acutely.

Across the region, the fateful application of crude oil in the hands
of Man is there for all to see: its empires and anarchies bound together
by the gleaming promise and diabolical curse of riches beyond compare. The story still unfolds, with only a few beacons of hope remaining
as the world emerges from the time that many will talk about but
increasingly fewer will recall, the era that will be memorialized as the
Age of Oil.

APPENDIX

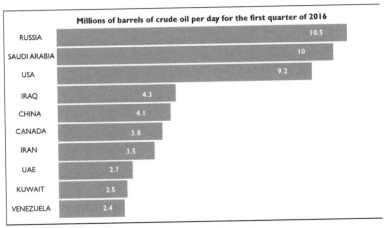

Top oil producers in the world.

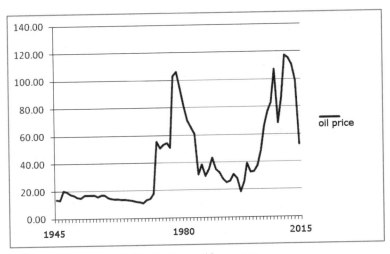

World oil prices ($) 1945–2015.

TIMELINE

1908   Oil is discovered at Masjid-i-Suleiman.

1914   The Ottoman grand vizier grants a 'concession' to the Turkish Petroleum Company (TPC); the First World War breaks out; British forces occupy Abadan.

1918   The war ends: British forces advance as far as Mosul.

1920   San Remo Oil Agreement.

1922   Meeting at Uqair between Ibn Saud, Percy Cox and Major Frank Holmes.

1923   On behalf of E&GS, Major Frank Holmes obtains an oil concession for Al Hasa, followed by a concession for the Neutral Zone the following year.

1925   The Turkish Petroleum Convention (TPC) is the first oil concession granted by the Iraqi government. The sheikh of Bahrain grants a concession to E&GS.

1927   TPC strikes oil at Baba Gurgur.

1928   Red Line Agreement; the Achnacarry ('As Is') Agreement.

1929   TPC is renamed the Iraq Petroleum Company.

1931   A revised Iraq convention is signed: IPC Mediterranean pipeline project to proceed.

1932   Bahrain Petroleum Company (Bapco) strikes oil on Bahrain Island.

1933   The Hasa concession is granted to Standard Oil of California (SoCal), which establishes the California Arabian Standard Oil Company (Casoc) to operate the concession; the Anglo-Persian concession in Iran is renegotiated with Reza Shah Pahlavi.

1934   The first Kuwait concession is granted to the Kuwait Oil Company.

1935   IPC pipelines to Haifa and Tripoli are inaugurated; the first Qatar concession is granted to Anglo-Persian/Iranian (later transferred to the IPC group); the Texas Oil Company joins the Hasa and Bahrain concessions.

1938   The first oil strikes on the Arabian mainland at Burgan (Kuwait) and Dammam (Saudi Arabia).

1939   The first Abu Dhabi concession is granted to the IPC group. Exploration is gradually suspended across the region after the outbreak of the Second World War.

1940   First oil strike in Qatar (Dukhan), air raids on Haifa and Bahrain.

1941   Golden Square coup in Iraq; Kirkuk oilfield occupied by Iraqi forces; the Germans arrive in Baghdad before the British regain control; Reza Shah Pahlavi abdicates; his son Mohammed succeeds to the throne.

1943–4   DeGolyer mission to assess the oilfields of the Middle East.

1944   Casoc renamed Arabian American Oil Company (Aramco); the Anglo-American Oil Agreement fails in the U.S. Senate.

1945	The war ends.
1947	India and Pakistan win independence.
1948	End of the Red Line Agreement; Jersey Standard and Socony-Vacuum join Aramco; the largest onshore oilfield in the world (Ghawar) is discovered.
1950	Saudi Arabia and Aramco enter a 50–50 profit-sharing agreement; Tapline is inaugurated.
1951	Mohammad Mossadegh nationalizes the Iranian oil industry; Anglo-Iranian abandons Abadan; the largest offshore oilfield in the world (Safaniya) is discovered.
1952	Iraq and IPC agree a 50–50 profit-sharing agreement.
1953	Mossadegh is overthrown in a CIA-backed coup.
1954	A consortium of Western oil companies enters Iran.
1955	British delegation withdraws from the Buraimi arbitration and a Saudi contingent is expelled from the oasis.
1956	Suez Crisis: destruction of the Syrian pumping stations.
1958	The first Abu Dhabi oil discovery (Umm Shaif); the July Revolution in Iraq; General Qasim seizes power.
1960	The Organization of Petroleum Exporting Countries (OPEC) is formed.
1962	First oil discovery in Oman at Yibal.
1963	The Ba'ath Party seizes power in Iraq; General Qasim is assassinated.
1966	Sheikh Zayed bin Sultan Al Nahyan replaces his brother Shakhbut as ruler of Abu Dhabi.
1967	Six-Day Arab–Israeli War: the export of oil to certain Western countries banned.
1971	The Tehran and Tripoli Agreements; Ghaddafi nationalizes BP in Libya.
1972	IPC assets are nationalized in Iraq.
1973	Arab–Israeli ('Yom Kippur' or 'Ramadan') War; OPEC oil embargo on Western countries.
1974	Oil embargo lifted; the start of Project Independence in the United States.
1979	All outstanding claims between the IPC group and Iraq are settled. Iranian Revolution; Iranian hostage crisis; U.S. bans Iranian oil imports.
1980	Iran–Iraq War begins (ending in 1988); Saudi Arabia completes its purchase of the private interests in Aramco.
1984	First oil discovery in Yemen at Arif.
1986	Saudi Arabia breaks ranks with OPEC; oil price collapses.
1990	Iraqi troops invade Kuwait.
1991	The U.S.-led coalition defeats Iraq.
1997	Kyoto Protocol signed, committing signatories to reductions in greenhouse gas emissions.
2003	Coalition forces invade Iraq and remove Saddam Hussein from power.
2011	The start of the Arab Spring.
2014	Saudi Arabia begins pumping oil to protect market share, particularly against rising U.S. shale oil production; oil prices fall.
2015	The Iran Nuclear Deal allows oil sanctions against Iran to be lifted.
2016	Saudi Arabia announces its 'Vision 2030', OPEC agreement to cut oil production.

GLOSSARY

agha – an equivalent title to 'sheikh' meaning chief or leader, e.g. Ali Agha

anticline – a convex fold in rock strata, typically in the form of an arch, with the oldest rocks at the core, and beds dipping away on either side

API – the American Petroleum Institute (API) classifies oil according to its specific gravity. Heavy crude has an API gravity of 22 degrees or less, medium crude between 22 and 38 degrees and light crude 38 degrees or more. Heavy oil is less attractive commercially than light oil because it is more difficult to process

Arab Zone – a late Jurassic oil-bearing rock formation found in Saudi Arabia and elsewhere in the Middle East. It is divided into four sections, A to D, with sections C and D being the most productive

Asmari – the name given to a prolific limestone oil reservoir in Iran

'arish – palm tree fronds used to build huts

bitumen – a thick, black substance such as tar or asphalt formed naturally from a mixture of heavier hydrocarbons

Cretaceous – geological period 145–66 million years BP

crude short – where an oil company does not have access to sufficient crude oil to meet its market needs

fellahin – peasant or labourer

grand vizier – the first minister of the Ottoman state

gravity meters – these measure variations in the earth's gravity and give geophysicists an idea of prominent rock uplifts and where sedimentary basins might be located

ghutra – traditional Arab headdress

Hajj – the annual pilgrimage to Mecca; *haji* being the title of someone who has performed it

heavy oil – see API

Ikhwan – Wahhabi militants of Saudi Arabia

imam – a religious leader

jebel – a mountain or hilly land

jihadi – a person involved in a war or struggle against unbelievers, a term commonly applied to Islamic terrorists

Jurassic – geological period 201.3–145 million years BP

Khuff – a rock formation containing substantial gas reservoirs

light oil – see API

mutasarrif – governor

naphtha – the former name for petroleum, derived from the Persian word *naft* for crude oil

Nedji – a person from the central Arabia emirate of the Nejd

Political Resident – the senior British representative in the Persian Gulf

posted prices – the notional price at which the oil majors sold their crude oil at the point of shipment

ras – a headland

Rub al-Khali – the great sand desert of southern Arabia, the 'Empty Quarter'

seyyid – an honorific title denoting a male descendant of the Prophet Mohammed

spudding in – a term used to describe the start of drilling of a new oil well, which often used to be accompanied by animal sacrifices to bring good fortune

stratigraphy – the study of rock strata, especially the age, distribution and deposition of sedimentary rocks

swing producer – an oil producer with large spare production capacity that can change global oil prices through the amount of oil they choose to sell on the market

Thamama – an oil-bearing rock formation in which the first offshore discovery of oil was made in the UAE, and later onshore at Murban

thobe – a traditional Arab robe

Trucial Coast or Trucial States – the seven sheikhdoms of the lower Gulf region: Abu Dhabi, Dubai, Ras al-Khaimah, Sharjah, Fujairah, Ajman and Umm al-Qaiwain. An eighth sheikhdom, Kalba, was incorporated with Sharjah in 1952. In the nineteenth century their rulers had entered into a truce with the British government to end piracy. In 1971 they became the United Arab Emirates (UAE)

vilayet – former Ottoman province

wadi – a dried-up riverbed or valley

wildcat well – an exploratory well drilled in an area where the subsurface geology is not certain

Acronyms

ADMA	Abu Dhabi Marine Areas Ltd
ADPC	Abu Dhabi Petroleum Company
AGIP	Azienda Generali Italiana Petroli
AIOC	Anglo Iranian Oil Company
Aramco	Arabian American Oil Company
Bapco	Bahrain Petroleum Company
BOD	British Oil Development Co. Ltd
BP	British Petroleum
Casoc	California Arabian Standard Oil Company
CPA	Coalition Provisional Authority
CFP	Compagnie Française des Pétroles, renamed Total in 1991
Elf	Energie Liquide de France
ERAP	Entreprise de recherches et d'activitiés petrolières
INOC	Iraq National Oil Company
IPC	Iraq Petroleum Company
ISIS	Islamic State in Iraq and Syria
KOC	Kuwait Oil Company
NIOC	National Iranian Oil Company
OPEC	Organization of the Petroleum Exporting Countries
PCL	Petroleum Concessions Limited
PDO	Petroleum Development (Oman) Ltd
PDQ	Petroleum Development (Qatar) Ltd
PDTC	Petroleum Development (Trucial Coast) Ltd
QPC	Qatar Petroleum Company
RAF	Royal Air Force
Socal	Standard Oil of California, later Chevron (with Texaco)
Socony	Standard Oil Company of New York, later Mobil
TPC	Turkish Petroleum Company
UAE	United Arab Emirates
USAAF	United States Army Air Force
WMD	weapon of mass destruction

REFERENCES

INTRODUCTION

1 Foreign Office to Wingate, 4 February 1918, 'Memorandum on British Commitments to King Hussein' [102v] (2/20), IOR/L/PS/18/B292, India Office Records, British Library.

1 A SCRAP OF PAPER, 1849–1918

1 William Kennett Loftus, 'On the Geology of Portions of the Turko-Persian Frontier, and of the Districts Adjoining', *Journal of the Geological Society*, XI (January 1855), pp. 247–344.

2 Arminius Vámbéry, *Travels in Central Asia* (London, 1864), p. 3.

3 Among those who were interested in Kitabchi's proposal were Calouste Gulbenkian and Henri Deterding of Shell, both of whom rejected it as being too speculative.

4 A series of articles in the Persian newspaper *Shafaq-i-Surkh* under the title 'The D'Arcy Scrap of Paper' was promised but never published: File 82/34 II (F 94) 'Anglo-Persian Concession' (18/362), IOR/R/15/1/636.

5 See Daniel Yergin, *The Prize: The Epic Quest for Oil, Money and Power* (New York, 2008), p. 142.

6 D'Arcy to the Foreign Office, 28 December 1908, IOR/L/PS/10/143/2.

7 Winston Churchill, *The World in Crisis* (New York, 1923), p. 134.

8 See Stephanie Cronin, 'The Politics of Debt: The Anglo-Persian Oil Company and the Bakhtiari Khans', *Middle Eastern Studies*, XL/4 (July 2004), pp. 1–31.

9 Anglo-Persian Oil Company Prospectus, file 1421/1908, Pt 4, 'Persia: Oil; Anglo-Persian Oil Co and Bakhtiaris', IOR/L/PS/10/144/2.

10 'The Land of the Bakhtiaris', *The Times*, 6 May 1910.

11 Yergin, *The Prize*, p. 144.

12 John Fisher, *Memories* (London, 1919), p. 217.

13 Yergin, *The Prize*, p. 141.

14 'Final Report of the Admiralty Commission on the Persian Oilfields', 6 April 1914, IOR/L/PS&S/10/410.

15 Robert Henriques, *Marcus Samuel* (London, 1960), p. 572.

2 CIRCLING SKIES, 1918–45

1 Sir John Cadman, 'A Journey through Bakhtiari Country', *The Naft* [Anglo-Persian Oil Company magazine] (1926).

2 Engert to the Secretary of State, 30 January 1922, cited in Michael A. Rubin, 'Stumbling through the "Open Door": The u.s. in Persia and the Standard-Sinclair Oil Dispute, 1920–1925', *Iranian Studies*, XXVIII/3–4 (Summer–Autumn 1995), p. 213.

3 Ibid.

4 Vita Sackville-West, *Passenger to Tehran* (London, 1926), p. 127.

5 *Sitara-yi Iran*, 28 November 1921, cited in Rubin, 'Stumbling through the "Open Door"', p. 210.

6 *Nahzat-i-sharq*, 12 February 1922, cited ibid., p. 213.

7 'Sir John Cadman's Bargain', *The Times*, 1 June 1933.

8 Cadman diary, BP 96659.

9 'Iran: 20th-century Darius', *Time*, XXXI/18 (25 April 1938), p. 18.

10 'Report on Oil Concession in North Persia', 12 September 1945, FO 371/45506, cited in M. Abdullahzadeh, 'The Kavir-i Khurian Oil Concession', *Journal of Persian Studies*, XXXIII (1995), p. 162.

11 'Oil in its Relation to the Middle East', IOR/R/15/1/700.

12 Stephen Hemsley Longrigg, *Oil in the Middle East: Its Discovery and Development* (London, 1961), p. 56.

13 'A Middle East Danger Point', *The Times*, 6 August 1941.

3 INTO THE GREAT UNKNOWN, 1945–71

1 James H. Bamberg, *The History of the British Petroleum Company*, vol. II: *The Anglo-Iranian Years, 1928–54* (Cambridge, 1995), p. 256.

2 Cited in Daniel Yergin, *The Prize: The Epic Quest for Oil, Money and Power* (New York, 2008), p. 436.

3 Sir Peter Ramsbotham, interviewed in 2001, British Diplomatic Oral History Programme, p. 13.

4 'fire-eating', in Roger Louis, *The British Empire in the Middle East 1945–1951: Arab Nationalism, the United States and Postwar Imperialism* (Oxford, 1984), p. 644; 'slippery', in Yergin, *The Prize*, p. 439.

5 *Baktar-e Emruz*, 18 July 1951, cited in Encyclopaedia Iranica, www.iranica online.org.

6 George McGhee, *On the Frontline in the Cold War: An Ambassador Reports* (London, 1997), p. 11.

7 Tehran to the State Department, 21 December 1950, cited in Bamberg, *The History of the British Petroleum Company*, vol II, p. 405.

8 Manucher Farmanfarmaian and Roxane Farmanfarmaian, *Blood and Oil: Memoirs of a Persian Prince* (New York, 2005), p. 241.

9 Clifton Daniel, 'British Warn Iran of Serious Result if She Seizes Oil', *New York Times*, 20 May 1951.

10 'Dr Moussadek's [sic] Collapse', *The Times*, 14 May 1951.

11 'Persia's Oil Plans', *The Times,* 24 May 1951.

12 Churchill to Lloyd, 24 May 1953, FO 371/104296.

13 'Mossadegh Here, Appeals to Americans to Back Iran', *New York Times*, 9 October 1951.

14 'Policy in Middle East', *The Times*, 8 October 1951.

15 Stephen Hemsley Longrigg, *Oil in the Middle East: Its Discovery and Development* (London, 1961), p. 170.

16 Neil Tweedie, 'Public Record Office: Shah's Party was too Tacky for the Queen', *The Telegraph*, 15 August 2001.

17 David Housego, 'Shah Laughs at Remark about Iraq', *The Times*, 14 October 1971.

4 THE OIL GAME, 1903–28

1 Correspondence between Nichols, Gilchrist and Walker, 15 September 1908, BP Archive ref: 72655.

2 Gabriel Garcia Márquez, *One Hundred Years of Solitude* (Buenos Aires, 1967), p. 165. Incidently, the town in question, Macondo, gave its name to the ill-fated Deepwater Horizon well that erupted in 2010.

3 Reproduced in *Foreign Relations of the United States* (FRUS), II, 1920, p. 662, U.S. Government Printing Office, Washington DC, www.digicoll.library. wisc.edu, accessed 15 February 2016.

4 See Scott Anderson, *Lawrence in Arabia: War, Deceit, Imperial Folly and the Making of the Modern Middle East* (New York, 2013), pp. 10–12.

5 Wilson to Foreign Office, 13 March 1918, IOR/L/PS/10/815.

6 Admiral Sir Edmond Slade, 'Petroleum Situation in the British Empire', 29 July 1918, CAB 21/119.

7 Hankey to Lloyd George, 1 August 1918, CAB 21/119.

8 Hankey to Geddes of the Admiralty, 30 July 1918, CAB 21/119.

9 Calouste Sarkis Gulbenkian, *Memoirs of Calouste Sarkis Gulbenkian With Particular Relation to the Origins and Foundation of the Iraq Petroleum Company*, 16 September 1945, U.S. National Archives, RG 59 890.G.6363/3-

148, 3, p. 17. The comment was a retort to French Prime Minister Clemenceau's famous remark, 'When I want oil I go to my grocer.'

10 Colby, *FRUS*, II, 20 November 1920, p. 669.

11 Davis to the Secretary of State (Lansing), 22 November 1919, *FRUS*, II, p. 260.

12 See James Barr, *A Line in the Sand: Britain, France and the Struggle that Shaped the Middle East* (London, 2011), pp. 154–6.

13 Calouste Gulbenkian to Nichols, 26 February 1925, 174–530A, BP Archive.

14 Initially the NEDC represented five U.S. oil companies but three withdrew, leaving only Jersey Standard and Socony-Vacuum.

5 BIRDS OF ILL OMEN, 1928–45

1 Nubar Gulbenkian, *Pantaraxia: The Autobiography of Nubar Gulbenkian* (New York, 1965), p. 102.

2 Mercier, letter to NEDC, 15 September 1931, Jersey Standard files, part 24-A., cited in Walter Adams et al., 'Retarding the Development of Iraq's Oil Resources: An Episode in Oleaginous Diplomacy, 1927–1939', *Journal of Economic Issues*, XXVII/1 (1993), p. 77 n. 20.

3 Meny to Mercier, 18 August 1930, CFP, 81.1/25, cited in Edward Peter Fitzgerald, 'Business Diplomacy: Walter Teagle, Jersey Standard, and the Anglo-French Pipeline Conflict in the Middle East, 1930–1931', *Business History Review*, LXVII/2 (Summer 1993), p. 223 n 23.

4 Cadman Diary, 23 February 1931, BP Archive ref: 70221.

5 Skliros to Morgan, 21 October 1931, Jersey Standard files, part 24-A, cited in Adams, 'Retarding the Development of Iraq's Oil Resources', p. 88 n 24.

6 Cited in Reynolds M. Salerno, *Vital Crossroads: Mediterranean Origins of the Second World War, 1935–1940* (New York, 2002), p. 17.

7 Cited in Nir Arielli, '"Haifa is Still Burning": Italian, German and French Air Raids on Palestine during the Second World War', *Middle Eastern Studies*, XLVI/3 (2010), pp. 331–47.

8 Report by the chiefs of staff, 1 November 1940, Records of the Cabinet Office, 'An Advance by the Enemy through the Balkans and Syria to the Middle East', 1 November 1940, CAB 66/13/11.

9 See Douglas Cole, 'A Difficult Five Weeks in Kirkuk', *IPC Society Newsletter*, no. 104 (October 1999), pp. 26–33.

10 Ibid., p. 30.

11 Churchill to Lloyd George, 1 September 1922, cited in Martin Gilbert, *Winston S. Churchill Companion*, vol. IV (London, 1977), part 3, p. 1724.

6 PUMPING DUST, 1945–71

1 This project should not be confused with the infamous construction of a canal to drain the Basra marshes in the 1990s, which was also known as 'The Third River'.
2 Wright to Lloyd, 8 February 1957, FO 371/128038.
3 Adeed Dawisha, *Iraq: A Political History from Independence to Occupation* (Princeton, NJ, 2009), p. 134.
4 'Iraq: In One Swift Hour', *Time*, LXXII/4 (28 July 1958), p. 25.
5 'Philip Pawson', *The Telegraph*, 15 June 2001.
6 Howard Page to the Senate hearings on Multinational Corporations (1974), XI/7, p. 309.
7 Stockwell to IPC, 22 September 1971, IPC 136011, BP Archive.
8 Tom Cholmondeley, 'Over a Barrel', *The Guardian*, 22 November 2002.

7 THE PLENTY QUARTER, 1920–44

1 Harold Dickson, *Kuwait and Her Neighbours* (London, 1956), pp. 268–78.
2 The seepage was well known, having been first investigated by Guy Pilgrim of the Geological Survey of India in 1905.
3 Literally, 'Allah sift the evil out of the English.' The account of this meeting is based on Chapter Eight in Ameen Rihani, *Ibn Sa'oud and Arabia: His People and his Land* (London, 1928); Dickson, *Kuwait and her Neighbours*, pp. 272–8.
4 File 8/7 I, Jidda Intelligence Report, 9 May 1933 (185/536), IOR/R/15/2/295.
5 File 61/6 IV (D 34), 'Bin Saud and Akwan [*sic*] Movement', 7 December 1920 (207/565), IOR/R/15/1/558.
6 Arnold Heim, 'The Question of Petroleum in Eastern Arabia', 5 September 1924, ETH-Bibliothek Archives Hs 494.
7 Cited in Archibald Chisholm, *The First Kuwait Oil Concession Agreement: A Record of the Negotiations, 1911–34* (London, 1975), p. 162, n. 59.
8 Thomas E. Ward, *Negotiations for Oil Concessions in Bahrain, El Hasa (Saudi Arabia), the Neutral Zone, Qatar and Kuwait* (New York, 1965), p. 108.
9 Aileen Keating, *Mirage: Power, Politics and the Hidden History of Arabian Oil* (New York, 2005), p. 252.
10 Angela Clarke, *Bahrain Oil and Development, 1929–1989* (Boulder, CO, 1990), p. 76.
11 Ibid., p. 130.
12 File 86/2 III (C 42) Political Resident to Sec. of State for Colonies, 4 June 1932, Bahrain Oil, Eastern and General Syndicate Limited, IOR/R/15/1/651.

13 File 61/11 IV (D 77), Political Agent to Political Resident, 17 January 1932, Hejaz-Nejd, Miscellaneous, IOR/R/15/1/567.

14 Wallace Stegner, 'Air Raid', *Aramco World*, XXI/1 (January–February 1970).

15 William E. Mulligan, 'Air Raid! A Sequel!', *Aramco World*, XXVII/4 (July–August 1976).

16 Wallace Stegner, 'Discovery! The Story of Aramco Then: The Time of the Hundred Men', *Aramco World*, XXI/2 (March–April 1970).

8 BIG AND LITTLE WHEELS, 1924–44

1 Stanton Hope, *Arabian Adventurer: The Story of Haji Williamson* (London, 1951), pp. 165–6.

2 Geological report, Cox and Shaw, July 1933, BP Archive ref: 078519.

3 Mylles to D'Arcy Exploration Co. Ltd, London, 12 May 1935, BP Archive ref: 067027.

4 Correspondence between the Political Agent and Sheikh Abdullah, January 1940, File 10/3 XI, 'Qatar Oil Concession', IOR/R/15/2/418.

5 File 10/13, APOC – Residency Agent to Political Agent, 6 October 1936, IOR/R/15/2/436.

6 Political Resident to Sec. of State for India, 25 May 1937, IOR/L/PS/12/233.

7 Penelope Tuson and Emma Quick, eds, *Arabian Treaties, 1600–1960* (Farnham, 1993), vol. III, p. 247.

8 Bertram Thomas, 'The South-eastern Borderlands of the Rub' Al Khali', *Geographical Journal*, LXXIII (1929), pp. 193–215.

9 G. M. Lees and K. W. Gray, 'The Geology of Oman and Adjoining Portions of South Eastern Arabia', 21 September 1926, BP Archive ref: 130863.

10 Lester S. Thomson, progress report, 10 December 1938, PC/27A (84), BP Archive.

9 CHASING THE ARAB ZONE, 1944–71

1 Daniel Yergin, *The Prize: The Epic Quest for Oil, Money and Power* (New York, 2008), p. 401.

2 'Memorandum Re: IPC', U.S. Senate hearings on Multinational Corporations (1974), XI/8, p. 124.

3 Louise Durham, 'The Elephant of All Elephants', *AAPG Explorer* (January 2005).

4 'Safaniya Field', *Aramco World*, XIII/7 (August–September 1962), pp. 3–7.

5 British Legation, Jedda to Eden, 29 December 1936, 'Arab Series – 1933–1939', File 8/15, IOR/R/15/2/310.

6 Parker T. Hart, *Saudi Arabia and the United States: Birth of a Security Partnership* (Bloomington, IN, 1998), p. 56.

7 File 1/A/5 III, 'Administration, Qatar affairs', IOR/R/15/2/143.

8 File 28/35, 'Denial programme, Qatar', IOR/R/15/2/729.

9 *Petroleum Week*, IV (1957), p. 24.

10 Loganecker, memorandum of 6 June 1952, *FRUS*, 1952–1954 (The Near and Middle East), p. 597

10 VOICES IN THE DARK

1 Wilfred Thesiger, Preface to *Arabian Sands* (London, rev. 1991), p. 5.

2 Ibrahim al-Rashid, ed., *Saudi Arabia Enters the World: Secret U.S. Documents on the Emergence of the Kingdom of Saudi Arabia as a World Power, 1936–1949*, part 1 (Salisbury, NC, 1980), pp. 201–3, cited in David Commins, *Islam in Saudi Arabia* (London, 2015), p. 1.

3 Wells, 7 April 1948, FO 624/130.

4 E. L. DeGolyer, 'Some Aspects of Oil in the Middle East', in *The Near East and the Great Powers*, ed. Richard N. Frye (Cambridge, MA, 1951), pp. 119–36.

5 Manucher Farmanfarmaian and Roxane Farmanfarmaian, *Blood and Oil: Memoirs of a Persian Prince* (New York, 2005), p. 241.

6 Steffen Hertog, *Princes, Brokers, and Bureaucrats: Oil and the State in Saudi Arabia* (New York, 2010), p. 28.

11 SISTERS AND BROTHERS, 1945–80

1 William N. Greene, *Strategies of the Major Oil Companies* (Ann Arbor, MI, 1985), cited in Edward Peter Fitzgerald, 'The Iraq Petroleum Company, Standard Oil of California, and the Contest for Eastern Arabia, 1930–1933', *International History Review*, XIII/3 (1991), p. 464 n. 75.

2 For reasons of national security, the Federal Trade Commission report was published in a redacted form in August 1952. At the same time, criminal proceedings were commenced against 21 oil companies but dropped five months later in favour of civil proceedings that were scaled back and eventually settled with several remaining defendants in 1968.

3 Earl Wilson, [Middlesboro, KY] *Daily News*, 24 April 1972. Although attributed to Getty, it is likely that the saying originated in the oilfields.

4 J. Vaughan, *The Failure of American and British Propaganda in the Arab Middle East, 1945–1957: Unconquerable Minds* (London, 2005), p. 215.

5 Oil was pumped along the full length of Tapline oil until 1982, and then to Jordan until 1990, when it was finally shut down. In 1982 a 727-mile pipeline was built across the Arabian Peninsula to Yanbu on the west coast. Today, while the main Iraqi pipelines are through Turkey and to the Persian Gulf, the Mediterranean pipelines lie in ruins, the victims of war and neglect.

6 Anthony Sampson, *The Seven Sisters: The Great Oil Companies and the World They Made* (London, 1975), p. 171.

7 Manucher Farmanfarmaian and Roxane Farmanfarmaian, *Blood and Oil: Memoirs of a Persian Prince* (New York, 2005), p. 341.

8 Sampson, *The Seven Sisters*, p. 174.

9 Daniel Yergin, *The Prize: The Epic Quest for Oil, Money and Power* (New York, 2008), p. 505.

10 'Two Sides in Iraq Oil Dispute Try Again', *The Times*, 30 May 1972.

11 'Buyers of Iraq Oil Likely to be Sued', *The Times*, 3 June 1972; 'Let the Iraqis Fall', Jungers to Ensor, 6 June 1972, in IPC 136014, cited in Brandon Wolfe-Hunnicutt, 'The End of the Concessionary Regime: Oil and American Power in Iraq, 1958–1972', PhD thesis, Stanford University, 2011, p. 257.

12 'Kissinger on Oil, Food and Trade', *Business Week*, 13 January 1975.

12 KINGS AND CARTELS, 1968–86

1 Memorandum of conversation, Shah, Ford and Kissinger, 16 May 1975, GRF-0134, U.S. National Archives, https://catalog.archives.gov.

2 'Kissinger to Press Shah on Oil Costs', *Washington Post*, 1 November 1974, cited in Andrew Scott Cooper, 'Showdown at Doha: The Secret Oil Deal that Helped Sink the Shah of Iran', *Middle East Journal*, LXII/4 (2008), p. 578.

3 Asadollah Alam, *The Shah and I: The Confidential Diary of Iran's Royal Court, 1969–1977* (New York, 1991), p. 535.

4 The Israelis nationalized the pipeline in 1979, resulting in legal proceedings for compensation that were only recently decided in favour of Iran; see Gregg Carlstrom, 'Israel Ordered to Pay Iran $1bn for Seizing Oil Pipeline', *The Times*, 15 August 2016.

5 Frederik Gerlach, telegram to the Department of State, 21 November 1978, U.S. National Archives ref: 1978RIYADHOIOOO.

6 The true extent of Saudi Arabia's reserves is debatable, and depends on how one calculates it. According to BP's latest review of world energy, the kingdom now holds about 16 per cent of the world's oil reserves.

7 David E. Long, 'Saudi Oil Policy', *Wilson Quarterly*, III/1 (1979), pp. 83–91.

13 A CAMEL RIDE TO ARMAGEDDON, 1980–2003

1 Robert Pear, 'Khomeini Accepts "Poison" of Ending the War with Iraq; UN Sending Mission', *New York Times*, 21 July 1988.

2 'Iraq: A Poisoned Dagger', *Time*, 30 July 1990.

3 'Iraq's Weapons of Mass Destruction: The Assessment of the British Government', www.fco.gov.uk/files, 24 September 2002; 'Iraq – Its Infrastructure of Concealment, Deception and Intimidation', www.number-10.gov.uk, 3 February 2003 The term 'dodgy dossier' appears to have been first used in the online magazine *Spiked*, in relation to the former dossier, in an article by Brendan O'Neill, 24 September 2002.

4 'UK Feared Americans Would Invade Gulf during 1973 Oil Crisis', *The Guardian*, 1 January 2004.

5 National Archives, Nixon Presidential Materials, National Security Council Files, Kissinger Telephone Conversation Transcripts, Box 23, Chronological Files.

6 *The Economist*, 17 January 1974, cited in the National Archives, Nixon Presidential Materials, NSC Files, Box 426, Backchannel Files, Middle East/ Africa, 1974, II.

7 Helms to Scowcroft, 22 January 1974, ibid.

8 Richard Dreyfus, 'The Thirty Year Itch', *Mother Jones*: www.motherjones.com, March/April 2003.

9 Paul Bignell, 'Secret Memos Expose Link between Oil Firms and Invasion of Iraq', *Independent*, 18 April 2011.

10 Dr Michael Klare, cited in Dreyfus, 'The Thirty Year Itch'.

11 'Strategic Energy Policy Challenges for the 21st Century', April 2001, www.cfr.org.

12 Ahmed Nafeez, 'Iraq Invasion was about Oil', *The Guardian*, 20 March 2014.

13 Blair to Bush, 12 September 2011, Chilcot report, www.iraqinquiry.org.uk, 6 July 2016.

14 Carne Ross, 12 July 2010, Chilcot report.

15 Dearlove to Manning, 3 December 2001, Chilcot report.

14 THE NEW ROME

1 *Wahid* is Arabic for 'one'. The old man was referring to the author's father, Mike Morton, and his colleague Ted 'Peewee' Melville. Email from Dr Alan Heward to the author, 26 September 2006.

2 See Terry Adams, 'Baghdad or Bust: Oil, War and People in Iraq', *IPC Society Newsletter*, no. 123 (July 2004), pp. 12–23.

3 'U.S. Companies Shut Out as Iraq Auctions its Oil Fields', *Time World*, 19 December 2009.

4 Vivienne Walt, 'Oil Exec. Who Charmed Kings and Dictators Killed in Plane Crash', *Time*, 21 October 2014.

5 Water is usually injected for two reasons: to maintain reservoir pressure and to improve the sweep oil ahead of the advancing water front.

6 Matthew R. Simmons, *Twilight in the Desert: The Coming Saudi Oil Shock and the World Economy* (Hoboken, NJ, 2005), p. 179.

7 Tom DiChristopher, 'OPEC Deal Shows Saudi Oil Strategy has Backfired, says John Kilduff', CNBC, 28 September 2016, www.cnbc.com, accessed 8 December 2016.

8 Halfdan Carstens, 'Some Basic Facts', *GEO ExPro*, XIII/5 (2016), p. 84, available at www.geoexpro.com, accessed 8 December 2016.

9 Nayla Razzouk, 'After 20 Years, OPEC Bids Farewell to Saudi Arabia Oil Chief', Bloomberg, www.bloomberg.com, 7 May 2016.

SELECT BIBLIOGRAPHY

Anaz, Ghanim, *Iraq: Oil and Gas Industry in the Twentieth Century* (Nottingham, 2012)

Anderson, Scott, *Lawrence in Arabia: War, Deceit, Imperial Folly and the Making of the Modern Middle East* (New York, 2013)

Barr, James, *A Line in the Sand: Britain, France and the Struggle that Shaped the Middle East* (London, 2011)

Chisholm, Archibald, *The First Kuwait Oil Concession: A Record of Negotiations, 1911–1934* (London, 1975)

Citino, Nathan J., *From Arab Nationalism to OPEC* (Bloomington, OH, 2002)

Clarke, Angela, *Bahrain Oil and Development, 1929–1989* (London, 1991)

Ferrier, Ronald W., *The History of the British Petroleum Company: The Developing Years, 1901–1932* (Cambridge, 1982)

Heard, David, *From Pearls to Oil: How the Oil Industry Came to the United Arab Emirates* (Dubai, 2011)

Kent, Marian, *Oil and Empire: British Policy and Mesopotamian Oil, 1900–1920* (London, 1976)

Kinzer, Stephen, *All the Shah's Men: An American Coup and the Roots of Middle East Terror* (Hoboken, NJ, 2008)

Longrigg, Stephen H., *Oil in the Middle East: Its Discovery and Development* (London, 1954, rev. 1961)

Owen, E. W., *Trek of the Oil Finders: A History of Exploration for Petroleum* (Tulsa, OK, 1975)

Penrose, E., and E. F. Penrose, *Iraq: International Relations and National Development* (London, 1978)

Pfeister, Sam L., *Solomon's Temple: Musjid-i-Suleiman and the Quest for Oil in the Middle East* (Georgetown, TX, 2014)

Sampson, Anthony, *The Seven Sisters: The Great Oil Companies and the World They Made* (London, 1976)

Sheridan, Don, *Fahud – Leopard Mountain: Oil Exploration in Oman and Libya in the 1950s* (Dublin, 2000)

Stegner, Wallace, *Discovery! The Search for Arabian Gold* (St Vista, CA, 2007)

Yergin, Daniel, *The Prize: The Epic Quest for Oil, Money and Power* (New York, 1991)

ACKNOWLEDGEMENTS

Empires and Anarchies is the result of more than a decade of reading and writing about oil in the Middle East. It started with research into my late father's travels as an exploration geologist and culminated in a study of the higher reaches of oil politics and diplomacy. There have been many experiences along the way, and I would like to thank the many people who selflessly helped me, including my father's colleagues who shared many insights into oil exploration and discovery. An immense debt of gratitude goes to my wife Gill for her patience and support, and for sharing a great adventure. I am also indebted to Dr Alan Heward and my brother Peter, who commented on the manuscript. I would like to thank Peter Housego and Joanne Burman for facilitating access to the BP Archive.

Finally, the spirit of my father D. M. ('Mike') Morton, who inspired me through the stories of his life, invests the pages of the book, unseen but always present. For someone who was able to roam around the region's deserts and mountains in search of oil, he would surely have looked on its present situation with mixed feelings: admiration for the benefits that oil wealth has brought and sadness for the turmoil it has wrought.

PHOTO ACKNOWLEDGEMENTS

The author and publishers wish to express their thanks to the below sources of illustrative material and/or permission to reproduce it.

Hamza Farouq Abbas: p. 232; BP Archive: pp. 18, 22, 26, 29, 32, 35, 40, 45, 46, 50, 55, 59, 78, 91, 112, 137, 162, 170, 175, 177, 181, 228; courtesy Cambridge University Press: p. 187; William Connolley: p. 221; DeGolyer Library, Southern Methodist University, Robert Yarnall Richie Collection: p. 154; ETH-Bibliothek Zürich, Bildarchiv/Arnold Heim: pp. 123, 127; Everett Collection Historical/Alamy: p. 193; Elliott/U.S. Navy: p. 211; Gerald R. Ford Library/U.S. National Archives: p. 203; The Gulbenkian Foundation: p. 75; David Holt: p. 67; Imperial War Museum: pp. 84, 103; *Illustrated London News*: p. 116; Imperial War Museum: p. 109; Iraq Petroleum Company: pp. 143, 158, 164; Library of Congress: pp. 81, 89, 97, 100, 104, 208; D. M. Morton: p. 146; © M. Q. Morton: pp. 8, 9, 225; National Archives (UK): p. 191; Franklin D. Roosevelt Presidential Library and Museum: p. 151; Joseph D. Mountain/Smithsonian Institute: p. 131; Homer Sykes/Alamy: p. 197; Harry S. Truman Library and Museum: p. 62; U.S. Air Force: p. 216; U.S. Department of State: p. 237.

INDEX

Jones, Alton 61
Jordan 174, 237

Kashani, Abul Qasim 56, 60
Kazemi, Bagher 61
Kennedy, John F. 115
Kerr, Dick, 149
Kerry, John *237*
Khamenei, Ali 12, 226
Khan, Antoine Kitabchi 21
Khan, Aziz *18*
Khan, Muhammed Karim *18*
Khomeini, Ayatollah Ruholla 205,
    206, 214
Khonsari, Muhammad Taqi 56
Khostaria, Arkady 36, 43–4
Kirkuk 90–91, *84*, 92, 94, 101, 102,
    114, 176
Kissinger, Henry 199, 202, 203, *208*,
    210, 218
Kurdistan 230
Kuwait 135–8, 175, 194, 200, 215–16, 218
Kuwait Oil Co. 49, 137, 185

Lawrence, T. E. 79
Lees, George Martin 127, 139, 144–5
Lermitte, Basil 142
Libya 189, 194, 195, 198, 213
Lloyd George, David 83, 85–6, 88
Loftus, William 16–17, 19
Longrigg, Stephen 45, 142, 143

Makki, Husayn 58
Mann, Alex 123
Margerie, Christophe de 232
Marshall, William 83
Masjid-i-Suleiman 16–17, 25–6, *26*, 33,
    44, *170*
Mattei, Enrico 183, 184, 186, 189
Melville, Edward 223
Mexico 50, 178
Miller, Robert *131*
Morgan, Jacques de 20, 22
Morton, D. M. ('Mike') 164, 223
Mossadegh, Mohammad 12, 48, 50,
    51, 52, 54–64, *62*, 66
Mosul 85–6, 88–90
al-Muhairi, Mohamed Abd 173
Mujahidin 13, 209

Mukalla *146*
Mussolini, Benito 99
Mylles, Charles 139

Al Nahyan, Shakhbut bin Sultan 143,
    159, 170
al-Naimi, Ali 234, 236
Nasser, Gamel 63, 111, 157, 190
Nazih, Hassan 206
Neutral Zone (Saudi Arabia/Kuwait)
    136, 188, 189
Nichols, Herbert 74, 76
Nicolson, Harold 40
al-Nimr, Nimr 227
Nixon, Richard 68, 202

Oman 143–5, 161–4, 223–4
Open Door principle 35–6, 87–9
Organization of Arab Petroleum
    Exporting Countries (OAPEC) 194
Organization of the Petroleum
    Exporting Countries (OPEC) 14,
    175, 192–6, 199, 201, 204, 213,
    234, 235
al-Otaiba, Mana Saeed 199

al-Pachachi, Muzahim 92
Page, Howard 191
Palestine 79–80, 107, 172
Paris Agreement (2015) 236
Parker, Alwyn 77
Partex 163, 198
Philby, Harry St John 131, 151
Phillips, Wendell 162
Pike, R. W. 146
Pilgrim, Guy 23, 144
Preece, John
Pretyman, Ernest 24

Qasim, Abdul al-Karim 113–15, *116*
Qatar 138–40, 155–8, 161, 176, 190,
    200, 204, 232
Qavan, Ahmad 61

Ras al-Khaimah 69, 161
Razmara, Ali 54, 56, 57
Razzak, Abdul 140
Red Line Agreement (1928) 92, 136,
    141, 148–9, 184